The criminal liability of corporations in English law

LSE research monographs 2

This series is published jointly with the London School of Economics and Political Science. It aims to make available research of originality and quality from the whole range of the social sciences, including all the fields and disciplines which are studied at the school. The intention is to provide a continuing outlet for serious scholarly work, and relatively quick publication. The books will be of interest to specialists in the various fields, irrespective of whether they are in universities, government departments, industries or elsewhere, as well as to libraries throughout the world.

Each monograph will be introduced with a foreword by a distinguished authority on the subject, whose aim will be to set the particular research in to the wider framework of the appropriate discipline. Forthcoming monographs include the following:

Changes in Subject Choice at School and University
Celia M. Phillips

Industrial Demand for Water: a Study of South-East England
Judith Rees

The Politics of Decontrol of Industry: Britain and the United States
Susan Armitage

The Administrative Functions of the French Conseil d'Etat
Nancy Rendell

The Concept of Responsibility in the Criminal Law
F. G. Jacobs

Six Studies of Indian Industry
Angus Hone

The criminal liability of corporations in English law

L.H. Leigh

B.A LL.B (Alberta) Ph.D

Lecturer in Law, London School of Economics and Political Science

London School of Economics and Political Science

Weidenfeld and Nicolson
5 Winsley Street London W1

SBN 297 17818 0
Printed in Great Britain by
Lowe & Brydone (Printers) Ltd., London

Contents

Preface

The invention of that curious creature, the corporation aggregate, being a legal 'person' separate from its members, was bound to create difficulties in the administration of justice. Developments in the criminal law have for some time exemplified those difficulties. The confusion of concepts which even today surrounds both judicial and legislative discussion of the 'nature' of corporate personality, the unsatisfying case law applying rules based upon vicarious liability (where the corporation is liable for agents) and 'personal' liability of the corporation (where some managers are regarded as its *alter ego*), and the problems of policy and practicability involved in the very enforcement of criminal sanctions against corporate bodies, have all led to the need for a new analysis of the law in its social setting. In days of increasing concentration of capital, when economic power resides in the hands of fewer and fewer corporations, it is a cause for concern that the law relating to these bodies—what Berle and Means called in 1932 the 'potential constitutional law of the new economic state'—should so often be obscure or outmoded.

The present volume is the first attempt to analyse comprehensively the state of English law dealing with the criminal liability of corporations. Moreover, it relates the existing law both to its own history and to its modern social background; and from that discussion it proceeds to review the possible directions which reforms might take. The work is based upon Dr. Leigh's Ph.D. thesis in the University of London. It is bound to be read by all those who are interested in the criminal law and in the legal and social problems connected with corporations, since its matter, and no less the author's own views, will without doubt now form a starting point for the continuing debate on this topic

K. W. Wedderburn,
Cassel Professor of Commercial
Law in the University of London

London School of Economics

Introduction

Corporate criminal liability is now an accepted principle of English criminal law. For several reasons this general principle is of some interest. It represents a complete reversal of the original common law rule. Until 1944 it was at least doubtful whether corporations could be made liable for offences involving *mens rea*. Corporations were successively made liable in cases of public nuisance, and for public welfare offences. They were not made liable for crimes of which *mens rea* was a necessary ingredient. When liability was finally imposed upon corporations, the bases upon which it was imposed, and the reasons underlying its imposition were not made apparent. Probably it was a response to violations of wartime regulations. It may well have represented a desire to bring within the ambit of regulations, all types of business organization. Certainly, there were a number of wartime cases in which violations of defence regulations occurred in respect of activities engaged in by corporations.

The development of corporate criminal liability is an interesting facet of a much larger development; namely, the assimilation of these bodies into the legal system generally. The appearance of the corporation as a common mode of business organization forced developments in several areas of the law. Their effect upon vicarious liability has been charted by Baty[1] and Fifoot.[2] Their subjection to the criminal law forms the subject of this thesis.

A further, and interesting aspect of this development is that it has, for the most part, been confined to legal systems deriving from English common law. In the United States, Canada, Australia, and even Nigeria,[3] corporate criminal liability is an accepted phenomenon. In Scots law, corporations, while liable for public welfare offences, have never been made liable for offences involving *mens rea*.[4] In the civil law systems, it is generally unknown.[5] Donnedieu de Vabres states, of French law, that the Cour de Cassation has excluded corporations from criminal liability except in the case of Revenue legislation, and where, as under Black Market legislation, penalties are of an *in rem* character, such as confiscation of property.[6] In Norway, liability is only imposed in respect of economic crimes.[7] The classic bars to criminal liability in English law long since surmounted; that corporations have no mind capable of entertaining a criminal intent, that they have no capacity to commit crimes, and that they are not generally amenable to other than pecuniary punishments, still prevail.[8] It is paradoxical that while

corporate criminal liability represents a common law development,
England was one of the last common law countries to adopt an explicit
rule that corporations were generally criminally liable. In comparison
with the United States and Canada, corporate liability is still, in English
law, in a state of infancy.

The fact that corporate criminal liability is in a state of infancy
makes an examination of a number of facets of the subject both
interesting and important. Accordingly, I have sought to trace its
history, to indicate how parallel developments in other areas of the law
have affected its development and to evaluate its significance both
doctrinally and practically. Because this book was originally conceived
as a London Ph.D. thesis and as such required to be a complete account,
a number of issues of largely historical significance were considered at a
length which their contemporary interest does not warrant. For the
truncated remnants of such discussion I apologise, remarking only that
the issues interested me, and in some instances, particularly in relation
to procedure, deal with problems which still arise in some areas of the
Commonwealth.

It is right to record a debt to several people. The greatest is undoubtedly
owed to Mr. J. E. Hall Williams, reader in criminology and my original
supervisor, who struggled through endless drafts, and to Professor
K. W. Wedderburn who succeeded him. This topic was suggested by
Mr. S. Prevezer, formerly reader in law at University College, who
endured my presence at a number of his LL.M. seminars. My external
examiner, Mr. R. N. Gooderson, Fellow of St. Catherine's College,
Cambridge, advanced a number of helpful suggestions of some of which I
have taken advantage. To all of them I am most grateful.

1   Baty, *Vicarious Liability* (1916)
2   Fifoot, *Judge And Jurist In The Reign Of Victoria* (1959) Chapter 3
3   See *Mandillas and Karaberis Ltd.* v. *Inspector-General of Police*, 1958 FSC 20
4   In *Clydebank Co-Operative Society Limited* v. *Binnie*, 1937 JC 17, the conviction
of the society of causing or permitting user of a vehicle as an express carriage
without the appropriate licence was upheld, but the case seemingly turns on
vicarious liability. See also *Shields* v. *Little*, 1954 JC 25
5   Mueller, 'Mens Rea And The Corporation' (1957) 19 U. Pitt. L. Rev. 21;
Andenaes, *The General Part Of The Criminal Law Of Norway* (1965) pp 246-247
6   *Traite De Droit Criminel Et De Legislation Pénale Comparée* (1946) pp 149-50
7   Andenaes, *The General Part Of The Criminal Law Of Norway* (1965) p 246
8   See note 6 also Stefani et Levasseur, *Droit Pénale Général Et Criminologie*
(1958) pp 232-233

Chapter 2

Early bars to the development of corporate criminal liability

The development of corporate criminal liability was impeded from the first by both conceptual and practical obstacles. Initially, it was said that a corporation had no mind, could not will, and so could not personally entertain the intent necessary to commit a crime. Similarly, before the development of vicarious liability, it was clear that a corporation lacked corporeal members, and could not therefore act physically. It was also said at a later date that corporations, other than charter corporations, were creatures endowed with such limited powers as were specified either by an incorporating statute or, if incorporated under the enabling provisions of the Companies Act by the objects set out in the memorandum of association. Powers were never explicitly conferred enabling the corporation to commit crimes. Therefore, it was said, the commission of any crime was necessarily *ultra vires* a corporation and could not be imputed to it. Finally, until recent times, no adequate system of procedure existed whereby a corporation could be made to appear and answer for its alleged crimes.[1] Over and above these objections, there existed a further and equally fundamental bar. As corporations act only through their officers, agents and employees, and cannot act *in propria persona*, corporate liability had necessarily to be vicarious liability. From an early period, it had been a fundamental principle of English common law, that a person could not be held vicariously liable for the crimes of another.[2]

Three of these bars are examined in this chapter, namely, the inability of a corporation to will, the notion that the commission of crimes was *ultra vires* the corporation, and the inadequacy of early procedure to deal with corporations accused of criminal offences. The manner in which liability developed, and in which the objection to corporate criminal liability as vicarious liability was overcome are dealt with subsequently.

Theories of corporate personality and their effect

The primary theoretical bar to liability lay in the lawyers conception of the corporation as an entity unable to think or to act for itself. In its time, no question was more vexed than that of the nature of corporate personality. The notion that the common law received the fiction theory of the corporation has long been discarded. Sir Frederick Pollock many years ago demonstrated that medieval precedents do not support that the common law viewed the corporation as a fictional entity lacking a mind or will of its own, and acting under tutelage.[3] It is now accepted that the common law declined to receive any theory of corporate personality at all.[4] Nonetheless, the corporation was seen as an entity in which reposed certain capacities relating to its function as corporation. It had no soul to damn and no body to kick.[5] Until the advent of vicarious liability, it had no arm with which to strike.[6] It could exercise certain capacities necessary to carry out its functions. It could sue and be sued in its corporate name, and it could hold and alienate property.[7] Certain corporations could pass by-laws regulating the prices of commodities in which its members dealt and enforce them by penalties and might, if these were judged oppressive '. . .and to the common hurt and damage of the people' be fined.[8] It was early held that, for what were conceived to be its proper purposes, the will of its governing body could be imputed to it.[9] Similarly, practical necessity shortly made it necessary for the courts to hold that a minor servant engaged in routine duties need not be authorised under seal to do so.[10]

Until vicarious liability developed and provided the key to liability, it was only natural that the corporation should not be held liable for misfeasance. In the meantime, questions of the essential nature of the corporation were of little concern. Such definitions of the corporation as were propounded were less definitions than statements of the powers with which corporations were endowed, and the functions for which they were incorporated. Among these are stated to be immortality, individuality enabling many persons to act as one, the ability to manage its own affairs, and to hold property. It was for the purpose of clothing bodies of men with these qualities and capacities that corporations were invented. These means enabled a perpetual succession of individuals to act for the promotion of a particular object, like one immortal being.[11]

In addition to drawing attention to the purposes for which corporations were invented, the common lawyers also attended to the manner of their government. Thus Blackstone refers to the corporation as a 'little republic' whose affairs were carried on by a governing board for the benefit of the members at large.[12]

Two things may be remarked. First, the early writers drew attention not to any essence of the corporation but to the functions which corporations were intended to serve and the powers with which accordingly, they were invested. There was also early attention to the manner in which they were governed.[13] If the term fiction was used of a corporation, it was used as a means of indicating that a corporation was not a man, but an abstraction. Corporate criminal liability was not substantially impeded by any theory that the corporation was a fictional being. When, in 1859, it was argued that a corporation, being a fiction, could not be held liable for a tort involving violence, Erle C. J. referred to the notion as '. . . more quaint than substantial.'[14]

The corporation as an abstraction

The notion that a corporation was an abstraction did however have an important consequence whic served to impede the imposition of liability. It could not act for itself. Physical acts had to be performed, not by the corporation, but in its name. Criminal liability, if imposed upon the corporation, had therefore to be vicarious liability. Vicarious liability had no place in English criminal law. To Lord Lindley, writing as a junior barrister the corporation was to be treated as a natural person so far as possible. Natural persons could be held vicariously liable for the torts of their servants or agents. They could not be held vicariously liable for the crimes of others. There was therefore, no analogy which could be drawn from a natural person and applied to a corporation in order to justify corporate criminal liability. In addition, Lord Lindley relied upon policy objections. The end of the criminal process is to impose not compensation, but punishment. In Lord Lindley's view, criminal punishment ought always to fall upon the culpable human actor who ought to be made to feel its incidence.[15] Forty years later, as a Lord of Appeal, he reiterated, in *Citizens Life Assurance Company* v. *Brown* the undesirability of introducing what he regarded as metaphysical subtleties.[16] Corporate liability for torts rested, he declared, upon the responsibility of a master for the acts of his servant.

The realist theory and its effect

For so long as a corporation could be regarded as only acting through agents, criminal liability if imposed upon a corporation, could only have been said to be vicarious liability. The realist theory of corporate personality may well have been indirectly responsible for introducing the notion of organic representation into English law. That it had any wider significance may well be doubted. While no English court adopted the realist theory outright, it did seemingly lead to the introduction of the language of organic representation to English law. In *Lennards Carrying Company* v. *Asiatic Petroleum Company Limited*[17] Lord Haldane was faced with the problem of determining under what circumstances, under the Merchant Shipping Act, 1894, a corporation could be said to be personally negligent. This was one of the few occasions in which vicarious liability was clearly not sufficient to do justice. Lord Haldane chose to say that the acts of the person or persons representing the controlling mind and will of the corporation were its acts. Lord Dunedin, by contrast, spoke of the corporation as being represented by such persons.[18] Essentially however, the organic theory of representation was imported as a device for a particular purpose. The realist theory as such was never adopted. Nor was the term 'organ' itself unknown when applied to the Board of Directors. It had been previously used to describe a relationship not aptly comprehended by the concepts of agency or trusteeship.[19] Similarly, *alter ego* has been used to describe the licensee's delegate under the Licensing Acts.[20] What Lord Haldane did was to analyse the control structure of a corporation in order to ascertain the appropriate analogy to the personal acts of a human being. He spoke in the language of German romanticism; while Lord Dunedin's language has a more familiar ring. At any rate, and whatever Lord Haldane's views of the nature of corporate personality may have been, they failed to effect the importation into English Law of any theory of corporate personality. The result may well have been to import into an existing body of case and statute law a device which exists uncomfortably with a body of doctrine based upon a contrary predicate.[21]

The corporation and its analogy to natural persons

The courts, in fact, have been content to treat corporations as nearly as possible as though they were natural persons. The inquiry with which the judges have dealt has been concerned not with the nature of corporations, but with what rights and liabilities they possess and to which they ought to be subjected. This question has not been approached from the vantage point of any *a priori* assumption regarding the nature of the entity. Both Professor Dewey and Professor Hart rightly remind us that this is a question which is largely irrelevant in the day to day solution of practical problems. We are reminded that the judges must decide 'how far the analogies latent in the law permit them to extend to corporations rules worked out for individuals when justice seems to demand it.'[22] There are limitations upon this technique, and these are two-fold. There is a question how far the analogy can extend, and secondly, whether, in a particular case, the interests of justice demand that it be drawn.

Limitations of treatment by analogy

We cannot draw an inference by analogy that the body of the human or humans who constitute its controlling organs, constitutes the body of the corporation. Clearly, in terms of existing legal concepts, that is not so. We do not sentence the corporation to death and carry out the sentence by hanging the controlling person in the corporate structure. The corporation is an abstraction and survives the death of those who act on its behalf. We are reluctant to say that a corporation can possess the professional knowledge of a pharmacist, for such knowledge cannot survive the natural person in whom alone it inheres.[23] Equally, we may be reluctant to hold that a corporation can commit rape, for we have difficulty relating it to a corporate purpose, and therefore cannot see that justice requires such a result. But we do say that a corporation can make a false return of one sort or another and, because the act can be said to be relevant to a corporate purpose, it does not seem absurd to charge the corporation with its commission. Of course the act itself is that of a natural person, but that result we have tacitly accepted. The lawyer's concern has been with vicarious mental states.

While the assertion or denial that corporate bodies possess a natural immanence are irrelevant to the actual workings of the legal system, two things can hardly be denied. The first is that to deal in terms of analogy and policy is not an entirely easy matter. In the absence of conceptual bars or imperatives, the question of technique in a system which is uncomfortable in verbalising policy questions becomes one of some subtlety. For example, we become dependant in large measure on devices used in statutory interpretation in order to find that a statute was or was not intended to apply to corporations. Again, distinctions which contradict the courts own reasoning may be employed. It is said that certain crimes, such as rape, can be committed only by individuals; but, if a corporation can defraud, why can it not rape? To this, no logical answer can be given. Secondly, the fact that we need not be concerned for the purposes of affixing personality with any supposed ontological attributes of the corporate entity does not mean that these alleged attributes can be ignored for the purposes of the criminal responsibility of corporations. Rather, it means that they are properly used as instruments of policy. Frequently they are founded on a valid insight into the workings of a group. A knowledge of the manner in which the corporation operates is basic to an appreciation of the value of applying the criminal sanction to it.

It is perhaps fortunate that the conceptual theories did not become masters, denying to the law a needed flexibility. The courts were largely content to meet new situations in a pragmatic fashion. In this context, the search for a corporate immanence seems not to have preoccupied them. If theories of corporate personality had an effect other than that of introducing the notion of organic representation as a useful device, it may have been that of emphasizing both the uses to which the corporate entity might be put, and the manner in which it functioned. No more definite statement than this can be advanced.

Ultra vires as a bar to liability

The doctrine of *ultra vires* was also advanced as a bar to corporate criminal liability. This doctrine, which was authoritatively enunciated in *Ashbury Railway Carriage Co. Ltd.* v. *Riche*[24] and which applied to companies incorporated by Special Act of Parliament or under the enabling Provisions of the Companies Act, imposed a limitation upon the capacity of such corporations. In brief, the doctrine provided that a company could not pursue objects other than those specified in its objects clause. Activities falling entirely outside the ambit of those specified in the objects clause were said to be *ultra vires* the company and, in respect of such activities, the company could not be made liable.[25] The rule which has been applied strictly in cases of contract was also advanced as an answer to the contention that a corporation could be made liable for torts involving malice which were committed by its officers agents and servants. Originally, the doctrine was advanced as an answer to the contention that a corporation could be made liable for torts involving malice which were committed by its officers, agents, and servants. In *Abrath* v. *North Eastern Railway Company*[26] Lord Bramwell stated that a corporation could not be held liable for torts in which malice or motive is an essential ingredient because it could only do that which is within its authorised powers. It could not authorise its agents to do that which is not within the limits of those powers. By its constitution and nature, it lacked the power to commit torts involving malice or motive and it therefore could not authorise the performance of such acts. The argument had a certain plausibility although Lord Selborne L. C. and Lord FitzGerald made it clear that they did not accede to it. The current of authority even at that date was against the contention. Nonetheless, the idea enjoyed a period of popularity in the United

States[27] and made a belated appearance in a New Zealand decision which put Lord Bramwell's argument in classic form.[28]

The rejection of *ultra vires* in tort and crime

In the law of tort however, Lord Lindley put the matter beyond doubt in *Citizens Life Assurance Company* v. *Brown*.[29] The corporation civilly was to be placed in the same postion as a human employer with respect to liability for the torts of his employees. All employers were liable for torts involving malice committed by their employees in the course of their employment. The corporation was in the same position. The courts thus adopted the view that the relevant inquiry was not directed towards the nature of the act in question, but to whether it was done in pursuit of objects competent to the corporation.

The *ultra vires* bar to holding a corporation criminally liable was simply dismissed by inference.[30] In none of the cases in which corporate criminal liability has been imposed was the matter argued.[31] The limitations urged by Lord Bramwell were in fact ignored. Most text-books of the period including *Pollock on Tort*,[32] rejected the contention, although Pollock himself as a *First Book of Jurisprudence* disclosed was not entirely consistent.[33] Maitland summed the matter up with his accustomed felicity[34] :

To serious minds there is something repulsive in the attribution of fraud or the like to the mindless *persona ficta.* The law would set a bad example if its fictions were fraudulent . . . [but] . . . even Savigny could not permanently prevail when the day of railway collisions had come. And so in England we may see the speculative doubt obtruding itself from time to time, but only to be smothered under the weight of accumulating precedents . . . '

It now seems clear that *ultra vires* will be taken as referring solely to capacity and that, if a criminal act is performed in pursuance of an activity *intra vires* the corporation, the corporation will be held liable in respect of it. Early American experience in which *ultra vires* did have an inhibiting effect, discloses that it might have been a considerable impediment to the imposition of liability.[35]

Procedural obstacles to liability[36]

The third impediment to liability is to be found in the procedure for compelling the appearance of corporations. Here the difficulties arose with respect to indictable offences. No such difficulty arose with respect of offences punishable on summary conviction. The Summary Conviction Act, 1848 specifically provided that the accused could appear by his counsel or attorney. In addition, by the Quarter Sessions Act, 1849 either the party or his attorney could sign a notice of appeal.

Certiorari procedure in indictable offences

Indictable offences posed greater difficulty. On assize the accused had to appear personally. A corporation could only appear by its attorney and accordingly was not triable at assizes. Furthermore, as it had no body, it could not be committed for trial. The system therefore was to prefer a bill before the grand jury. If a true bill were returned and the matter remitted to assize it was then necessary to remove the indictment, by *certiorari*, to the Kings Bench.[37] There *ex gratia curia* the corporation could appear and plead by its attorney. Trial could be either in London or, it would seem, at *nisi prius*.[38] When once the indictment had been preferred before the Kings Bench, that court could compel the corporation to appear. The procedure was analogous to that employed against a natural person. In the case of a natural person the body could be attached by successive writs of *capias, alies* and *pluries capias* with outlawry as a last resort.[39] A similar procedure was invoked against the corporation. Initially, writs of *venire facias* and *distringas* were issued in an amount thought sufficient to ensure the corporation's appearance. If this proved insufficient *alias* and *pluries* writs of *distringas* could issue. The culmination was the issuance of a distress infinite by which the entirety of the corporation's assets could be attached. The courts were by no means hesitant about using this machinery.[40]

The effect of the judicature act, 1873

This mode of procedure continued, with minor changes, until 1925. The Judicature Act of 1873 made courts of Oyer, Terminer, and Gaol Delivery part of the High Court and thereafter indictments could be removed from Assize to the King's Bench Division by order rather than by *certiorari*. The Crown Office Rules however, retained the old procedure for corporations. Rule 13 preserved the system of removing indictments against bodies corporate into the King's Bench Division. The order was obtained upon the filing of an affidavit stating that an indictment had been found against the corporation and that it was unable to appear in the court below. The order was then granted as a matter of course upon an *ex parte* application.[41]

Inconveniences of unreformed procedure

The inconveniences of this procedure were apparently not felt until 1922 when the case of *Rex* v. *Daily Mirror Newspapers Limited* was decided.[42] The company was charged with an offence contrary to section 34 of the Representation of the People Act, 1918. Grand Juries had been suspended for the duration of the First World War by the Grand Juries (Suspension) Act, 1917. Under that act, an indictment could only be properly presented if the person against whom it was sought to present the indictment had been committed for trial, or the consent or direction in writing from a judge of the High Court for the presentment of an indictment had been given, or the consent or direction of one of the Law Officers had been obtained. In this case however, the Crown sought to rely upon an alleged committal of the corporation. It was held that a corporation could not be committed for trial because, by the Interpretation Act, 1889, committal involved the detention of the accused in custody. As a matter of statutory interpretation it was held that a corporation was incapable of being committed for trial. Committal procedure did not therefore lie against it. As no notice had been given of an intention to present an indictment against the corporation, that procedure could not be invoked.[43] The tenor of the courts decision also indicated that the position with respect to offences punishable either on summary conviction or on indictment was far from clear. The Summary Jurisdiction Act, 1879 provided that an accused had the option when charged with an offence (other than assault) for which the maximum penalty was a term of imprisonment greater than three months to elect whether to be tried summarily or by a court composed of a judge and jury. If he chose the latter course the magistrates were to hold a preliminary inquiry with a view to committing the offender for trial. However, although this had been done and had passed without comment in *Rex* v. *Ascanio Puck & Co.*[44] such procedure in future would have been impossible. As a result, the Criminal Justice Act, 1925 provided improved machinery.

The Criminal Justice Act, 1925

At this point, it may be helpful to give a brief account of the provisions of the *Criminal Justice Act*, 1925. Where a corporation was charged with an indictable offence the examining justices, if satisfied that evidence sufficient to put the corporation upon trial had been adduced, could make an order empowering the prosecutor to present a bill in respect of the offence named in the order. For the purposes of any enactments referring to committal for trial such order was to be deemed to be a committal. Where the grand jury at assizes or quarter sessions returned a true bill against the corporation the corporation could appear and plead by its representative, before the court of assize or quarter sessions. In cases falling within section 17 of the Summary Jurisdiction Act, 1879 the corporation was enabled, by its representative, to claim to be tried by a jury. A corporation was empowered to appoint a representative by a simple statement in writing signed by the managing director of the corporation. In 1933 however, the grand jury was abolished[45] and thereafter a bill could only be preferred before the court if the corporation had been committed for trial, or if a bill had been preferred with the consent or by the direction of a justice of the high court, or pursuant to an order made under section 9 of the Perjury Act, 1911.

1   See the discussion in Glanville Williams, *Criminal Law; The General Part* (2nd ed 1961) pp 854-857, and Welsh, 'The Criminal Liability Of Corporations' (1946) 62 LQR 345

2   *Rex* v. *Huggins* (1730) 2 Ld Raym 1574

3   Pollock, 'Has The Common Law Received The Fiction Theory Of Corporations' (1911) 27 LQR 219; Maitland, *Introduction* to Gierke, *Political theories of the middle age* (1900) pp xxx-xxxi

4   Hart, 'Definition And Theory In Jurisprudence' (1954) 70 LQR 37; Dewey, 'The Historical Background To Corporate Legal Personality' (1926) 25 Yale LJ 655

5   A statement attributed to Lord Thurlow and cited in Glanville Williams, *Criminal Law; The General Part* (2nd ed. 1961) at page 856

6   per Green C. J. in *State* v. *Morris and Essex Railway Company* (1850) 23 NJL 360

7   Blackstone, *Commentaries,* Book 1 pp 475-476 gives a convenient summary of corporate powers in the 18th century

8   19 Hen. VII c. 7; an early example of monopoly control

9   *Rex* v. *City of London* (1682) 8 St. Tr. 1039 at page 1146

10   *Cory* v. *Matthews* (1701) 1 Salk. 191. The medieval conception of corporations as incapable of acting save by others (see *The Case of Sutton's Hospital* (1612), 10 Co. Rep. 23a and *Tipling* v. *Pexall* (1614), 2 Bulst. 233) led to occasional practical results as in the latter case where the issue was in what manner a special supplicavit could be addressed to a corporation.

11   Kyd, *A Treatise on the Law of Corporations* (1793), Introduction to Vol 1 p 13, and see *Trustees of Dartmouth College* v. *Woodward,* 4 Wheat. 518; 4 L. Ed. 629 (1819)

12   Blackstone, *Commentaries,* Book 1, pp 468, 475-476

13   Thus, for example, the principle of majority rule was early recognised.

See *Hascard* v. *Somany,* 1 Freem. KB 504 (1693); Kyd, *A Treatise on the Law of Corporations* (1793) vol 1, pp 308-309; Smith, *The Wealth Of Nations* (Modern Library Edition, 1937) p 699 gives a vivid, if partial, account of their government

14 *Green* v. *London General Omnibus Company* (1859) 7 CB (n.s.) 290

15 Lindley, 'On The Principles Which Govern The Criminal and Civil Liabilities of Corporations' (1857) 2 Juridical Society Papers 31

16 [1904] AC 423 at page 428

17 [1915] AC 705

18 [1915] AC 705 at page 715 per Lord Dunedin

19 *Gluckstein* v. *Barnes* [1900] AC 240 at page 257 per Lord Robertson

20 *Worth* v. *Brown* [1890] 40 Sol. J. 515

21 See the discussion in chapter 7

22 'Definition And Theory In Jurisprudence' (1954) 70 LQR 37

23 *Pharmaceutical Society* v. *London and Provincial Supply Association Limited* (1880) 5 App. Cas. 857. An illustration of limitations upon the technique is provided by *Unit Construction Company Ltd.* v. *Bullock* [1960] AC 351

24 (1875) LR 7 HL 653

25 See the discussion in chapter 5

26 (1886) 11 App. Cas 247

27 Note, 'Criminal Liability Of Corporations' (1914) 14 Col. L. Rev. 242, but as is there indicated, the adoption of such a view would have meant that any wrongful act would have been *ultra vires* the corporation and hence the corporation could never have been liable in either tort or crime. It is interesting that the only writer approving Lord Bramwell in *Abrath*'s case was Baty, *Vicarious liability* (1916). Brice, *Ultra vires* (3rd ed. 1893) dismissed Lord Bramwell's remarks in a footnote on page 435

28 *O. F. Nelson and Co. Ltd.* v. *Police* [1932] NZLR 367

29 [1904] AC 423

30 *Harker* v. *Britannic Assurance Co. Ltd.* [1928] 1 KB 766

31 See the discussion in chapter 4

32 Pollock, *The Law Of Tort* (7th ed. 1904) pp 58-59

33 Pollock, *A First Book of Jurisprudence* (1929) at page 126 arguing that a corporation could not commit crimes because it could not authorise their commission.

34 Maitland, *Introduction,* Gierke, *Political theories of the middle age* (1900) at page xxxix

35 Note, 'Criminal Liability Of Corporations' (1914) 14 Col. L. Rev. 242

36 Curiously this procedure still seems to be applicable in Victoria. See Gowans, Hon. Mr. Justice. 'Some Experiences in Criminal Trials in Relation to Company Offences' (1966) 39 ALJR 328

37 *Regina* v. *Birmingham and Gloucester Railway* (1842) 3 QB 223

38 *Certiorari* was the normal manner of applying to change the venue of trial. See Blackstone, *Commentaries,* Bk. 4, p 320

39 Blackstone, *Commentaries,* Bk. 4, p 318

40 Short & Mellor, *Crown Office Practice* (2nd ed. 1908) p 98. There, *Regina* v. *Birkenhead Street Railway,* July 22, 1862, unrep. is cited. The corporation not

appearing after a venire and distringas, Willes J. was prepared to issue distringas for £1000, rather than the £100 requested by the prosecution

41 Short & Mellor, *Crown Office Practice* (2nd ed. 1908) p 20

42 [1922] 2 KB 530

43 The Assizes and Quarter Sessions Act, 1908 section 1 (5) provided that notice had to be given to the proper officer of intention to present an indictment at least five days before the commission day or days appointed for holding Quarter Sessions

44 (1912) 76 JP 487

45 Administration of Justice (Miscellaneous Provisions) Act, 1933, and see *Rex* v. *H. Sherman Ltd.* [1949] 2 All ER 207

Chapter 3

The development of corporate criminal liability

Initially, liability was confined to prosecutions for nuisance. Later there arose a fairly wide liability in prosecutions for the recovery of a penalty for failure to abide by statutory provisions. Then came liability for what are now termed public welfare offences. In the meantime the courts had held that civilly, intent and malice could be inputed to the corporation. This strand of authority was to blend together with vicarious liability, and, perhaps under the guise of the theory of organic representation, to lead to corporate criminal liability. In all this, legislation relating to statutory interpretation was to play a permissive role. The impetus for this development is difficult to find. We can identify factors conducing to the imposition for liability in nuisance. Liability for public welfare offences arose because corporations were introduced into fields of business in respect of which regulatory legislation existed. Tortious liability rested upon an amalgam of factors among which scholars identify the notion that the master can usually pay while the servant cannot, that a master must conduct his business with due regard for the safety of others, that he profits from the servants employment, and that by employing the servant he has at least provided a *sine qua non* without the injury would not have occurred.[1] All these are largely irrelevant to the criminal law. Statements enunciated in the field of torts were however to become accepted as principles applicable to the field of criminal law, with but isolated protests.[2] It is accordingly difficult to explain what factors influenced the final result although the chain of reasoning employed seems tolerably clear. In this chapter the growth of corporate criminal liability to 1915 is examined, at which point the stage had fairly been set for the culmination of the process.

Early liability for nonfeasance

The lack of a *mens rea* personal to the corporation, its inability to perform a physical act, and its inability to appear in person, were no doubt sufficient to cause Holt C. J. to hold that a corporation could not be indicted, but that the particular members of it could be.[3] To this general statement, one exception had however even then to be made. An indictment lay against a corporation in respect of failure to perform a public duty resulting in a nuisance.[4] The history of group liability has been traced by Mr. Carr to the frankpledge.[5] The liability of corporations however derives its real impetus from liability for nonfeasance in cases of public nuisance. Corporations were indictable for non-performance of duties laid upon them by charter, prescription, or statute, when non-performance resulted in a public nuisance. Such a prosecution was seen not as in essence a criminal proceeding, but as a means of enforcing the performance of a public duty.[6] No *mens rea* was required and, as the gist of the offence lay in a failure to eradicate the nuisance, no question of ascribing an act to the corporation arose. That the real complaint was of inaction on the part of the corporation's officers and servants was not adverted to. Further, policy really required that the corporation be made amenable for the duty to repair lay upon the corporation, and not upon its individual members. As the object of the prosecution was not the punishment of the defendant but the removal of the nuisance it was not necessary that the defendant be in personal attendance at the time that judgment was pronounced. The penalty was a fine, a penalty which could be imposed upon the corporation although it was recognised that were the corporation insolvent, the remedy would be altogether ineffectual.[7]

Accordingly, group liability for nonfeasance may be found as early as the seventeenth century.[8] Most such cases dealt with counties or unincorporated boroughs, such bodies for long being treated in the same manner as corporations.[9] There seems little doubt however that where highways or bridges were situated within an incorporated town, the town was liable for non-repair.[10] Gradually liability was extended to the canal companies as well. Both these and municipal corporations were of a type upon which duties such as the repair of roads and bridges and and the clearing of navigable waterways were commonly imposed. In a number of eighteenth century cases, liability was either imposed or stated to be capable of imposition.[11] Similarly the text writers were of opinion that such an indictment would lie.[12] Chitty's *Practical Treatise* gives several precedents of indictments for failure to repair highways and bridges, one of which is an indictment against a canal company.[13]

In 1840, the practice of centuries was challenged. In *Regina* v. *Birmingham and Gloucester Railway* the corporation was indicted for disobeying an order of the Justices, confirmed at Quarter Sessions, directing it to remove a bridge which it had erected over a road.[14]

Parke B., on Assize indicating that the sole difficulty was one of appearance, directed that the matter be removed by *certiorari* to the Queen's Bench. Before the Queen's Bench counsel for the corporation relied strongly upon two points, first, that the corporation was not indictable, a proposition based on the case of *Suttons Hospital* and the *Anonymous* case before Holt C. J.[15] and, secondly, that a corporation if it were indictable, must have named individuals joined with it so that the fine, in any event, could be paid. The Crown was prepared to admit that an indictment for misfeasance would not lie, but contended that to deny liability for nonfeasance would be at variance with the practice of centuries.

The court overruled the demurrer. In the same year it had held that the mindless incorporeality of the corporation was no answer to an action for trespass committed by the corporation's servant.[16] The tendency of the decisions, it held, was to equate corporations with natural persons. The *Anonymous* case applied only to felony or to cases involving personal violence such as riots or assaults.

Liability for misfeasance

The growth of vicarious liability in tort proceeding on the fiction of an implied command made possible the imposition of liability for misfeasance in the case of public nuisance.[17] While at the end of the eighteenth century the text writers were of opinion that the growing body of law relating to vicarious liability had no application to corporations, this view failed to survive the appearance, in significant numbers, of railway, canal, and other bodies corporate.[18] In the late eighteenth and early nineteenth centuries, corporations were held vicariously liable in trover,[19] trespass,[20] and negligence.[21] The growing familiarity of the body corporate in the ordinary life of the community made it necessary to fit the corporation within some framework of liability. An impetus existed for the imposition of liability for misfeasance; vicarious liability provided the necessary device.

The point arose in *Regina* v. *Great North of England Railway Company*.[22] The company was indicted for cutting through and obstructing a highway with its railway line. It had failed to build a bridge over the highway in accordance with the statutory requirements. The Crown argued that the case was analogous to a mere trespass to land, that an indictment would lie in respect of it, and that 'The tendency of modern decisions has been to make corporations civilly as well as criminally, amenable like individuals'.[23] The court's attention was drawn to the application of vicarious liability to the corporation in tort. The corporation was convicted.[24] Lord Denman C. J. for the court drew attention to the difficulty of distinguishing in many cases between wrongful acts and omissions. It is, he held,[25]

as easy to charge one person or a body corporate with erecting a bar across a public road as with the non-repair of it; and they may as well be compelled to pay a fine for the act as for the omission.

Accepting that a corporation could not be guilty of treason, felony, offences against the person or perjury, he stated that the reason for excluding such liability was that these offences derived their character from the guilty mind of the offender and at any rate were violations of the social duty belonging to natural persons. A corporation, he states[26]:

. . .which, as such, has no such duties, cannot be guilty in these cases: but they may be guilty as a body corporate of commanding acts to be done to the nuisance of the community at large.

In the final analysis Lord Denman CJ put his judgment firmly on the basis of policy. He agreed that the individuals who voted the order or who executed the work could be prosecuted. This had in fact been done in *Rex* v. *Medley*.[27] The duty not to cause a nuisance was imposed on the corporation. One may at least surmise that, in punishing the corporation, Lord Denman CJ felt it necessary to make an example for the public benefit of a form of business organisation for which wide distrust was felt. Declining to impose liability solely upon the human actors involved, he stated[28]:

But the public knows nothing of the former [the directors] ; and the latter, if they can be identified, are commonly persons of the lowest rank, wholly incompetent to make reparation for the injury. There can be no effectual means for deterring from an oppressive exercise of power for the purpose of gain, except the remedy by an indictment against those who truly commit it, that is, the corporation acting by its majority: and there is no principle which places them beyond the reach of the law for such proceedings.

Corporate liability for misfeasance in cases of public nuisance was thus firmly established. No objections to ' . . . the invisibility of the body aggregate, the impossibility of arresting it, its inability to appear, its incapacity for punishment . . .'[29] had been taken until very late and these had not prevailed.

Lord Denman's statements serve to remind us that the corporation was still regarded with suspicion as a repository of both economic and political power. The eighteenth century economists had taught that the corporation was both an inefficient and irresponsible mode of business organisation and in so doing, had fostered an attitude of suspicion which lingered for many years.[30] In particular it had been urged by Adam Smith that not only were directors irresponsible, but that shareholders did little to govern the corporation's conduct.[31] This common assumption explains what Baty called a confusion of thought on the part of Lord Denman CJ.[32] It seems clear that Lord Denman in imposing liability upon the corporation sought to impose a check upon those in control of its management by imposing a responsibility upon its members. His judgment could be rationalised by pointing to the shareholders' power to elect careful directors. Such a statement is clearly akin to the rationale once advanced in order to explain a master's vicarious liability in tort; that the master was responsible for the actions of his servants because he had the selection of them.[33]

Another and cogent reason for imposing liability upon the corporation was supplied by an American court. An indictment for nuisance raised, in some cases, the question of destruction of corporate property. To mitigate the nuisance might involve the destruction of corporate property. It would obviously be unjust to order the destruction of the corporation's property in its absence. Were only the workmen involved impleaded this result might well have occurred.[34]

It is probable that, even in 1846, the assumption that shareholders could be forced to employ their undoubted powers in order to force management to abide by the law, upon which Lord Denman CJ proceeded was unworkable. It was early recognised that, in the case of large corporations, the shareholder could have no real voice in daily management; that the directors had to be entrusted with an ample measure of discretion, and that as a practical matter a change in the government of the corporation could only be effected in the case of gross mismanagement. The argument that shareholders could or would exercise a close supervision over the activities of management was essentially spurious.[35] This was to become more evident during the nineteenth century as corporate membership became ever more diffused.[36]

In the result, by 1850, a corporation could be indicted for public nuisance and for failure to perform a public duty laid on it by statute

but not for treason, felony, perjury, or offences against the person.[37]
The nineteenth century saw a steady expansion of liability within these
limits.

Legislative extensions of liability

Parliament was responsible for the next practical extension of liability;
the subjecting of corporations to penalties under various of the clauses
acts for failure to abide by their terms. In addition to these however,
there is a statute of 1827 which apparently was intended to have an even
wider effect. Section 14 of the Act, which dealt with the administration
of justice in criminal cases, provided in part that in such cases the word
'person' should include 'corporation'.[38] Seemingly, this statute could be
read as rendering corporations *prima facie* liable for most statutory
offences. That this was the intention of Parliament seems improbable.
It was suggested by counsel in *Mutual Loan Agency* v. *Attorney-General
of New South Wales* that Parliament intended corporations to be made
generally liable for all indictable offences punishable on summary
conviction. [39] No cases have been found to support this contention.
That a corporation was generally considered to be a person within the
meaning of statutes was a generally accepted principle at common law.[40]
This interpretation provision merely confirmed the rule. It did not for
example enable a corporation to sue as a common informer; an action
which would, Lord Coleridge CJ stated, be against its nature.[41]
Grant whose work on corporations remains the most detailed source of
information on early corporation law mentions no extension of corporate
liability as attributable to this statute. On the whole it seems likely that
no more was intended than to confirm the common law rule. It is
probable that the principal reason for including corporations within the
definition section was to bring corporate property within the protective
ambit of the criminal law. While no definite information has been found
upon the point it is noteworthy that for some time provisions penalising
forgery did not extend to cases wherein the offence was committed with
intent to defraud a corporation.[42] Furthermore, there are cases in which
the issue was whether the corporation was entitled to the benefit of
certain statutory provisions.[43] It seems reasonable to assume that the
main purport of the section in its application to corporations was to
establish that they were persons against whose property offences could be
committed.

Liability under the clauses acts

Corporate liability was however provided for under a number of

statutes dealing primarily with the regulation of certain undertakings
carried on by bodies corporate. These acts regulated the activities of
corporations carrying out public utility functions. The first half of the
nineteenth century saw the growth of canal, railway, and municipal
undertaking corporations, in significant numbers. Initially governed by
individual private acts, uniform control was eventually secured by the
passing of public general acts imposing a common legislative pattern.
Examples are the Gasworks Clauses Act, 1847, the Town Improvement
Clauses Act, 1847, the Waterworks Clauses Act, 1847, the Harbours,
Docks and Piers Clauses Act, 1847, the Cemeteries Clauses Act, 1847,
and the well known Railway Clauses Consolidation Act, 1845.

A primary object of the legislation was to ensure that the activities
with which they dealt should be carried on with as little inconvenience
to the public as possible. The method of control adopted was to penalise
non-compliance with the statutory provisions by a penalty, either
recoverable by action[44] or imposed by the Justices.[45] In general the
matters dealt with were such as fell broadly within the rubric of
nuisance.[46] In addition to the provision of specific penalties a saving
clause continuing the liability of undertakers to indictments for nuisance
was a common feature.[47] The acts sought to provide a code governing the
rights and liabilities of undertakers engaged in public utility ventures.
Their importance lies not so much in extending the theoretical boundaries
of corporate criminal liability as in subjecting certain areas of business
activity to a detailed scheme of administrative control. One effect of
them however, was to render the indictment for nuisance a much less
frequently sought remedy in practice. Furthermore, the intervention of
equity in granting injunctions to restrain public nuisance completed the
process,[48] for by it, the offending party could be ordered to abate. It
thus gave the plaintiff a more ample and speedier remedy.

Liability under public welfare legislation generally

The latter half of the nineteenth century saw further incursions by the
legislature into the general regulation of business activities, in the public
interest.[49] To most of these statutes, corporations were subject. As
corporate activities burgeoned into most fields of enterprise, corporations
naturally became subject to statutes regulating their conduct. Whereas,
before the Companies Acts of 1855 and 1862 corporate activities were
broadly speaking, confined to banking, insurance, railways, municipal
undertakings, mining, and manufacturing, thereafter corporate enterprise
invaded most other fields as well.[50] By 1893, Mr. W. S. Gilbert could

suggest that England was in a fair way to being governed upon the joint stock principle.[51] Furthermore the decision in *Salomon* v. *Salomon and Co. Ltd.* by demonstrating that incorporation could be attained with but one true beneficial owner, and its legislative aftermath the Companies Act, 1907, made commonplace the appearance of corporations formed to carry on businesses which formerly had been regarded as the exclusive preserve of the sole proprietorship or the partnership.[53]

The result was an increasing spate of convictions against corporations for violations of regulatory legislation, as, in increasing numbers, corporations became subject to their terms. For the most part cast or interpreted as offences of strict liability their applicability to corporations was taken for granted. Decisions began to appear in which the accused was a body corporate; yet most turned upon miscellaneous points of construction. Accordingly, in addition to the existing liability to indictment for nuisance,[54] and to summary conviction for the contravention of statutory provisions relating to nuisance,[55] corporations were held liable for offences under the Factories Acts,[56] the Sale of Food and Drugs Acts,[57] the Public Health Acts,[58] the Coal Mines Regulation Acts,[59] and the Merchandise Marks Act.[60] With one exception, corporate liability for public welfare offences was attained without serious argument. That exception concerned offences involving *mens rea* in respect of which it was desired to hold corporations vicariously liable as master.

The foundation of a more extended liability: liability for torts involving malice

The extension of vicarious liability to a corporation where the offence involved required *mens rea* developed from a line of decisions holding that a corporation could be held to be vicariously liable in respect of torts, committed by corporate servants, involving malice. While the battle swirled for some time, it was gradually established that corporations could be held liable for all torts whether or not malice was a necessary ingredient. Corporate liability for malicious prosecution was established in 1900,[61] for libel in 1904,[62] and for slander in 1911.[63] Liability rested, it was said, upon the ordinary principles of the law of master and servant. As has been noted, the objections raised in particular by Lord Bramwell in *Abrath* v. *North Eastern Railway* were simply ignored.[64]

The effect of the interpretation act, 1889

Another factor conducing to a more widespread rule of liability was the definition of 'person' contained in the Interpretation Act, 1889. Section 2(1) provided:

In the construction of every enactment relating to an offence
punishable on indictment or on summary conviction, whether contained
in an Act passed before or after the commencement of this act, the
expression 'person' shall, unless the contrary intention appears, include
a body corporate.

It is probable that this section sought to introduce no wider rule of
liability than was formerly the case. It did no more than replace the
interpretation section in the 1827 Act dealing with the administration of
criminal justice.[65] Nonetheless its appearance in a general interpretation
statute made it more readily accessible. It is likely that Parliament
contemplated that except for summary conviction offences and indictable
offences punishable on summary conviction, a 'contrary intention' would
appear. This conclusion is based upon two considerations. The first is
that no writer of authority writing at the time when the Interpretation
Act was passed contemplated that the effect of the section would be to
extend liability for all, or even most statutory offences, to corporations.[66]
Nor was such a possibility contemplated by the judges.[67] A similar
inference arises from statutes under which corporations were made
liable in respect of indictable offences punishable on summary conviction.
One such statute, the Explosives Substances Act, clearly contained
provisions directed at occupiers of premises used for storing or making
explosives and the Act itself recognised that such occupiers might be
corporations.[68] Similarly, the Sale of Food and Drugs Act, 1875
provided that offences might be prosecuted either on indictment or on
summary conviction. It seems unlikely that Parliament had offences other
than these in mind.[69]

Liability for public welfare officers involving intent

A combination of these two strands: of vicarious liability in tort and of
the rule of statutory interpretation, combined to extend liability for
offences involving *mens rea* in respect of which employers were vicariously
criminally liable, to corporations. In *Pearks, Gunston and Tee Limited* v.
Ward[70] the Corporation was charged with the strict liability offence of
selling adulterated milk. The argument against liability was founded on
sections of the relevant Act conferring a defence where the adulteration
was non-fraudulent. While the Court was prepared to concede that some
difficulty could arise in the latter area, it nonetheless held the corporation
liable.[71] In *Chuter* v. *Freeth and Pocock Limited*[72] the Court went
further, holding a corporation liable under the Sale of Food and Drugs
Act for giving a false warranty. In the case of a vicarious liability offence,

the corporation could give a warranty through its agents and through them believe or not believe that the statements contained in it were true.

The ambit of liability by 1915

It is thus clear that by 1915 corporations were held liable for nuisance, whether at common law or under statute, for failure to perform statutory duties, for minor offences of strict liability, and for offences to which vicarious liability was recognised as applying, whether or not *mens rea* was required for their commission. Liability did not however, extend to offences, regarded as truly criminal in character, of which it was said that *mens rea* was a necessary ingredient.[73] Before such an extension could take place, it was necessary to hold in some fashion that a corporation could be taken to act personally rather than by procuration. Until that could be done and a company could truly be said to have a mind, it could not be made generally amenable to the criminal law. Furthermore, at this period no procedural reform had been undertaken; a corporation still could not be committed for trial, and if the penalty were corporal could not be made to suffer it.[74] Whereas in other jurisdictions a mind had been imputed to the corporation for criminal purposes[75] and procedure had been reformed to provide a specific mode of proceeding against corporations[76] resulting in fairly widespread corporate criminal liability, in England corporate criminal liability remained in a state of infancy.

1   A very full discussion is James, 'Vicarious Liability' (1954) 28 Tulane L. Rev. 161
2   See Glanville Williams, *Criminal Law; The General Part* (2nd ed. 1961) p 862
'For all that appears, the legal development has been motivated by little more than a crude personification of the group'
3   *Anonymous Case* (1701) 12 Mod. 559
4   *Regina* v. *Saintiff* (1705) 6 Mod. 255
5   Carr, *Law Of Corporations* (1902) pp 85 ff
6   Chitty, *A Practical Treatise On The Criminal Law*, vol 3 (1816) p 574; *Regina* v. *Stephens* (1865) LR 1 QB 702, 709
7   *The King* v. *Severn & Wye Railway Co.* (1819) 2 B. & Ald. 645
8   Lambarde, *Eirenarcha, or of the office of the Justices of the Peace* (1619) pp 477 and 609
9   In 1788, In *Russell* v. *Men of Devon* (1788) 2 TR 667, Lord Kenyon CJ held that only a corporation could be sued in its aggregate name, although he noted that indictments had successfully been brought against the inhabitants of a place collectively
10   *Rex* v. *Inhabitants of Dorset,* KB Easter Term, 1825, noted 77 ER 1442
11   *Mayor of Lynn* v. *Turner* (1774) 1 Cowp. 86; *The King* v. *Mayor and*

Corporation of Liverpool (1802) 3 East 86; *The King* v. *Corporation of Stratford upon Avon* (1811) 14 East 348; *The King* v. *Severn & Wye Railway Company* (1819) 2 B. & Ald. 645; *Mayor and Burgesses of Lyme Regis* v. *Henley* (1834) 1 Bing. NC 222

12 Kyd, *The Law Of Corporations* (1793) vol 1, pp 225-226

13 Chitty, *A Practical Treatise On The Criminal Law* (1816) vol 3, pp 600-601 contains a precedent for such an indictment

14 (1842) 3 QB 223; and on Assize (1840) 9 C. & P. 469

15 *The Case of Suttons Hospital* (1612) 10 Co. Rep. 23a; *Anonymous Case* (1701) 12 Mod. 559

16 *Yarborough* v. *Bank of England* (1812) 16 East 6

17 The early history of vicarious liability is traced in Holdsworth, *History of English Law* (1925) vol 8, pp 472-79; Wigmore, 'Responsibility For Tortious Acts; Its History", in *Select Essays In Anglo-American Legal History* (1909) vol 3, p 474, 527 *seq*

18 Fifoot, *Judge And Jurist In The Reign Of Victoria* (1959) draws attention to the effect that the appearance of bodies corporate had on the development of vicarious liability in tort

19 *Yarborough* v. *Bank of England* (1812) 16 East 6; *Smith* v. *Birmingham and Staffordshire Gas Light Company* (1834) 1 A. & E. 526, in which the early case of *Cory* v. *Matthews* (1701) 1 Salk. 191 is cited with approval

20 *Maund* v. *Monmouthshire Canal Company* (1842) 4 M. & G. 452

21 *Matthews* v. *West London Water Works Company* (1813) 3 Campb. 403

22 (1846) 9 QB 315

23 (1846) 9 QB 315 at page 319

24 The trial at Durham Assizes appears to have been at *Nisi Prius*

25 (1846) 9 QB 315 at page 326

26 (1846) 9 QB 315 at page 326

27 (1834) 6 C. & P. 292

28 (1846) 9 QB 315 at page 327

29 per Green, C. J. in *The State* v. *Morris and Essex Railroad Company,* 23 NJL 360 (1850)

30 Hunt, *The Development Of The Business Corporation In England, 1800-1867* (1936) pp 153-157 notes that even in the 1860's freedom of incorporation was viewed askance by many persons

31 Smith, *The Wealth Of Nations* (Modern Library edition, 1937) pp 699-700

32 Baty, *Vicarious Liability* (1916) p 67

33 James, 'Vicarious liability' (1954) 28 Tulane L. Rev. 161 at pages 165-169

34 *The State* v. *Morris and Essex Railway,* 23 NJL 360 (1850) *Commonwealth* v. *Pulaski County Agricultural and Mechanical Association* 17 SW 442 (Ky.) (1891)

35 Spencer, 'Railway Morals and Railway Policy', Edinburgh Review, vol C, pp 420-21, cited by Hunt, *The Development Of The Business Corporation In England, 1800-1867* (1936) who at page 135 considers that the picture of a corporation as a representative democracy is only accurate as applied to the affairs of a small corporation which is, in effect, an incorporated partnership

36 See Jeffray, 'The Denomination And Character Of Shares' in: Carus-Wilson, ed. *Essays In Economic History* (1954) vol 1, p 344

B

37 *Regina* v. *Great North of England Railway Company* (1846) 9 QB 315; *King of the Two Sicilies* v. *Willcox* (1851) 1 Sim. NS 301; Grant, *Law Of Corporations* (1850) p 284

38 An Act for further improving the administration of justice in criminal cases in England, 7 & 8 Geo.IV c.28

39 (1909) 9 CLR 72 at page 79 per Cullen KC *arguendo*, for the corporation

40 *Cortis* v. *The Kent Waterworks Co.* (1827) 7 B. & C. 314

41 *St. Leonard's Shoreditch Guardians* v. *Franklin* (1878) 3 CPD 377, in which it was said that a corporation could not take the affidavit required to sue as a common informer

42 Grant, *The Law Of Corporations* (1850) p 66 n.2

43 See *Mayor & etc. of Hereford* v. *Morton* (1866) 31 JP 56 in which the question arose whether the corporation could claim the benefit of an act penalising persons who should break gas lamps; *Boyd* v. *Croydon Railway Company* (1838) 4 Bing. NC 669 in which the issue arose whether, in an action brought against a corporation under a private act, the corporation was a person and so entitled to the benefit of a section providing that any person against whom an action was brought was entitled to 20 days prior notice that action was intended

44 Railway Clauses Consolidation Act, 1845 section 54 by which the corporation was to forfeit £20 for every day during which, it having interfered with an existing road, it had failed to substitute another road, such penalty to be recovered by action in any of the superior courts

45 Railway Clauses Consolidation Act, 1845, sections 57, 58, 59, 64, 65, and 114; Waterworks Clauses Act, 1847 sections 45, 61, 62, 64, and 95; Cemeteries Clauses Act, 1847, section 20; Harbours, Docks and Piers Clauses Act, 1847 sections 15, 39 and 92

46 Thus the Railway Clauses Consolidation Act, 1845 imposed penalties for; failure to repair and restore roads, to make sufficient approaches to Bridleways and Footways, for failure to screen turnpike roads, for failure to repair bridges and fences, and for using engines not so constructed to consume their own smoke. The Waterworks Clauses Act, 1847, penalised the permitting of substances used in the making of gas to flow into the works, the Cemeteries Clauses Acts, 1847 penalised proprietors for permitting offensive matter from the cemetery to flow into streams, the Harbours, Docks and Piers Clauses Act, 1847 penalised undertakers who neglected to repair watchouses

47 e.g. Gasworks Clauses Act, 1847 sec.29; Wordsworth, *Railways, Canal, Water, Dock, Gas and other companies* (1851)

48 It was originally held that Courts of Equity could not grant an injunction to restrain the commission of a nuisance because the matter was cognizable at law, *Semple* v. *London and Birmingham Railway Co.* (1838) 1 Ry. & Can. Cas. 480. In *A.G.* v. *United Kingdom Electric Telegraph Co.* (1861) 30 Beav. 287 it was held that equity could intervene in the first instance where the information was brought by the Attorney-General to restrain a public nuisance

49 See Dicey, *Law And Opinion In England* (1905) pp 259-302 for a general account of the rise of welfare legislation

50 Hunt, *The Development Of The Business Corporation In England* (1936) pp 145-159

51 Gilbert, *Utopia Ltd.* cited by Hunt, *The Development Of The Business Corporation In England* (1936) p 159
52 [1897] AC 22
53 Cohen of Walmer (Lord) *One Hundred Years Of Limited Liability Companies In England* (1957) p 12
54 *Regina* v. *Birmingham and Gloucester Railway* (1846) 9 QB 315
55 *Patterson* v. *Chamber Colliery Co.* (1892) 56 JP 200; *Armitage Ltd.* v. *Nicholson* (1913) 108 LT 993; *Star Omnibus Co. (London) Ltd,* v. *Tagg* (1907) 97 LT 481; *Herbert* v. *Leigh Mills Company Limited* (1889) 53 JP 679
56 *Pearson* v. *Belgian Mills Co.* [1896] 1 QB 244; *Crabtree* v. *Commercial Mills Spinning Co. Ltd.* (1911) 75 JP 6; *Crabtree* v. *Fern Spinning Company Limited* (1901) 85 LT 549
57 *Starey* v. *Chilworth Gunpowder Company* (1890) 24 QBD 90; *Pearks, Gunston & Tee Ltd.* v. *Ward* [1902] 2 KB 1; *Star Tea Company Limited* v. *Neale* (1909) 73 JP 511
58 *Regina* v. *Ascanio Puck & Co.* (1912) 76 JP 487
59 Remarks of Fletcher Moulton LJ in *David* v. *Britannic Merthyr Coal Company* [1909] 2 KB 146, aff'd [1910] AC 74, *sub. nom. Britannic Merthyr Coal Company* v. *David*
60 *Starey* v. *Chilworth Gunpowder Co.* (1890) 24 QBD 90
61 *Cornford* v. *Carlton Bank* [1900] 1 QB 22
62 *Citizens Life Assurance Company Limited* v. *Brown* [1904] AC 423
63 *The Corporation of Glasgow* v. *Lorimer* [1911] AC 209
64 (1886) 11 App. Cas. 247
65 The Interpretation Act, 1889 repealed section 14 of the earlier act
66 Stephen, *Digest Of The Criminal Law,* does not mention corporate liability in either the 1st ed. (1877) or the 6th ed. (1904). *Russell on Crimes* (7th ed. 1909) deals with the *Interpretation Act,* and states 'It would seem that the common law rule affords a good guide as to the intention of a statute. At common law, corporations are indictable for nuisance and breach of public duty . . . .' Harris, *Criminal law* (5th ed. 1889) and 6th ed. 1892 simply repeats the common law rule, in the same language as that used in the 1st ed. 1877. Kenny, *Outlines Of Criminal Law,* (1902) points out that despite the *Interpretation Act,* corporations cannot be indicted for major crimes because they cannot be made to suffer a corporal punishment. The limit to corporate criminal liability was, in his view, a limitation to those offences for which the punishment provided was a fine. But Kenny, though he seems to admit of an ampler liability than other writers, regarded the Interpretation Act merely as a restatement of the common law rule
67 Before 1889 it was recognised that in construing statutes the word 'person' included 'corporation' unless a contrary intention appeared. In *Pharmaceutical Society* v. *London and Provincial Supply Association* (1880) 5 App. Cas. 857, Lord Blackburn stated that he did not regard the presumption as a strong one. Other judgments illustrative of contemporary attitudes are *South Hetton Coal Company* v. *North-Eastern News Association,* [1894] 1 QB 133 at p 141; *MacNee* v. *Persian Investment Corporation,* (1890) 44 Ch. D. 306; *Mayor of Manchester* v. *Williams,* [1891] 1 QB 94; *Metropolitan Bank* v. *Pooley,* (1885) 10 App. Cas. 210, and above all, *Rex* v. *Grubb,* [1915] 2 KB 683 where it was

assumed that a corporation could not commit larceny

68 Explosives Act, 1875 section 91, and note that the expression 'occupier' is defined by section 108 to include a body corporate. Similarly, 'canal company' and 'railway company' are defined in like manner. By section 92, where a person is accused before a court of summary jurisdiction of an offence, the penalty for which exceeds £100, the accused may object to being tried before a court of summary jurisdiction, and the court must then proceed as though the offence were triable on indictment. The Sale of Food and Drugs Act, 1875 section 28 contains a saving power permitting proceedings by indictment against offenders. Furthermore, by the Summary Jurisdiction Act, 1879 section 17(2), where the possible penalty exceeded three months inprisonment, the accused could elect to be tried by indictment. This was done in *Rex* v. *Ascanio Puck & Co. Ltd.* (1912) 76 JP 487, in respect of an offence under the Public Health (London) Act, 1891. The procedure was not shown to be impossible until *Rex* v. *Daily Mirror Newspapers* [1922] 2 KB 530. Indeed, Rowlatt J. did not accede to an argument that a corporation could not elect to be tried on indictment

69 No discussion of the section appears in the Parliamentary Debates which supports the inference that the section was not intended to enlarge the then existing boundaries of corporate criminal liability. It is submitted that the construction placed upon the section by Kenny, and in *Russell on Crimes* was correct

70 [1902] 2 KB 1

71 [1902] 2 KB 1 at page 11 per Channell J.

72 [1911] 2 KB 832

73 *Regina* v. *Bradlaugh* (1885) 14 QBD 667

74 *Rex* v. *Grubb* [1915] 2 KB 683

75 American courts had taken the first steps in this direction. See *United States* v. *MacAndrews & Forbes Company,* 149 Fed. 823 (1906); Canfield, 'Corporate Responsibility for Crime' 14 Col. L. Rev. 469 (1914). The Canadian Supreme Court, in *Union Colliery Company Limited* v. *The Queen* (1900) 31 Can. SCR 81, left open the question whether or not ' . . . under the present state of the law and its constantly broadening and widening jurisprudence on the subject of the civil and criminal liability of bodies corporate, they are capable of committing the offence.' In 1905, the Ontario Court of Appeal in *Rex* v. *Master Plumbers and Steam Fitters Co-Operative Association Limited et al.* (1905) 14 OLR 295 held that a corporation could be convicted of conspiracy in restraint of trade under section 520 of the Criminal Code, 1892. The general amenability of corporations to the Criminal Code was not however, established beyond doubt until *Rex* v. *Fane Robinson Ltd.* [1941] 3 DLR 409

76 e.g. Canada, where procedure was first reformed in 1886. The history of procedural reform is considered in Lagarde, 'Assignation Et Procès Des Corporations En Matière Pénale' (1964) 24 La Revue du Barreau, 61

Chapter 4

The attainment of corporate criminal liability

It was to be nearly thirty years before corporate liability was extended beyond offences of strict and vicarious liability. By 1945 the law developed in such a manner as to define clearly the position of the board of directors as a governing organ of the corporation and so to furnish a justification and a rationale for the imposition of corporate criminal liability. It will be convenient, before examining this development, to examine the manner in which corporate criminal liability came to be accepted as a general principle of English criminal law. It is therefore proposed to examine the line of decisions which established liability. In a subsequent chapter the theoretical basis upon which liability purportedly rests will be discussed.

The foundations of liability: the effect of Mousell's case

The key to the development of corporate criminal liability is the decision in *Mousell Brothers Limited* v. *London and North-Western Railway Co.*[1] Mousell Brothers Limited were charged with fraudulently avoiding the payment of freight charges contrary to the Railway Clauses Consolidation Act, 1845. The fraud had been perpetrated by the company's branch manager and a clerk at the Manchester office. The prosecution pressed for conviction urging not that the corporation was vicariously liable for the acts of its officers, agents and servants, but that it could only act through its officers and was personally liable for their actions. The Interpretation Act, 1889 was relied on to show that it was intended by Parliament that corporations should, in general, be criminally liable. The Divisional Court convicted the corporation holding it to be vicariously liable for the acts of its branch manager, and in the course of so doing, delivered the classic judgment indicating in what circumstances a master would be subject to vicarious liability. It did not hold the corporation personally liable, because, as Lord Reading CJ explained, it was not suggested that the directors were privy to the fraud.[2]

It is often urged that *Mousell*'s case is a milestone on the path to corporate criminal liability.[3] So indeed it was, but in a sense more significant than that which is attributed to it. An appreciation of this however, depends upon a close examination of the test of vicarious liability propounded in it and an analysis of the later decisions. The test, propounded by Atkin LJ, is in the following terms[4]:

> ... while *prima facie* a principal is not to be made criminally responsible for the acts of his servants, yet the Legislature may prohibit an act or enforce a duty in such terms as to make the prohibition or the duty absolute; in which case the principal is liable if the act is in fact done by his servants. To ascertain whether a particular Act of Parliament has that effect or not regard must be had to the object of the statute, the words used, the nature of the duty laid down, the person upon whom it is imposed, the person by whom in ordinary circumstances it would be performed, and the person upon whom the penalty is imposed.

The significance here lies in the delegation aspect of the test; the inquiry towards the nature of the duty and the person by whom it would normally be performed. This as will be seen was the prime consideration adopted by the Courts in dealing with corporate criminal liability.

For a time however it appeared that corporations would not be made criminally liable. Notwithstanding the procedural reforms contained in the Criminal Justice Act 1925, an indictment for manslaughter in *Rex* v. *Cory Brothers Limited* was quashed in 1927, the court characterizing the statutory provisions as mere machinery.[5] Winn castigated this decision as contrary to the tenor of the Criminal Justice Act.[6] It is submitted that this view was mistaken.[7]

The trend towards full liability

In 1939, a significant change in judicial opinion occurred. In *Triplex Safety Glass Company* v. *Lancegay Safety Glass (1934) Limited*[8] Du Parcq LJ, following Canadian authority,[9] upheld a claim of privilege by the defendant to a libel action. This decision involved a finding that a corporation could be convicted of criminal libel, and therefore could rely upon the privilege against self-incrimination. It has been argued that this decision is of little moment because a corporation could always have been convicted of criminal libel, that being one of the exceptional cases in which vicarious criminal liability was imposed.[10] This argument, however, fails to give the judgment its due emphasis for whatever view the Court of Appeal might have taken, it seems clear that its decision related to personal liability.[11] In one sense, this decision is of limited importance; there was no attempt to extend the bounds of liability.

Lord Blackburn had, many years before, indicated that corporations might be punished for libel.[12] The primary interest of the judgment lies in its acceptance that those elements which might suffice to found civil liability could equally suffice to found criminal liability.[13]

Advances occurring as a result of war regulations

Marked advances in this field occurred during the Second World War, probably as the result of fairly widespread violations of wartime regulations.[14] A line of little known decisions began to establish the general amenability of corporations to the criminal law.[15]

These cases seem to have had little direct effect. Occurring in wartime, little care was lavished upon them. They are not cited in later decisions. It is difficult to say whether they represent a wide application of vicarious liability or the application of some notion of personal liability. They may well however have contributed to an atmosphere in which the idea of widespread corporate liability for crimes involving a mental element was gaining acceptance. No more affirmative statement than this is warranted.

It was in fact in 1944 that corporate criminal liability became firmly established in English criminal law. It is instructive to examine the three decisions responsible for this development. It is interesting to note how much these cases depend upon earlier authority relating to vicarious liability for offences involving intent.

The attainment of full liability: the 1944 cases

The first of these cases was *D.P.P.* v. *Kent and Sussex Contractors.*[16] This case involved two charges. The first was that the company with intent to deceive, made use for the purposes of the Motor Fuel Rationing (No 3) Order, 1941, of a fortnightly vehicle record in respect of a specified vehicle, which was false in a material particular in that it mis-stated the journeys and mileage done by the vehicle over a specified period. The second charge was that the company, in furnishing the form, made a statement which was false in a material particular contrary to Regulation 82 of the Defence (General) Regulations, 1939. The document which was forwarded from the company was signed by its transport manager.

The justices found that the offence included a mental element, that a corporation could not entertain a criminal intent, and that therefore the company could not be made criminally liable for the offence. The prosecution appealed.

The Divisional Court directed the magistrates to convict the company. Viscount Caldecote CJ, who delivered the leading judgment treated as clear law the proposition that a corporation can possess guilty knowledge and can form an intention to perform a criminal act. Apart from certain established exceptions, such as treason, and offences in respect of which the only penalty is capital or corporal, ' . . . there are a number of criminal offences of which a company can be convicted'.[17] Vicarious liability was said to be ' . . . beside the real point which we have to decide, which is, I repeat, whether a company is capable of an act of will or of a state of mind, so as to be able to form an intention to deceive or to have knowledge of the truth or falsity of a statement'.[18] In finding that the intention of a corporation's officers can be imputed to the company as its intention, he states that ' . . . although the directors or general manager of a company are its agents, they are something more. A company is incapable of acting or speaking or even of thinking except insofar as its officers have acted, spoken or thought'.[19]

Clear though the decision seems to be, it nonetheless left several questions unresolved. To begin with it is by no means clear that the court intended to lay down any rule respecting criminal liability generally; it may in fact have been thinking primarily of 'quasi-criminal' or summary offences. In support of this interpretation the repeated statement in the judgment of Lord Caldecote CJ that as the mental elements of the offences were set out in the applicable statutory instruments, no question of *mens rea* arose, may be cited.[20] This was implicitly to construe *mens rea* as requiring moral wickedness. Secondly, one may point to the citation of cases dealing with vicarious liability for summary offences involving intent as fairly applicable to the case; a feature of all the judgments.[21]

Mousell's case is distinguished as referring to vicarious liability.[22] More interesting is the use to which *Mousell*'s case was put by Hallett J. The following extract illustrates its influence on this area of the law. Hallett J states[23]:

By s. 98 [of the Railway Clauses Consolidation Act] every person being the owner of goods passing on the railway, must give to the collector an exact account of certain particulars. That seems to me to correspond to the requirement of the Motor Fuel Rationing Order that every person desiring to obtain coupons must give the information required by the Board of Trade. By s. 99 if any such owner gives a false account with intent to avoid payment he is liable to a penalty.

Similarly, in the present case, if any person gives false information for
the purposes of the Motor Fuel Rationing Order, with intent to deceive,
he is liable to a penalty.

He then cites Lord Atkin's remark that in *Mousell*'s case the intent of
the servant was sufficient to found liability because the servant there
was the person who had to deal with the particular matter. 'Those words',
states Hallett J 'seem to me eminently applicable to the present case'.[24]
MacNaghten J places the case on the same footing.[25]

It is not surprising that one writer felt that this and following decisions
related primarily to revenue legislation.[26] The most interesting feature
however, lies in the use to which *Mousell*'s case was put and not least to
the manner in which it was misunderstood. That case clearly related to
the vicarious criminal liability of corporate masters as well as to natural
persons. It admitted a clearer line between the personal and the vicarious
liability of corporations than Lord Caldecote contemplated.[27]
Furthermore it impliedly denied that delegation was the critical feature
of corporate personal liability. The fact that the responsible officer was,
in *D.P.P.* v. *Kent and Sussex Contractors*, the transport manager within
whose (delegated) sphere compliance with the relevant Statutory Orders
fell was clearly a deciding factor. The decision is hardly an authority
favouring a clear distinction between personal liability and vicarious
liability. It virtually denies that such a distinction can validly be drawn.

On balance it seems likely that the court failed to appreciate the
extent to which it was altering the generally accepted position; that
corporations could not be made liable for crimes involving criminal intent.

The question was treated more perceptively in the next case, *Rex*
v. *I.C.R. Haulage Ltd.*[28] The appellant company was charged at Assizes
with a common law conspiracy to defraud. A preliminary objection was
taken that an indictment alleging a common law conspiracy to defraud
would not lie against a company. The submission was not accepted and
the company was duly convicted and fined. The Court of Criminal
Appeal was called on to deal only with the question whether, in law,
a corporation could be held guilty of a common law conspiracy;
whether, in other words, the indictment was bad on its face. The court
held that the indictment was good. Although at least one case dealing
with quasi-criminal offences was relied upon, the decision is clear.
Mousell's case was treated as beside the point. It was correctly said to
deal with the vicarious liability of corporations. Stable J., further said,
again correctly, that[29]:

It did not decide that in no circumstances a criminal intention in the mind of a servant or agent can be imputed to a principal who is a limited company.

Much reliance was put on the *Triplex* case[30] and upon *D.P.P.* v. *Kent and Sussex Contractors Ltd.*[31] as establishing that a limited company can entertain a criminal intent.

In the result the case clearly establishes two propositions. The first is that a distinction exists between personal and vicarious liability as respects corporations. The second is that in the appropriate circumstances, the state of mind and the actions of an agent may be the state of mind and acts of the company. It is clearly impossible to go beyond this. It cannot be said that an underlying doctrine such as the notion of organic representation appears. Whether there is evidence that the state of mind and actions of a corporate agent are to be imputed to the corporation[32]:

. . . must depend on the nature of the charge, the relative position of the officer or agent, and the other relevant facts and circumstances of the case.

In this case the human agent was the managing director, probably the most important figure in the managerial hierarchy of the limited company and one in respect of whose position and functions neither the concepts of agency nor trusteeship gives an adequate explanation.[33]

Limitations to liability are further dealt with. The potential ambit of liability indicated by Stable J is unquestionably wide. Manslaughter, it was said, may now be a crime in respect of which a corporation can be convicted.[34] Such limitations as exist are said to be those arising from the nature of the entity such as perjury, ' . . . an offence which cannot be vicariously committed . . . '[35] and bigamy which can only be committed by a natural person. To the extent that this judgment conceives of corporate liability as a species of vicarious liability, it must conceive the distinction between the two to rest upon a distinction in the status of various classes of corporate agents, based probably upon the extent to which their action represent an attribution of corporate powers.[36]

The third of this celebrated triumvirate of cases is *Moore* v. *I. Bresler Ltd.*[37] The company, its secretary, and the manager of its Nottingham branch, were charged under the Finance (2) Act, 1940 that they did, with intent to deceive, publish a document which was false in a material particular. Unlike the preceding cases, the acts were done by the company's officers with intent to defraud the company. Certain sales had been made in fraud of the company and the forms submitted by the company's officers, purportedly on its behalf under the Act, were false. Their intention was to defraud the company and conceal the fraud by deceiving the revenue. On this basis, Quarter Sessions discharged the company holding that the sales in respect of which returns were made were not made by the officers of the company as its agent or with its authority.

The Divisional Court held that the company must be convicted. Although the sales were fraudulent and the returns made as a means of concealing the fraud, the secretary and manager were, it was held, acting within the scope of their authority in making the sales. In making the returns required under the Finance Act they were clearly acting as officers of the company. Both Lord Caldecote CJ and Humphreys J stressed the agency element; that the officers were acting within the scope of their authority as agents of the company. Furthermore they were the proper officers to make those returns. It was held that their actions in doing so were the actions of the company. Humphreys J indeed stated that[38]:

It is difficult to imagine two persons whose acts would more effectually bind the company or who could be said on the terms of their employment to be more obviously agents for the purposes of the company than the secretary and general manager of that branch and the sales manager of that branch.

The company, he stated, could only act through agents. In law the sales were made and returns forwarded within the company's authority. On the principles of vicarious liability, of the liability of master for the acts of his servant committed within the scope of the servants employment, the conviction was justified. That Humphreys J in fact spoke the language of vicarious liability seems clear. Birkett J, agreeing, relied on *D.P.P.* v. *Kent and Sussex Contractors* a decision which, it has been argued, is permeated with concepts of vicarious responsibility.

The result of the 1944 cases and later authority

The result of these cases has been not clarity, but confusion. The basis for the now established concept of corporate criminal liability is not yet entirely clear. *Moore* v. *J. Bresler Ltd.* has been criticized as carrying over into the criminal law, the harsh rule of vicarious liability

applicable to public welfare offences.[39] Yet the criticisms have been
put on markedly different, though superficially similar, footings,
reflecting a basic difference of views on the proper bases of liability.
At any rate, the only judgment which distinguished clearly between
personal and vicarious liability is *Rex* v. *I.C.R. Haulage Ltd.*, and that
decision is too general in its terms to lead to any firm conclusion
respecting the conceptual bases of liability.[40]

There has been some clarification in subsequent cases. It is clear that
liability will now be imposed where the officer of the company occupies
a superior position in the corporate structure and exercises managerial,
though perhaps delegated, functions. *James and Sons Ltd.* v. *Smee* was a
welcome re-affirmation that there is a difference between liability personal
to the corporation and vicarious liability.[41] The company was charged
with permitting user of a motor vehicle in contravention of the Motor
Vehicles (Construction and Use) Regulations, 1951. The fault was that
of a minor servant. The majority of the court held that the company
must be acquitted. There was no evidence that any responsible officer
of the company had permitted user in contravention. The servant's
knowledge could not be imputed to the company as its knowledge; in
which respect there was no difference between a corporation and any
other master.

Other cases are less illuminating. In general, until recently there has
been little judicial discussion of the elements of corporate liability or
of its nature and purpose. In *Davies Turner and Co. Ltd.* v. *Brodie* the
company was acquitted of aiding and abetting the commission of an
offence. The acts allegedly constituting the aiding and abetting were
done by a branch manager. Policy questions were not discussed, the
court holding that he lacked *mens rea.*[42] In *Poultry World Ltd.* v. *Condor*,
the company was acquitted of aiding and abetting the statutory offence
of advertising the sale of wild birds. It was found that the human agent,
the advertising manager, lacked *mens rea.*[43] His place in the corporate
hierarchy was not investigated, and it seems to be implied that the
company might have been held liable for his acts. *National Coal Board* v.
Gamble presents the unfamiliar spectacle of the court inadvertently
exercising an advisory jurisdiction. The Board was convicted of aiding
and abetting the commission of a statutory offence; the acts in question
being those of a minor servant exercising delegated authority over one
aspect of the Board's operations. The Board expressly accepted
responsibility for the servant's conduct. The case is noteworthy for
Devlin J.'s warning that it might be necessary in the future to discuss

the permissible boundaries of vicarious liability.[44] *Reg* v. *Blamires Transport Services Ltd.* presented the strange spectacle of a conviction against a corporation where the managing director was the person alleged to have conspired with it, and with certain of its minor servants, to commit summary offences contrary to the Road Traffic Act.[45]

Modern developments: a possible adoption of the Alter Ego Theory

In several recent cases there has been some clarification of the applicable doctrines. In *Reg* v. *Stanley Haulage Ltd.*,[46] Judge Chapman attempted to put the issue of identification on a satisfactory footing by holding that a corporation could be held liable where the authority employed by the officer in question was managerial and where his decisions over the relevant aspect of corporate affairs could be made without further reference to his superiors. In *John Henshall (Quarries) Ltd.* v. *Harvey*[47] the Divisional Court held that the fact that the performance of a function had been delegated to a servant was not enough to impute the servant's *mens rea* to the corporation.[48] Adverting to a dictum by Denning L. J. in *H. L. Bolton Co. Ltd.* v. *T. J. Graham & Sons Ltd.*[49] (which draws on *alter ego* sources) Lord Parker CJ held that a distinction had necessarily to be drawn for the purpose of imputing liability between some person representing the brains of the company as for example a director, the managing director, the secretary or other responsible officer, and a mere servant. In *Magna Plant Ltd.* v. *Mitchell* where a corporation was charged with 'permitting' use of a vehicle where all the parts and accessories of the vehicle were not maintained in a safe condition, the Divisional Court declined to hold the company liable for the fault of a mechanic and a depot engineer. Lord Parker CJ reiterated that a corporation is to be held liable only for ' . . . The acts of responsible officers forming the brain, or in the case of an individual, a person to whom delegation in the true sense of delegation of management has been passed'.[51]

A most interesting feature of these decisions, and of a recent decision on corporate conspiracy, *Regina* v. *McDonnell*,[52] is that virtually for the first time the courts are commencing consciously to apply the *alter ego* doctrine of corporate representation. Mr Welsh, relying on *Lennards Carrying Company Ltd.* v. *Asiatic Petroleum Company Ltd.*[53] urged that liability should be predicated on the actions of persons wielding corporate powers by direct attribution.[54] Only thus, he argued, could corporate liability fail to be vicarious liability. It was urged that, relying on *Lennards* case, the actions of the primary representatives

of the corporation could be said to be personal to it. It may well be
that a more exact formulation of the conditions under which criminal
liability may be imposed upon corporations will be possible in the future.
The result of recent decisions, dealt with in detail later in this study,
would seem to indicate that the actions of officers may be ascribed
personally to a corporation where the function being exercised and in
respect of which liability is to be imposed is a managerial function,
and where the officer concerned enjoys all relevant powers of control
over that aspect of business to which it relates.[55] The conscious adoption
of the *alter ego* doctrine is relatively new.[56] It could impart much more
certainty into this area of the law.[57]

A summary of the English decisions

At this point some attempt may be made to summarize the effect of
these decisions. It is clear that corporate criminal liability has been
received as a general principle of criminal law. It is also clear that such
liability is to be seen as personal, that is, that there exists a difference
between it and vicarious liability as that is commonly understood. In some
cases seemingly, a corporation may be either personally or vicariously
liable for the actions of virtually the same officials. It is not clear however,
on what basis corporate liability is to be distinguished from vicarious
liability. It could be said that a corporation is personally liable for the
acts of its agents, servants and officers simply because they are such and
acting within the scope of their employment or agency. To advance such
a propostion would be to concede no differentiation between the two
concepts of corporate liability and vicarious liability.

There would seem now to be two cases in which corporate criminal
liability may be imposed. It may be imposed in respect of actions
commanded by the board of directors as the brain, or by a responsible
officer enjoying managerial functions. The problem in the latter case is to
identify first, what may be termed a managerial function and secondly,
who may be said to be a responsible officer. The cases for the most part
lead to the inference that at least as respects the actions of higher
managerial officials, corporate liability is to be taken as personal.[58]
It cannot be said with confidence upon what basis the latter distinction
is made, nor can it yet be said what authority such an official must have
or what capacity he must be exercising in order to impute his acts to
the corporation as its acts. Unless this be known however, there is a
marked danger, as will be seen, that corporate liability and vicarious
liability will be in practice virtually indistinguishable. In the English

cases no elucidation of the managerial structures of accused corporations
seems really to be undertaken. The inquiry is at best rather a crude one,
and this tends to cause confusion, a possibility enhanced in the light of
the influence of *Mousell's* case[59] in this area of the law. With the sole
example of *Rex* v. *I.C.R. Haulage Ltd.* to the contrary[60] all the cases in
which corporations have been held criminally liable and in which the
bases of such liability have been adverted to, have involved officers
exercising a wide delegated authority and acting within the scope of
such delegation. *D.P.P.* v. *Kent and Sussex Contractors* involved a
transport manager who submitted on behalf of the corporation returns
relating to the operation of the company's vehicles. *Moore* v. *I. Bresler
Ltd.* involved the company secretary and the branch manager who
submitted fraudulent returns. The submitting of returns was a secretarial
function. *Reg.* v. *Stanley Haulage Ltd.* involved the actions of a depot
transport manager acting in relation to requirements relating to the
operation of vehicles. Equally revealing perhaps, are the cases in which
the corporation was found not guilty because its officers lacked *mens rea*.
In these cases too, the human actor was a managerial officer acting within
the scope of his delegated authority. In *John Henshall (Quarries) Ltd.* v.
Harvey the Divisional Court discusses the question as one of position
and function. Not every servant is competent to bind the corporation
personally by his actions. He must represent the brains of the company.
A learned commentator in the *Criminal Law Review* remarks that no
question of vicarious liability arose in *Reg.* v. *Stanley Haulage Ltd.*[61] ;
it is far from certain that this view is correct. In that case as in others,
did not the court essentially have regard to 'the nature of the duty laid
down, the person upon whom it is imposed, the person by whom it
would in ordinary circumstances be performed, and the person upon
whom the penalty is imposed'?[62] The danger which Mr. Welsh foresaw,
that corporate liability could become indistinguishable from vicarious
liability, is only gradually being averted.[63] It may be that corporate
liability is personal liability or imputed liability as distinct from vicarious
liability.[64] It is possible to suggest conceptual bases upon which such a
distinction between corporate liability and vicarious liability could be
maintained. As this study shows however, they are in many respects
similar phenomena, deriving from the same root.[65] Certainly the
case law for the most part indicates that the species of liability known as
corporate criminal liability differs from vicarious liability insofar as the
court requires the human actor to occupy a rather special postion in the
corporate hierarchy; a position which involves the exercise of a superior

executive function in respect of an area of corporate activities to which a statute imposing criminal sanctions relates.

1   [1917] 2 KB 836
2   [1917] 2 KB 836, at pages 842, 844
3   See *Rex* v. *Fane Robinson Ltd.* [1941] 3 DLR 409, and Glanville Williams, *Criminal Law: The General Part* (2nd ed. 1961) p 274
4   [1917] 2 KB 836, 845
5   [1927] 1 KB 810
6   'The Criminal Responsibility of Corporations' (1927) 3 Camb. LJ 398
7   Writers of authority do not seem to have contemplated any extension of liability. See *Russell on Crime* (9th ed. edited by Ross, 1936) vol 1 at page 46; Kenny, *Outlines of Criminal Law* (15th ed. edited by Phillips, 1936) at pp 74-75. It is probable that the provisions of the Criminal Justice Act 1925 were intended to make the Summary Jurisdiction Act 1879 fully operative. Support for the opposite view could be derived from the director's liability clauses in a number of statutes which seemed to contemplate corporate criminal liability by implication. For an account, see Lieck 'Corporations as Criminals', (1924) 88 JP 197
8   [1939] 2 KB 395
9   *Webster* v. *Solloway Mills and Co.* [1931] 1 DLR 831
10   See Gower, Modern Company Law (2nd ed. 1957) p 137
11   [1939] 2 KB 395 at p 408
12   *Pharmaceutical Society* v. *London and Provincial Supply Association* (1880) 5 App. Cas. 857
13   See *D.P.P.* v. *Kent and Sussex Contractors* [1944] All ER 119
14   Apart from the cases discussed herein, one might also refer to *Rex* v. *Sorsky* [1944] 2 All ER 333, and to *Berney* v. *A.G.* (1947) 116 LJR 983, and to the special provisions in the Defence Regulations dealing with crimes committed under the aegis of a corporation. See S.R. & O. 1942, No 501
15   *Stevens and Steeds Ltd.* v. *King* [1943] 1 All ER 314; *Board of Trade* v. *Woods, Cruh and Clark Dennis and Co. Ltd.* (1944) 8 Jo. Cr. L. 85; *Williams Brothers Direct Supply Company Ltd.* v. *Cloote* (1944) 60 JLR 270; *London Computator Ltd.* v. *Seymour* [1944] 2 All ER 11
16   [1944] KB 146
17   [1944] KB at page 151
18   [1944] KB at page 151
19   [1944] KB at page 155
20   [1944] KB at pp 150-152
21   [1944] KB at page 156 per MacNaghten J. and at page 158 per Hallett J.
22   [1944] KB at page 154 per Lord Caldecote CJ
23   [1944] KB at page 158
24   [1944] KB at page 159
25   [1944] KB at page 156
26   (1945-46) 19 A. LJ 51; but cf. (1944) 18 A. LJ 199
27   See remarks of Lord Reading CJ in [1917] 2 KB 835, 842 in which it is implied that if the directors of *Mousell Brothers Limited* had been party to the fraud, the corporation might have been personally liable

28 [1944] KB 551
29 [1944] KB 551 at page 556
30 [1939] 2 KB 395
31 [1944] KB 146
32 [1944] KB at page 559
33 See the discussion in chapter 7
34 [1944] KB at page 556
35 [1944] KB at page 554
36 It seems impossible to go farther than this and to say that any organic notion
was expressly adopted. *Lennards Carrying Company Ltd.* v. *Asiatic Petroleum
Company Ltd.* [1915] AC 705 was not cited, nor were the possibly applicable
decisions on the doctrine of common employment such as *Rudd* v. *Elder Dempster
& Co.* [1933] 1 KB 556, or *Fanton* v. *Denville* [1932] 2 KB 309. See further,
Burrows, 'The Responsibility of Corporations under Criminal Law' (1948)
1 Jo. Crim. Sci. 1 at pages 9-11
37 [1944] 2 All ER 515
38 [1944] 2 All ER at page 517. Again the analysis is essentially that of *Mousell's*
case [1917] 2 KB 836
39 See Welsh, 'The Criminal Liability Of Corporations' (1946) 62 LQR 345;
W.J.D. 'The Criminal Responsibility Of Corporations' (1946) 62 Sc. L. Rev. 212;
Glanville Williams, *Criminal Law: The General Part* (2nd ed. 1961) p 859
40 See reference no 41
41 [1955] 1 QB 78
42 [1954] 1 WLR 1364
43 [1957] Crim. LR 803
44 [1958] 3 All ER 203
45 [1963] 3 All ER 170—the conspiracy aspects of this decision are dealt with
in chapter 5
46 [1964] Crim. LR 221
47 [1965] 2 QB 233
48 It seems clear from this that *National Coal Board* v. *Gamble* [1959] 1 QB 11
was wrongly decided and would not now be followed
49 [1957] 1 QB 159 at page 172
50 [1966] Crim. LR 395
51 Transcript of judgement. The case has not been fully reported
52 [1965] 3 WLR 1138
53 [1915] AC 705
54 Welsh, 'The Criminal Liability Of Corporations' (1946) 62 LQR 345
55 See the discussion in chapter 7
56 This view derives some incidental support from Burrows, 'The Responsibility
of Corporations under Criminal Law' (1948) 1 Jo. Crim. Sci. 1. Certainly, the
cases decided in 1944 contain no mention of the *alter ego* theory
57 See the discussion in chapter 7
58 Hence the advocacy by Welsh in 'The Criminal Liability Of Corporations'
(1946) 62 LQR 345 of the *alter ego* doctrine as the proper basis of liability
59 [1917] 2 KB 836
60 [1944] KB 551
61 [1964] Crim. LR 221

62 Wording employed by Atkin LJ at [1917] 1 KB 836, 845
63 Although here, the effect of *Reg.* v. *McDonnell* [1965] 3 WLR 1138 and
John Henshall (Quarries) Ltd. v. *Harvey* [1965] 2 QB 233 may well be to establish
a basis upon which a meaningful distinction, even if merely a distinction of degree
rather than of kind, may be maintained
64 See Friedmann, *Law In A Changing Society* (1959) p 193
65 See the discussion in chapter 6

Chapter 5

Corporate criminal liability: a general view

While it is clear that corporations can be held liable for most criminal offences, neither the ambit of such liability nor the bases upon which it proceeds are clear. In England as in most common law jurisdictions, these matters have never been fully canvassed. It is therefore difficult to indicate with precision the conditions governing the ascription of liability to corporations, the nature of the defences open to a corporation to a criminal charge, or the probable incidence of liability.

Much of the discussion in this area reflects a desire to import into the field of corporate criminal liability, specifically 'corporate' factors. An insistence that the principle of identification applies in determining for whose actions a corporation shall be held liable dervies from a desire that a corporation shall be punished only for a 'corporate' act. The argument that before a corporation may be held liable the human actor involved must have intended to benefit the corporation springs from the same root. Arguments based on the doctrine of *ultra vires* derive from this source. So also do arguments against holding a corporation liable for conspiracy where the person with whom the entity is alleged to have conspired was the managing director or the Board of Directors of the corporation. If corporate criminal liability were truly corporate crime, it could be conceded that as the minds of these persons represent the mind of the corporation, no two minds were available for the purposes of conspiring together.

Because the status, the character, and the functions of corporate criminal liability are in doubt, confusion arises. It is not clear what the imposition of such liability seeks to achieve. It is not clear in what respects its aims differ from those of vicarious liability. For all that appears corporate criminal liability is a mere device, invented in order to hold corporations liable for crimes in respect of which there is a bar to the imposition of vicarious criminal liability. While these matters are discussed in detail in a later portion of this work, some of the confusion caused by a failure to articulate basic policy considerations can readily be demonstrated. The uncertain desiderata underlying the employment of

the doctrine of identification derive from an uncertainty respecting
the aims of corporate criminal liability. If, like vicarious liability, it is
essentially directed towards ensuring that the management of a
business will police the enforcement of legislation by its employees,
there is little point in restricting the ascription of liability to the actions
of persons wielding primary authority over the corporation. It would be
more sensible to adopt the solution of the American Federal Courts and
impose liability in respect of the actions of any person enjoying a
delegated authority over the matters to which the acts in question
relate.[1] On the other hand, if it is desired to ensure that the management
of a corporation will not wilfully employ its assets and forms in violation
of the criminal law, liability can meaningfully be predicated on the actions
of the primary representatives of the company. Unless however, the
policy question be asked and answered, it is difficult to provide a
convincing formulation of the conditions governing liability, the defences
to liability, and its probable incidence.

In the light of these considerations the field can further be explored.
What follows, so far as the nature of the cases permits, is a general
survey of corporate criminal liability.

In this chapter an examination of the conditions under which liability
is ascribed to corporations is undertaken. Certain aspects of corporate
conspiracy which involves the question of the corporate mind are
examined. Limitations to liability are examined at length, including
limitations arising from the doctrine of *ultra vires,* from statutory
interpretation, and from the nature of the offences concerned. An
examination of the present procedure used in the criminal courts is
undertaken. Finally some remarks are ventured with respect to the
probable incidence of corporate criminal liability in practice. In effect,
this chapter is concerned with a general survey of the field.

Conditions under which liability is ascribed to corporations: entities liable to criminal prosecution

In English law the sole entity to which criminal liability may be
ascribed is the corporation. Other forms of commercial organisation
such as the partnership[2] or the trade union, though for some purposes
invested with some attributes of legal personality, are not considered
to be persons, and cannot therefore be subjected to liability. It is of
course possible to alter this rule by statute. Under sections 15 and 16 of
the Trade Unions Act 1871 a registered trade union incurs fines and
penalties for failure to maintain a registered office and to file annual

returns. Similarly, trade unions and employers associations can be tried
on summary conviction for certain offences contrary to the Prices and
Incomes Act 1966. Proceedings are brought in the name of the body,
the fine if any is to be paid from its funds, and the procedural provisions
relating to corporations are to apply.[3] Corporations, whether domestic
or foreign, may be held liable.[4] Curiously perhaps, little differentiation
has been made between various types of corporation for the purposes of
criminal liability. The fact that corporations alone are made liable as
entities, even as respects public welfare offences, illustrates the *ad hoc*
character of legal development in this area. In America by contrast
Congress has imposed liability upon unincorporated business
organisations in respect of a wide range of summary offences.[5]

Persons in respect of whose actions liability may be ascribed

The human actor in respect of whose actions liability may be ascribed
to a corporation must occupy a superior position in the corporate
structure. He may be a person acting under the authority of the Board of
Directors, or he may be the managing director, or he may be a person
enjoying a wide delegated authority over some aspect of the corporation's
business. It has been intimated that in order for liability to be ascribed
to the corporation, the officer in question must enjoy a *de facto* primary
authority over the subject matter of the offence.[6] In general, he must
represent the brains of the company.[7] He must be someone of whom the
courts can say that his acts were the acts of the company.[8] This formula
invests the court with a very considerable discretion.[9] It has been said
that the doctrine of identification should be applied only to the actions
of those officers who govern the company under its constitutional
documents.[10] The courts have never adopted so restricted a view. They,
having regard to the circumstances of the case, the character and
magnitude of the company's business, and the authority delegated by the
Board of Directors to the managing officers of the company, seek to
determine whether the actions of the person involved can be said to be
the actions of the company.[11] As was said in an early Canadian case,
Rex v. *Canadian Allis-Chalmers Limited*[12]:

What the rank or position of the officer or employee or other agent
would have to be in order that his negligence might be deemed to be that
of a corporation cannot be stated generally; what would be said in the
case of a 'one man' company might be quite inaccurate in the case, say,
of a railway company whose lines extend across a continent; but in every

case the evidence must be such as to justify a finding that the company—
the employer—was negligent, or there can be no conviction.

It is not possible at the present time to state the conditions under which
liability will be ascribed to the company with any greater precision. It
is argued, in a later portion of this study, that the courts really seek to
ascribe liability to the corporation in respect of the actions of some person
whose standing in the corporation is sufficiently high that his actions
are likely to reflect an underlying corporate policy.

Course of employment and corporate benefit as factors governing liability

It is clear that before liability will be imposed upon the corporation
the human actor involved must have been acting within the scope of his
authority from the corporation.[13] Otherwise, his acts cannot be taken to
be corporate actions at all.[14] The doctrine of identification has never, in
the English courts, been taken to mean that some person is the
corporation.[15] It rather means that in certain circumstances the actions
of corporate officers may be taken to be those of the corporation.[16]

It is not clear whether the imposition of liability depends upon any
intention by the officer concerned to benefit the corporation. An
argument that intention to benefit the corporation must exist before the
corporation will be held liable is attractive if one seeks to impose liability
only in respect of acts and omissions which are truly 'corporate'. There
is Canadian and American authority which holds that corporate criminal
liability cannot be imposed unless the human actor concerned intended
to benefit the corporation.[17] Such a view might well commend itself to
an English court, in spite of the decision in *Moore* v. *I. Bresler Ltd.* to
the contrary.[18]

Must the activity be *intra vires* the corporation?

It has previously been explained that the courts did not adopt the idea
that all crimes as such are *ultra vires* the corporation. It has been held
tacitly that where a crime is committed in the course of activities which
are *intra vires* the corporation, the corporation is criminally liable for
them. The remaining area of dispute is whether, when a crime is committed
in pursuance of an object which does not fall within corporate powers, the
corporation may be held liable.[19] Assume for example that a given
corporation is empowered to operate a freight carrying service only. Is the
corporation liable if, while operating an *ultra vires* passenger service, its
driver is permitted to use the vehicle in contravention of statutory

provisions relating to road traffic? To this question no certain answer
can be given.

It is as well to define the term at the outset, because an examination
of the authorities discloses that *ultra vires* has been used in several senses,
not all of them strictly accurate. The doctrine of *ultra vires* is a limitation
upon corporate capacity and applies in respect of corporations
incorporated under Act of Parliament, or under the enabling provisions
of the Companies Acts.[20] The objects clause, contained in the instrument
of incorporation, delimits the business activities which the corporation is
entitled to pursue. Activities which fall outside the objects clause cannot
be competently undertaken by the corporation and are therefore said to
be *ultra vires;* that is, outside the area in which the corporation is regarded
as acting. *Ultra vires* is not a rule of illegality. It is not a rule that the
pursuit of objects falling outside the objects clause is for that reason
illegal, although the particular acts may in fact be so. It means that the
pursuit of activities outside the scope of powers conferred by the
incorporating documents are not regarded as the corporation's acts.[21]
Within its permissible area of operation, in the pursuit of objects
competent to it, there is no doubt that a corporation can commit offences
for which it will be held liable.

It has never been decided whether or not a corporation will be held
liable for crimes committed in the pursuit of *ultra vires* activities. The
application of the *ultra vires* rule in contract has been rigid. It has been
held, not only that a corporation cannot be held liable upon a contract
entered into for a purpose *ultra vires* the corporation, but that even a
judgment obtained against a corporation in respect of an *ultra vires*
contract is not sacrosanct unless it embodies a decision on the issue of
ultra vires.[22] Logically, one would expect the same result to follow in the
case of both torts and crimes. This view has indeed found academic
support. Professor Goodhart, for example, argues that a corporation could
not be held liable for a tort committed in the course of an *ultra vires*
activity because it could not competently employ servants to carry out
that activity. It would follow that, because the corporation was not
carrying out the activity complained of, its servants would not be acting
in the course of their employment with it.[23] The like view is taken in
several works of repute.[24] Professor Goodhart's opponents in general deny
that the rule applies in tort or crime. Their analytical bases for doing so are
at least questionable. Under the orthodox theory of *ultra vires* it is difficult
to argue that a company (other than a charter corporation) possesses a
power to act *ultra vires* but no privilege to do so. If *ultra vires* acts are

regarded as mere nullities it would follow that the corporation has no capacity whatever in connection with such transactions.[25] The most recent edition of *Salmond on Torts*, albeit in a grudging footnote, concedes the logic in Professor Goodhart's view but considers that development is likely to be based on policy grounds.

The position in English law regarding the *ultra vires* limitation

There is no clear rule in English law. It has been decided that where the activity is *ultra vires* the corporation, the human actor cannot be said to have an implied authority from the corporation to act as he did.[26] The issue where the actor had express authority from the corporation has not as yet arisen before the English courts.

In *Mill* v. *Hawker*[27] the existence of a limitation to liability in tort based upon the *ultra vires* rule was apparently recognised. All the members of the court were prepared to recognise that where ' . . . the act is *ultra vires* and is not, and cannot be in contemplation of law, a corporate act at all . . .' the corporation could not be held liable.[28] In *Campbell* v. *Paddington Corporation*,[29] a contrary view was taken. That case is unsatisfactory because, while the court spoke of *ultra vires*, the question was really one of illegality. In the *Taff Vale* case[30] Farwell J at trial delivered a dictum stating that a trade union, like a corporation, might be liable where unlawful acts are performed in the carrying on of the lawful purposes of the association. This dictum was not commented upon on appeal and was probably recognised as correct. No more modern English case dealing with this problem has been found. In two recent decisions in contract, *Anglo-Overseas Agencies Ltd.* v. *Green*[31] and at trial in *Bell Houses Ltd.* v. *City Wall Properties Ltd.*,[32] *ultra vires* contracts are treated as nullities incapable of conferring rights and imposing liabilities on either party thereto. In the latter case, in the Court of Appeal, Salmon LJ doubted whether once a company had performed its part of an *ultra vires* contract the other party could set up the point that the contract was *ultra vires* the company and so avoid payment. The harsher view seems more consistent with authority.[32a]

It should be noted that there exists an older line of authority which might well be relied on as a device to surmount the *ultra vires* limitation. The leading case is *Doolan* v. *Midland Railway Company*.[33] Lord Blackburn in a dictum suggested that a company could not set up its own lack of capacity to an action brought against it in respect of the negligent loss during carriage of the plaintiff's goods. It seems clear that the dictum in *Doolan* v. *Midland Railway Company* is at variance with

the modern *ultra vires* rule.[34] Nonetheless, it has been relied upon in
New Zealand in order to permit recovery in tort where the acts
complained of were done in pursuance of an *ultra vires* activity. In
Blunden v. *Inhabitants of the Oxford Road District*[35] and in *Northern
Publishing Company* v. *White*[36] the courts seized upon *Doolan*'s case as
authority for holding the corporation liable, notwithstanding that in
each case the activity was admittedly *ultra vires*.

Little assistance can be gathered elsewhere. In the United States it has
been held that the *ultra vires* doctrine is restricted in operation to
contracts and has no application to crime.[37] There however, the rule is
seen as an agency limitation on the power of directors and not as a rule
affecting corporate relations with third parties.[38] In Canada it has been
held that *ultra vires* does not apply in tort or in crime.[39] The reasoning is
not entirely satisfactory. In *Barreau de Richelieu* v. *St. Jean Automobile
Ltée*,[40] a case involving the unlawful practice of law by the accused
corporation, the court held that the corporation could not rely on the
doctrine of *ultra vires* as a defence. It held that the actions of its director
were the personal actions of the corporation. This begs the question
whether the corporation could be said to be acting at all. It overlooks
the point that a corporation cannot confer on its governing member
powers greater than it possesses.[41] In a trade union case, *Tunney* v.
Orchard,[42] in the Supreme Court, Rand J has expressed a dictum that a
corporation is not liable where the actions complained of were performed
in the course of an *ultra vires* activity.[43] The British Columbia Court
of Appeal has also expressed its adherence to this principle.[43] In
Australia, at any rate in tort, an *ultra vires* limitation exists.[44] Its
recognition has been placed on the grounds that to permit liability would
be to subvert the protection accorded to shareholders by the *ultra vires*
doctrine.

It is difficult to predict the final result of this controversy. It may well
be significant whether the question of the ambit of the *ultra vires* doctrine
arises first in a criminal case, or in the law of tort. The end to be served in
imposing liability for tort, compensation to injured persons, is clear. The
utility of imposing a criminal sanction is less so. The actual offender may
presumably still be apprehended. Professor Gower adopts such an
argument, urging that such liability is questionable as not serving the
functions of deterring those in control of the corporation.[45] This, if true,
is surely true of corporate criminal liability generally. Nonetheless, it is
an argument which is not entirely devoid of appeal. Furthermore it is
in the case of public welfare offences that the arguments in favour of

punishing the master rather than the servant are strongest.[46] Here, *ultra vires* is unlikely to be urged as a defence. It is hardly likely that a corporation will submit the question of the competence of the activities in which it engages to the magistrates or to the Divisional Court as a matter of defence.

The problem is hardly one of frequent occurrence. This infrequency, taken together with the general ability to prosecute the human agent, may make the courts reluctant to impair the logical symmetry of the rule. Hence unless the first attack on the *ultra vires* rule is mounted in a tort action it is unlikely that criminal liability will be imposed in respect of crimes committed in the course of an activity *ultra vires* the corporation.

The *ultra vires* rule itself has been eroded. The substratum rule has long since been avoided in practice by objects clauses which specify that all the objects are to be original in character.[47] Furthermore, the Court of Appeal in *Bell Houses Ltd.* v. *City Wall Properties Ltd.*[48] by upholding objects cast in a subjective form which permitted the company to carry on any other trade or business which in the opinion of the board of directors could be advantageously carried on by the company in connection with or as ancillary to the objects enumerated in the articles appears to have enabled companies virtually to surmount *ultra vires* limitations entirely. Judicial control over management acting in pursuance of ancillary powers can now only be of a very loose character. Corporate powers need now be subject to few limitations, and the incidence of the application of the doctrine is likely to be even more capricious in the future.[49]

Finally, it should be noted that these problems may shortly be legislated out of existence. The Jenkins Committee has recommended that the *ultra vires* rule in relation to contracts should be modified by permitting a third party who has contracted with the company in good faith to recover, notwithstanding that the contract was *ultra vires* the company.[50] This recommendation if implemented, may give an impetus to arguments that the *ultra vires* rule has no application outside the law of contract. It will not affect the rule that the directors can have no greater powers conferred upon them than the corporation possesses. It will in effect raise an estoppel against the company precluding it from denying that it had power to enter into a given contract. From this the courts might be prepared to raise a disguised form of estoppel against the corporation in cases of tort and crime, notwithstanding that an *ultra vires* act would still be susceptible of analysis as not representing an exercise of corporate powers. In the light of recent dicta, it is not inconceivable that reliance might be had on the realist theory of corporate personality in order to justify the result.[51]

Other factors in attributing corporate guilt

Most of the other factors relating to the impostion of corporate criminal liability can best be dealt with as limitations. It is therefore intended to give a brief account of the crimes for which corporations can be held liable, with special attention to conspiracy as involving the issue of the corporate mind, and then to deal with limitations to liability.

Offences of which corporations may be held liable

Corporations can now be held liable for many, and perhaps most offences. The earliest head of corporate criminal liability consisted in failure to perform a duty laid on the corporation which gave rise to a public nuisance.[52] Later this was extended to misfeasance resulting in public nuisance.[53] Usually these situations are now dealt with by injunction.[54] A corporation can be liable for criminal libel.[55] There seems no doubt that corporations can be parties to offences, even under the old law as principal in the second degree to felony, and this notwithstanding their lack of physical presence.[56] Corporations are commonly held liable for all manner of summary offences. As these are directed for the most part to the regulation of various aspects of trade and commerce, they form by far the most important head of corporate criminal liability.[57] There is a considerable list of offences in respect of which it has been said that corporations may be liable. In England, corporations have been convicted of conspiracy to defraud,[58] and to commit summary offences.[59] They have been convicted of aiding and abetting the commission of regulatory offences.[60] It has been virtually decided that corporations may be guilty of manslaughter.[61] This has occurred in the Commonwealth.[62] Corporations have also been held liable for contempt of court.[63] Professor Glanville Williams suggests that corporations can now be convicted of those offences against the state which are punishable by a fine.[64]

In Canada, a similar picture emerges. Corporations have been convicted of conspiracy to defraud and obtaining money by false pretences,[65] of conspiracy in restraint of trade,[66] of running a lottery,[67] of corrupt dealings with government,[68] of keeping a disorderly house,[69] and of offences concerning trading stamps.[70] American examples abound. A list by no means exhaustive, shows that corporations have been convicted of conspiracies in restraint of trade,[71] of the unlawful giving of rebates in interstate commerce,[72] of fraudulent sales of mining stock,[73] of conspiracy to defraud under the financial guaranty provisions of the Federal Housing Act,[74] of fraudulent conversion,[75] larceny,[76] violations of price control legislation,[77] violations of fair labour practices legislation,[78] violations of Sunday Observance legislation,[79] 'criminal syndicalism',[80] depositing obscene written matter in the mails,[81] violations of the Espionage Act,[82] sedition,[83] and assault, battery and libel.[84] Virtually the sole limitation suggested has been treason, and this has been doubted.[85]

One of the striking features disclosed by an examination of the cases has been the low incidence of decisions relating to what might be called traditional crimes. No English case has yet imposed liability for crimes of violence or for crimes against the state. In practice liability generally relates to certain types of commercial fraud or violations of regulatory legislation. Those traditional areas of the law in which corporations have appeared as the accused, such as fraud or obscene libel, involved offences closely related to the business activities of the corporation. It seems fair to infer that corporations, in general, are prosecuted only where the offence was closely related to the business affairs of the corporation.

Liability for contempt of court

One might here venture a few remarks on corporate liability for contempt of court. In addition to its importance to publishers, it has also recently become important with respect to restrictive trade practices.

The liability of persons who publish matter tending to interfere with the due administration of justice in criminal matters extends to corporations. Furthermore, the editor as well as the publisher is vicariously liable for all that appears in the publication.[86] It is thus possible to fine the publishing corporation, the editor of the publication, and the reporter who submitted the material.[87]

More interesting questions arise where attachment is sought for a contempt which consists in failing to obey an order of the court.[88] Under Order 52, Rule 4 dealing with attachment for disobedience to an order of the court, the corporation may be fined.[89] In addition, its officers may be attached.[90] The order goes not against the officers, but against the company. Liability on the part of the officers for contempt of court results not because they have been named in the order, but because by assisting the breach of an order they have aided in the resulting contempt of court.[91] The order which it is sought to enforce must be directed to the company. If the order is in positive terms requiring the company to do something, it must be served upon the company and upon any officers whom it may be desired to attach for failure to carry out its terms. If the order is prohibitory, service is not necessarily a condition precedent to attachment. It is sufficient if the person whom it is desired to attach had actual notice of it and assisted in its breach. Seemingly, such a person will be liable to attachment whatever his position, be it that of officer, member, or servant of the company.[92]

As stated, proceedings for attachment are likely to become of importance under the Restrictive Trade Practices Act. In *In re Galvanized Tank Managers Agreement*[93] several major steel firms were fined for breach of an undertaking not to enforce a price-fixing agreement which had been declared not to be in the public interest. The court indicated that in future an order for attachment would be issued to any individual who appeared to have wilfully participated in or aided and abetted a breach of any undertaking.

Liability for conspiracy

Conspiracy involves the entire problem of the corporate mind. It is trite learning that two minds are required for conspiracy. Even today, husband and wife cannot be convicted of conspiring together because in law they are but one person and are regarded as possessing one mind.[94] Now similarly, can it be argued that the corporation has a mind separate and apart from that of its Board of Directors or managing director? The corporation can only think as its officers have thought. Their decisions are those of the corporation. Their deliberations must for most purposes represent the thought processes of the corporation. If these high officials are to be identified with the corporation it seems a distinct *non sequitur* to hold that they can conspire with it. The identification theory, whatever it means, at least connotes that actions of the board or of high managerial agents are to be treated as the actions of the corporation for the purposes of the criminal law. If these persons represent the corporation, how can they conspire with it? It would seem clear that no conspiracy could exist in such a situation and this disposition of the matter finds support in certain English[95] and Canadian authority,[96] and in the American Federal Courts.[97]

Some decisions appeared to suggest either tacitly or explicitly that a charge of conspiracy between a corporation and its managing director would lie, thereby raising the issue whether a corporation could ever avoid a conspiracy charge in cases where a senior officer directed or permitted the commission of an offence.[98] In an Ontario decision the Court held that a charge of conspiracy between a corporation and its controlling officer would lie on the footing that the officer acted in two capacities and that a conspiracy could exist between the two capacities of the same mind.[99] The Ontario case raised directly the question of the permissible limits of corporate conspiracy.

Fortunately, the problem seems to have been resolved by the decision of Nield J in *Regina* v. *McDonnell* at Bristol Assizes.[100] The accused was charged on an indictment containing ten counts, two of which alleged conspiracies between himself and two companies with which he was associated.

The defence moved initially to quash the conspiracy counts in the indictment. Both counsel agreed at the outset that the accused was at all material times the sole person in either of the two companies who was responsible for any of the acts of the company. It was agreed that no other person had any authority to act for the company or was responsible for the acts of the company. He was the sole person alleged to have committed an offence.

Nield J quashed the conspiracy charges. Adverting to Lord Haldane's well known remarks in *Lennards Carrying Company* v. *Asiatic Petroleum Company Limited*,[101] as the foundation of corporate criminal liability, and to the dicta of Denning LJ in *H. L. Bolton (Engineering) Co. Ltd.* v. *T. J. Graham & Sons Ltd.*[102] he concludes that while the company is an entity separate from its *alter ego,* its liability is predicated on an identification of the actions of its *alter ego* with it.[103] Thus clearly, there were two persons involved. It could not, however, be said that there were two minds involved. Clearly a corporation can conspire. It is not however, possible to convict it of conspiracy with its *alter ego.* While according persuasive authority to *Regina* v. *Electrical Contractors Limited*,[104] Nield J declined to follow the court's reasoning. He states[105]:

> In the particular circumstances here, where the sole responsible person in the Company is the Defendant himself, it would not be right to say that there were two persons or two minds. If it were otherwise, I feel that it would offend against the basic idea of a conspiracy . . . and I think it would be artificial to take the view that the company, although it is clearly a separate entity, can be regarded here as a separate person or a separate mind . . .

His lordship concluded that[106]:

. . . the true position is that a Company and a Director cannot be convicted of conspiracy when the only human being who is said to have broken the law or intended to do so is the one Director, and that is the Defendant in this case.

In the event, the conspiracy counts were quashed.

The same principles would surely apply if more than one director or indeed the board were charged with conspiring with their company. Presumably a conspiracy could lie where a director, acting on his personal behalf of another company, conspired with the managing director or the board.

Conspiracy between parent and subsidiary companies

Acute problems of corporate conspiracy can also occur in the parent-subsidiary context. On one view, parent and subsidiary corporations certainly can conspire together. Each is a separate legal entity, and for most purposes is treated as such.[107] Provided that each has a separate organisation and its own management, there would appear to be no difficulty in holding that such corporations could conspire together, and that for the most part is the clear result in the United States and Canada.[108] Were there no exceptions to the rule that each corporation is to be treated as a separate legal entity, the result could be accepted with equanimity. The result might appear to be somewhat unreal. Such a legal rule, if stated baldly, would appear to ignore the fact that a subsidiary is so because it is under the control of its parent corporation. Its use is to conduct a facet of business on behalf of the parent which the parent for one reason or another finds it less convenient to conduct under its own corporate aegis. In fact, the subsidiary's major policy decisions in respect of which the conspiracy will probably be alleged, will accord with those of the parent. It would also seem to place a premium, at least so far as the criminal law is concerned, on organising in terms of separate departments within an entity, rather than organising in separate legal entities.[109] The accident of organisation within an enterprise would become of great importance.

Here again however, there is another and plausible answer. The concept that a company is a separate legal entity has not prevented the courts from looking, in certain ill-defined circumstances, to the question of ultimate control. On occasion a parent corporation and its subsidiaries have been regarded as units conducting a single enterprise.[110] To some extent, the Companies Acts of 1948 and 1967 recognise the validity of

the enterprise analysis in its provisions relating to group accounts.[111]
Business circles too are aware of the utility of the enterprise analysis in
the parent-subsidiary context.[112] If the enterprise analysis be accepted,
it can be said that major decisions taken on behalf of the parent and
subsidiary represent the decisions and agreement not of two rigidly
separate entities, but of a single enterprise, and that what goes before
represents not the thought processes of the separate components, but
rather of the enterprise as a whole. Decision making in the enterprise
consists of a joint deliberative and consultative process.[113]

There are no decided English cases on this point. Canadian and
American decisions indicate that parent and subsidiary can conspire
together in restraint of trade. Reliance has been had on the separate
legal entity doctrine, and on the fact that in some price-fixing meetings,
subsidiaries were separately represented.[114] The United States Supreme
Court in particular has held that the existence of a conspiracy in restraint
of trade is a finding not precluded by the ' . . . corporate interrelationship
of the conspirators'.[115] Arguments that parent and subsidiary were ' . . .
mere instrumentalities of a single manufacturing unit . . . '[116] have not
been accepted. Yet the contrary view has been strongly expressed. In
Timken Roller Bearing Company v. *United States*,[117] Justice Jackson
dissenting, held that the fundamental issue ' . . . concerns a severely
technical application to foreign commerce of the concept of
conspiracy',[118] and pointed out that to allow a finding that a conspiracy
in restraint of trade existed would attach considerable weight to the
organisational mode adopted by the defendant corporation.[119] Curiously,
in the light of earlier decisions the Supreme Court, in *Sunkist Growers
Inc.* v. *Winckler and Smith Citrus Products Co. et al.*[120] (a civil action
for treble damages under the *Sherman* anti-trust act) declined to hold
that an agricultural co-operative society and its wholly owned subsidiary
could conspire together to restrain and monopolize interstate commerce
in citrus fruits. These entities, the petitioners, claimed that certain
exemptions from the anti-trust laws applied to them. The court in
upholding the claim observed that under statute the growers could have
banded together in one association without incurring liability. That they
had banded together into separate associations did not alter the position.
The two entities could not be considered to be independent so as to be
able to conspire together in violation of the law. To hold otherwise,
Justice Clark stated[121]:

. . . would be to impose grave legal consequences upon organizational distinctions that are of de minimis meaning and effect to these growers who have banded together for processing and marketing purposes within the purview of the . . . acts.

American and Canadian courts appear in attempting to enforce restraint of trade legislation not to have been greatly concerned with the niceties of the law of conspiracy.[122] On balance however, it seems likely that an English court would hold notwithstanding the possibility of employing an enterprise analysis and restricting liability for conspiracy to the human agents involved, that parent and subsidiary corporations can conspire together. It is unlikely, where both parent and subsidiary have their own Boards of Directors, that the courts would hold that there were no two independent minds for the purposes of conspiracy. It may however transpire that in some situations the courts will be faced with the choice of appearing to violate the separate legal entity principal, or appearing to violate the fundamental rule that at least two independent minds are required for the crime of conspiracy. This would clearly occur if, for example, the management of parent and subsidiary were vested in the same person, or the same board.[123]

Can a corporate 'mind' be pieced together?

This question arises from an examination of an American decision, *Inland Freight Lines* v. *United States*.[124] The corporation was charged with knowingly and wilfully keeping and preserving false drivers' logs as part of the corporation's records. No single agent or representative of the corporation had actual knowledge of the falsity of the records. One agent had knowledge of the contents of the logs, while another had knowledge of the contents of the drivers' trip records. A knowledge of both would have revealed the falsity of the records. It was held that the separate knowledge of both agents could be blended together in order to fashion one guilty mind. This particular result is unlikely to occur in England. Civilly, in *Armstrong* v. *Strain*,[125] the matter was decided otherwise. The Court of Appeal there held that a dishonest purpose can never be present in the case of an innocent division of ingredients. The same result would probably follow in a criminal case.

Limitations to corporate criminal liability

While, in *Rex* v. *I. C. R. Haulage Ltd.*[126] Stable J indicated that corporations could be held liable for most offences, whether under statute

or at common law, the question of limitations received little discussion.
It is by no means certain that the ambit of corporate criminal liability
will be governed entirely by logical factors. It is possible that the courts,
motivated by instinctual feelings rather than by a process of logical
reasoning, will restrict the ambit of liability considerably. Stable J
stated that some offences are, by their very nature, incapable of being
committed by corporations. Otherwise, limitations to liability depend
largely on issues of statutory construction. It is not urged of most
offences that they possess an immanence which renders their ascription
to corporations impossible. As a result the question of limitations becomes
a question of the techniques which can be adopted in restricting liability.
The efficacy of these techniques depends, not upon their intrinsic merits,
but upon whatever judicial views underly their employment. In general
the most potent inhibition to liability lies in a finding that a statute
creating an offence was not intended to apply to corporations; a search
for an application of the provision of the Interpretation Act, 1889 which
directs that penal statutes shall apply to corporations unless a contrary
intention appears.[127] In addition there are sundry other limitations.
Certain corporations enjoying a status as Crown instrumentalities are
not criminally liable. Finally, certain miscellaneous provisions do exclude
corporations or types of corporation expressly from their ambit.

The search for a contrary intention

The most potent defence available to a corporation is that the statute
creating the offence was not intended to embrace corporations. The
search is for a contrary intention within the meaning of the Interpretation
Act, 1889. Such an intent is clearly indicated when the statute imposes
a penalty which cannot be imposed upon a corporation. In such a case
it is said that the corporation is not intended to come within its terms
because it is not to be expected that the court will embark upon a trial
at the conclusion of which it can make no effective order.[128] As the
limitation is upon conviction rather than upon the corporation's ability
to commit the offence a natural person can be charged as a party to it.[129]
In Scotland, where the Crown moves for sentence, a conviction has been
made against a corporation in respect of an offence bearing a corporal
penalty only.[130]

    This defence is subject to serious limitations. Most offences are now
finable.[131] Most modern statutes now provide penalties of a fine in
addition to, or in lieu of, imprisonment. It was early held that where a
statute imposed a penalty of fine or imprisonment, the statute was

intended to embrace corporations which were to be punished so far as was possible.[132] Eventually, the same result was attained after a series of conflicting decisions where the statute provided penalties of fine and imprisonment, it being said that a corporation was to be held liable to the extent that it could be held liable. Thus, after a series of conflicting decisions on enactments in this form, it was held that a corporation could be held liable under the Sunday Observance Act, 1781, of the offence of keeping open a house of public entertainment on Sunday. The penalty provided was both a fine and treatment as a rogue and vagabond.[133] The same rule applies in Australia and in the United States.[134] In Northern Ireland it was held that a corporation might be liable for permitting the use of a heavy vehicle when no policy of insurance covering its use was in force. The applicable penalties included an automatic disqualification from holding a driving licence.[135]

Liability for offences of violence

Certain offences however, primarily crimes of violence, formed one of the earliest stated exceptions to corporate criminal liability.[136] No conviction in respect of them has yet been made, although it now seems clear that corporations may be held liable for manslaughter.[137] Of course convictions for this offence have been made in other jurisdictions.[138] Manslaughter is however a crime of violence which requires no act of violence. Criminal negligence in the failure to perform a duty will suffice to found liability.[139] Furthermore, in some cases even where an act is concerned, it may well be anterior to the harm. An example would be the setting of a man trap or the erection without warning of an electrified fence around property.[140] It may be that a court would feel that properly, liability for other crimes of violence, ought to be ascribed only to natural persons. This feeling might be particularly strong were it felt that the actions concerned had little relevance to corporate purposes. Much might, on this argument, depend on the context in which the crime first arose before the courts. Relevance to corporate purposes might clearly be present if, for example, an aggravated assault were committed by a plant policeman against a picketing striker.[141] On the other hand one might have reservations about convicting a corporation if, for example, its managing director assaulted some person who was in the process of making a take-over bid for the company.

A court could, in the case of some offences of violence, justify a finding that the corporation was not intended to be brought within the

terms of a statute by the use of other canons of statutory construction.
It could, for example, hold that the statute was intended merely to enact
an existing common law rule. This has occurred in the United States.
In *People* v. *Rochester Railway and Light Company*,[142] a charge of
manslaughter, the New York Court of Appeals held that the statutory
provision was intended to relate to natural persons only. The act defined
the offence in the same manner as it was defined at common law;
namely, the killing of one human being by another. Adopting a
construction *noscitur a sociis* the court held that 'another' meant
another human being. In *State* v. *Pacific Powder Corporation*[143] the
Oregon Supreme Court reached the same result. The corporation was
charged with manslaughter by negligence. Its employee had left a lorry,
loaded with explosives, near a wooden building. The building caught
fire causing the explosives to ignite. The resulting explosion killed a
person in the vicinity. The court noted that only one State, New Jersey,
has specifically provided for corporate liability for homicide and other
crimes of violence. It held that the Oregon statute was not apt to do
this. Corporations were not specifically mentioned in it. Furthermore,
manslaughter was not defined by the statute. In determining that the
statute was not intended to apply to corporations, the court relied
upon a common law definition of manslaughter as the killing of one
human being by another. It then concluded that the statute was intended
to apply only to natural persons.

A historical construction cast in terms of the genus 'human' could
be adopted under the Offences Against the Person Act, 1861.[144]
That act was passed before corporate criminal liability became widespread.
It could be said to enact the common law rule.[145] Furthermore, the act,
in several sections, speaks of an offence committed by one person upon
'any other person'.[146] Common law definitions, particularly of murder,
manslaughter and assault, do not envisage the commission of such crimes
by corporations. These factors, while not in themselves entitled to
great weight do afford a technique upon which a court, determined to
inhibit liability, might rely.

In addition, there are sundry instances of statutes having been held
not to apply to corporations. This is the case where, for example, the
practice of a learned profession is involved. It has been said that such
statutes are directed to natural persons who alone can obtain or fail
to obtain the necessary qualifications.[147] This has not prevented the courts
from issuing injunctions forbidding corporations from representing
that they carry on such a profession.[148]

Crimes which cannot be committed by corporations

It is assumed, in *Rex* v. *I. C. R. Haulage Ltd.*[149] that there exist some offences which a corporation cannot commit. These are offences which cannot be committed vicariously.[150] Thus offences such as bigamy and perjury cannot be committed by corporations. Bigamy is a clear exception because the definition of marriage is, not surprisingly, cast in terms of natural persons. Perjury raises more difficult issues. It may readily be conceded that perjury in the face of the court cannot be committed by a corporation because a person called as a witness is sworn in his natural capacity. In this respect the reasoning of Willmer and Davies L JJ in *Penn-Texas Corporation* v. *Anstalt and Others*[151] is to be preferred to that of Lord Denning MR in *Penn-Texas Corporation* v. *Murat-Anstalt*(2).[152] In the former case, in considering the Foreign Tribunals Evidence Act, 1856, Willmer and Davies L JJ state that a corporation can be ordered to produce documents as a party rather than as a witness in the proceedings. In the latter case, the Court of Appeal held that, on the true construction of the act an order to produce documents could be directed only to a witness. Pearson LJ limits the duty of a corporation to one of production of documents in its possession. Lord Denning MR while conceding that a corporation cannot be called to give evidence generally, held that it could be called upon to produce documents. A witness called to produce documents can however[153] ,

... be truly described as a witness called to produce documents and give evidence as to their possession or custody; but as a matter of practice, when no question arises as to possession or custody, he is not required to be sworn.

This implies that a company, giving evidence as to the possession or custody of documents by its proper officer, itself gives evidence. Accordingly it could, seemingly, commit perjury. It is doubtful whether a court would accept this conclusion, a concomitant of which seemingly must be that the officer is not a witness and so is not personally liable. It might well be said that where evidence of possession and custody of documents produced by a corporation had to be given, the officer giving the required testimony alone could be convicted, he being sworn in his personal capacity and not as the corporation. In such circumstances, had the company directed the officer to perjure himself, there seems little doubt that the company could be convicted of subornation of perjury.[154] Similarly, there is authority indicating that a company could be guilty of aiding and abetting bigamy.[155] Furthermore, there are variants of perjury which could readily be committed by a corporation. There seems, for example, no reason why a corporation could not wilfully use a false affidavit for the purposes of the Bills of Sale Act, 1878, contrary to section 2(2) of the Perjury Act, 1911,[156] or knowingly and wilfully make a false statement in a book of account contrary to section 5 thereof, or attempt to procure the registration of some person as qualified to pursue a vocation, contrary to section 6 of the act.

Perjury and bigamy apart it is by no means clear to what offences the above limitations apply. It is certainly difficult to appreciate what ambit may be accorded to the vicarious liability limitation. Vicarious liability, like all liability, is ascribed. There is nothing immanent in most crimes which prevents their ascription to a corporation. As Winn pointed out, there are circumstances in which rape could be ascribed to a corporation. One could have recourse to the dogma that English criminal law does not admit vicarious liability. This is however, one of the barriers which corporate criminal liability seeks to surmount by ascribing guilt to the corporation personally. That it has not done so entirely convincingly may be seen from the remarks of Stable J in *Rex* v. *I. C. R. Haulage Ltd.* to which attention has already been drawn.[157] Were a limitation to liability recognised on the footing that certain offences in respect of which vicarious liability is not permitted could not be ascribed to corporations, then corporations could not be held liable for major offences. It would represent a concession that corporate criminal liability is merely vicarious liability.

Relevance to corporate purpose as a limiting factor
The real limitation which these suggestions seek to convey is that to convict a corporation of rape or certain other sexual offences would seem absurd. This in turn must be because such offences cannot be seen as having relevance to corporate purposes. Although a person, a corporation is also, for the most part, a commercial device. Unless the actions in question have relevance to corporate purposes, to hold a corporation liable in respect of them hardly seems sensible. A court would have difficulty in visualising their having been committed on the corporation's behalf.[158]

Anomalous defences based on statute
Certain limited defences based on statutory construction occasionally

appear. The character of certain incorporated clubs and some co-operative societies as members clubs has occasionally acted as a defence. It has for example been held that an incorporated club need not possess a liquor licence. The court, equating an incorporated club to an unincorporated club, held that the members were, in both cases, joint owners of the club property so that there was in law no sale to them.[159] On the other hand, in *Wurzel* v. *Houghton Main Delivery Service Ltd.*[160] the court refused to go behind the facade of incorporation. The corporation was charged that it carried goods for hire or reward without having the appropriate carriers licence. It argued that it was essentially a members club delivering only to its own members. Each of them, it was argued, had an interest in the property, and the club was therefore not carrying other persons goods for hire or reward. The court, declining to follow its decisions on liquor licensing, held that the corporation was a separate legal entity. It alone therefore had a property interest in the goods carried. The members of a corporation could not be treated in the same fashion as the members of a club. This seems clearly correct. One basic principle of company law is that no shareholder has a personal right of property in any goods possessed by the corporation. The defence allowed in the liquor licensing cases was clearly anomalous.

Other reported instances of anomalous defences include a Canadian case in which an incorporated society which showed films on Sunday to fully paid members of the club was held not to be liable under the Canadian Lords Day Act of exhibiting on Sunday for hire or reward.[161] There is an American decision in which it was held that anti-trust legislation was not intended to affect municipal corporations.[162] It cannot be deduced from these cases that the type of corporation involved is generally a relevant factor in corporate criminal liability.

Statutory provisions excluding certain corporations

Certain statutory provisions expressly exclude certain corporations from their ambit. Here again, one can cite only instances. Restrictions on dealers in securities under the Prevention of Fraud (Investments) Act, 1958[163] are expressed not to apply to certain corporations such as the Bank of England and Building Societies. Similarly certain corporations are exempted from the Protection of Depositors Act, 1963.[164]

Liability of crown corporations

There is an important limitation as respects corporations functioning as agents of the Crown. These share in the historic immunity of the Crown to criminal process. The Crown and its agents are not bound by a criminal statute, unless an intention that they shall be clearly appears. At the same time, it is by no means clear which public corporations will be found to partake of this immunity. If the statute specifically provides that the corporation functions as an agent of the Crown it will not be criminally liable.[165] Otherwise, the answer to the question whether a corporation functions as an agent of the Crown depends upon such matters as the independance of the entity and the degree of control exercised by the appropriate minister over such matters as finance, policy, and the appointment and dismissal of staff. Where the body possesses substantial attributes of independance, status as a public servant does not confer immunity as an agent of the Crown.[166] Dr. Friedmann suggests that the industrial or commercial type of public corporation, such as the National Coal Board, or British Rail, or the airways corporations do not share in Crown immunity.[167] To this list may be added the British Broadcasting Corporation.[168] The situation is gradually being clarified by statute, and it is to be hoped that this process of clarification will continue.[169]

Pre-incorporation crimes and the effect of dissolution

Two further limitations may be mentioned briefly. Clearly, a corporation cannot be held liable for crimes committed by its promoters before incorporation.[170] Dissolution of a corporation abates any prosecution commenced against it.[171]

Procedure applicable to corporations

Modern procedure applicable to the trial of corporations, both summarily and on indictment, is contained in a number of statutes of which the most important is the Magistrates Courts Act 1952.[172] Schedule II of that Act contains most of the relevant provisions. By section 3 of that schedule and section 29 of the Criminal Justice Act 1967 the corporation may appear by a representative[173] who may enter a plea to the charge, make a statement to the examining justices in answer to the charge, and who may consent or object to summary trial or claim trial by jury. Section 29 of the Criminal Justice Act 1967 further provides that a company which wishes to plead guilty and be tried without appearing before the Court may give a written notification or information accordingly[174] by a director or its secretary. The notification need not be under seal nor is any particular form of validation required. Where no representative appears any requirement in the Act that anything shall be done in the presence of or read or said to the representative shall not

apply nor shall any requirement that the consent of the accused be
obtained for summary trial apply.[175] If the trial is to proceed by
indictment, the court shall proceed to hold a preliminary inquiry. At
the conclusion thereof, if the court is of opinion that there is sufficient
evidence to put the corporation on trial it shall commit it accordingly.[176]
By section 1 of Schedule II, the court commits the corporation by an
order in writing empowering the prosecutor to prefer a bill of indictment
in respect of the offence named in the order. It was held in *Rex* v.
H. Sherman Ltd.[177] that the existence of such an order is a condition
precedent to the preferment of an indictment. The order must be made by
the magistrates before the bill of indictment is signed by the Clerk of
Assize. It may be noted that there still exists a power to prefer a bill
of indictment by the direction or with the consent of a judge of the High
Court, notwithstanding that committal proceedings have not taken
place.[178] On a trial on indictment the corporation may on arraignment
enter a plea of guilty or not guilty by its representative. If the corporation
does not appear, or on appearance fails to enter a plea, the court shall
enter a plea of not guilty.[179]

By section 6 of Schedule II, section 10(2) of the Magistrates Courts
Act, 1952 applies to corporations. Where the corporation is committed
for trial at Quarter Sessions, and the next Quarter Sessions for that county
or borough are to be held within five days, the court may commit the
corporation to the next Quarter Sessions but one. By Schedule II,
section 2, it is provided that the bill of indictment may include either
in substitution for or in addition to counts charging the offence for
which the corporation was committed, any counts founded on facts or
evidence disclosed in the preliminary inquiry or founded on the depositions
taken before the justices.[180] Section 9 of Schedule II deals with the
position where a corporation is charged jointly with an individual with
an offence before a magistrates court. If the offence is one which may be
tried summarily with the consent of the accused, the court shall not
proceed to summary trial unless each accused consents to be tried
summarily. If the offence is a summary offence, but one for which the
accused may claim trial by jury, the court shall not try either of the
accused summarily if the other exercises the right to trial by jury.

One point with respect to offences tried summarily may be noted.
Section 19(4) of the Magistrates Courts Act does not apply to
corporations.[181] Therefore, a corporation which consents to be tried
summarily for an offence specified by Schedule I cannot be committed to
Quarter Sessions under section 29 of the Act for sentence if the court

c*

is of opinion that it cannot award an adequate sentence. The court need not, by reason of section 19(2), grant the accused corporation an election if, having regard to the nature of the case and the adequacy of the punishment it can impose, it feels the case is properly one to be tried on indictment.

One final point may be noted. A corporation, like an individual, may make formal admissions before or during trial. Such admissions if made before trial must be made in writing and purport to be signed by a director or manager or the secretary or clerk or some other similar officer of the body corporate.[182] Apparently, oral admissions made before trial on behalf of a corporation need not be approved by its counsel or solicitor.[183] Oral admissions at trial seemingly can be made by a corporation's representative.[184]

1   See the discussion in chapter 7
2   Under the Quebec Civil Code, partnerships are legal entities. For an instance of criminal liability imposed upon a partnership, see *Prices Board* v. *Cote* (1946) 5 CR 237
3   Prices and Incomes Act 1966, sections 13, 16, 22
4   *Lewis* v. *Crafter* [1942] SASR 36; *McNabb* v. *Edmonson & Co. Ltd.* [1941] VLR 193; *Home Benefits Pty. Ltd.* v. *Crafter* (1939) 61 CLR 701
5   See discussion in the *Model Penal Code*, T.D.4, Notes at pp 155-156
6   *Regina* v. *Stanley Haulage Ltd.* (1964) 114 L. Jo. 25
7   *Rex* v. *I. C. R. Haulage Ltd.* [1944] KB 551; *John Henshall (Quarries) Ltd.* v. *Harvey* [1965] 2 QB 233; *Regina* v. *McDonnell* [1965] 3 WLR 1138
8   It is interesting that, in the two most recent cases, *John Henshall (Quarries) Ltd.* v. *Harvey* and *Regina* v. *McDonnell*, the *alter ego* theory as propounded in *Lennards Carrying Company* v. *Asiatic Petroleum Company Ltd.* [1915] AC 705 has been consciously applied. In turn this throws doubt upon earlier decisions, and in particular, *National Coal Board* v. *Gamble* (1958) 42 Cr. App.R. 240
9   Thus there remains considerable dispute over what officers can be said to be the *alter ego* of a corporation. Glanville Williams, *Criminal Law; The General Part* (2nd ed. 1961), considers that a branch manager could be said to be the *alter ego* of a corporation. See *Regina* v. *Stanley Haulage Ltd.* (1964) 114 L. Jo. 25, and the discussion in chapter 7
10   Welsh, 'The Criminal Liability Of Corporations' (1946) 62 LQR 345, and see Downey (1959) 22 MLR 91
11   *Rex* v. *I. C. R. Haulage Ltd.* [1944] KB 551
12   (1923) 54 OLR 38 at page 46 per Rose J
13   See *Regina* v. *Stanley Haulage Ltd.* (1964) 114 L. Jo. 25; *Rex* v. *I. C. R. Haulage Ltd.* [1944] KB 551
14   See the discussion in chapter 7 with respect to the *alter ego* doctrine
15   Compare *Tunstall* v. *Steigmann* [1962] 2 WLR 1045 with *Barreau de Richelieu* v. *St. Jean Automobile Ltée* [1957] Que. S. C. 360

16 See *Regina* v. *McDonnell* [1965] 3 WLR 1138
17 *Regina* v. *Howard Smith Paper Mills Ltd.* [1954] OR 543; *Standard Oil Company of Texas* v. *United States*, 307 F 2d. 120 (1963)
18 [1944] 2 All ER 515
19 With respect to *ultra vires* as a general bar see chapter 2
20 *Bonanza Creek Gold Mining Company* v. *The King* [1916] 1 AC 566
21 *Ashbury Carriage Company* v. *Riche* (1875) LR 7 HL 653. Pollock called it a doctrine of constitutional limitations. See 'Has The Common Law Received The Fiction Theory Of Corporations' (1911) 27 LQR 219
22 *Great Northern Railway Company* v. *Charlebois* [1899] AC 114 (PC); *In re Jon Beauforte Ltd.* [1953] Ch. 131
23 Goodhart, *Essays In Jurisprudence And The Common Law* (1931) p 91 seq
24 Street, *The Doctrine Of Ultra Vires* (1930) p.259; Clerk & Lindsell, *On Torts* (12th ed. edited by Armitage, 1961) p 94; *Palmer's Company Law* (21st. ed. edited by Schmitthoff (1968)) p 129
25 See Harno 'Privileges and Powers of a Corporation And The Doctrine of Ultra Vires', 35 Yale LJ 1 (1925); Salmond, *Law of Torts* (14th ed. edited by Heuston, 1965) pp 611-613; Street, *Law Of Torts* (3rd ed. 1963) p'475. The argument advanced in Winfield, *On Torts* (7th ed. edited by Jolowicz, 1963) does not really meet Goodhart's point which is that a company cannot act beyond the powers accorded to it in its objects clause.
26 *Poulton* v. *London and South-Western Railway* (1867) LR 2 QB 534; *Ormiston* v. *Great Western Railway* [1917] 1 KB 598
27 (1874) LR 9 Ex. 309
28 LR 9 Ex. 309, 321 per Kelly CB dissenting. Kelly CB in fact took a wider view of the Boards powers than the majority and would have held it liable
29 [1911] 1 KB 869
30 *The Taff Vale Railway Company* v. *The Amalgamated Society of Railway Servants* [1901] AC 426, 433 per Farwell J
31 [1961] 1 QB 1
32 [1965] 3 WLR 1065 and on appeal [1966] 2 QB 656
32a The dictum has been distinguished in *Re Staines U.D.C. Agreement*, [1968] 3 all ER 1. See also *Re K.L. Tractors Ltd.*, (1961) 106 CLR 318; *Breckenridge Speedway Ltd.* v. *The Queen*, (1967) 64 DLR (2d) 488 per Porter JA
33 (1877) 2 App. Cas. 792, 806 per Lord Blackburn
34 Street, *The Doctrine Of Ultra Vires* (1930) p 259
35 [1902] NZLR 593
36 [1940] NZLR 75
37 *Joplin Mercantile Co.* v. *United States*, 213 Fed. 296 (1914) aff'd 236 US 532; *Massa* v. *Wanamaker Academy of Beauty Culture Inc.* 80 NYS (2d) 923 (1948) *United States* v. *Mirror Lake Golf And Country Club Inc.*, 232 F. Supp. 167; *State* v. *Shouse*, 177 So. 2d 724 (1965)
38 Hornstein, *Corporation Law And Practice* (1959) vol 2, p 38
39 *Adams* v. *The National Electric Tramway and Lighting Company* (1893) 3 BCR 199 (but this is seemingly to be regarded as a case on illegality); Wegenast, *The Law Of Canadian Companies* (1930) p 133
40 [1957] Que. SC 360
41 See the discussion in chapter 7

42 [1957] SCR 436 at page 446
43 *Upholsterers International Union of North America No. 1* v. *Hankin & Struck Furniture Ltd. et al.* (1964) 49 WWR (ns) 33
44 *Egan* v. *Barrier Branch of the Amalgamated Mines Association and Others*(1917) 17 SR (NSW) 243; *Williams* v. *Hursey* (1960-61) 103 CLR at p 128-9 per Menzies J.
45 Gower, *Modern Company Law* (2nd ed. 1957) p 93
46 See the discussion in Chapter 9
47 In *Cotman* v. *Brougham* [1918] AC 514 the practice was deprecated, but without result.
48 [1966] 2 All ER 674
49 See Wedderburn, 'The Death of Ultra Vires?' (1966) 29 MLR 673
50 *Report of the Company Law Committee* (1962) Cmnd. 1749, para. 42
51 Especially in the light of recent decisions of the Court of Appeal, and in particular, *Penn-Texas Corporation* v. *Murat-Anstalt* (2) [1964] 2 All ER 594; *Willis* v. *Association of Universities of the British Commonwealth* [1964] 2 WLR 946 The paradoxical character of these developments has been discussed by Professor Wedderburn in 'Corporate personality And Social Policy: The Problem Of The Quasi-Corporation' (1965) 28 MLR 62 at pp 70-71
52 *Regina* v. *Birmingham and Gloucester Railway* (1842) 3 QB 223
53 *Regina* v. *Great North of England Railway Company* (1846) 9 QB 315
54 *Attorney-General* v. *P. Y. A. Quarries Ltd.* [1957] 2 QB 169
55 *Triplex Safety Glass Ltd.* v. *Lancegaye* [1939] 2 KB 395
56 *Lewis* v. *Crafter* [1942] SASR 36; *Provincial Motor Cab Company* v. *Dunning* [1909] 2 KB 599, but the particular decision in that case can no longer be supported. See Glanville Williams, *Criminal Law; The General Part* (2nd ed. 1961) at page 275
57 *Model Penal Code,* TD 4, Notes at page 150
58 *Rex* v. *I. C. R. Haulage Ltd.* [1944] KB 551
59 *Regina* v. *Blamires Transport Services Ltd.* [1963] 3 WLR 496; *Regina* v. *Stanley Haulage Ltd.* [1964] Crim. LR 221
60 *Ackroyds Air Travel Ltd.* v. *D. P. P.* [1950] 1 All ER 933; and see *John Henshall (Quarries) Ltd.* v. *Harvey* [1965] 2 QB 233
61 *Rex* v. *I. C. R. Haulage Ltd.* [1944] KB 551
62 *East Crest Oil Company Limited* v. *The King* [1944] 3 DLR 535; rev'd on other grounds [1945] SCR 191; *Union Colliery Company* v. *The Queen* (1900) Can. SCR 81; *Rex* v. *Bennet & Co. Pty. Ltd.* 1941 TPD 194
63 e.g. *Regina* v. *Odhams Press* [1956] 3 WLR 796
64 Glanville Williams, *Criminal Law; The General Part* (2nd ed. 1961) at page 861
65 *Rex* v. *Fane Robinson Ltd.* [1941] 3 DLR 409
66 e.g. *Regina* v. *Howard Smith Paper Mills Ltd.* [1954] OR 543; *Regina* v. *Electrical Contractors Ltd.* (1961) 27 DLR (2d) 193
67 *Rex* v. *Foothills Recreation Association* [1941] 2 DLR 203
68 *Regina* v. *Sommers et al.* (1958) 124 CCC 241; *Regina* v. *H. J. O'Connell Ltd.* [1962] Que QB 660
69 *Rex* v. *Hudsons Bay Company* (1915) 9 WWR 522
70 *Regina* v. *Loblaw Groceterias Co. (Man.) Ltd.* (1960) 34 CR 214
71 See the recent General Electric Company Case, cited by Donnelly, Goldstein & Schwartz, *Criminal Law* (1962) pp 1087-1089 for a striking example
72 *New York Central and Hudson Railroad* v. *United States,* 212 US 481 (1909)

73 *United States* v. *Cotter*, 60 F 2d 689 (1932)

74 *C.I.T. Corporation* v. *United States*, 150 F 2d 85 (1945)

75 *People* v. *Canadian Fur Trappers Corporation*, 248 NY 159 (1928)

76 *People* v. *Tyson*, 50 NYLJ 1829 (1914); *Magnolia Motor and Logging Corporation* v. *United States*, 264 F 2d 950 (1959)

77 *United States* v. *Armour and Co.* 168 F 2d 342 (1948)

78 *United States* v. *Carter et al.* 311 F 2d 934 (1963)

79 *States* v. *Carney*, 177 NE 2d 799 (1960)

80 *United States* v. *American Socialist Society*, 260 Fed. 885 (1919)

81 *United States* v. *New York Herald Co.* 159 Fed. 296 (1907)

82 *United States* v. *Nearing*, 252 Fed. 223 (1918)

83 *State* v. *Workers Socialist Publishing Co.* 185 NW 930 (1921)

84 *State* v. *Rowland Lumber Co.* 69 SE 58 (1910)

85 Mullen, *The Development And Rationale Of Corporate Criminal Liability* (1951) unpublished thesis, New York University, p 44

86 *Regina* v. *Evening Standard Co. Ltd.* [1954] 1 QB 578

87 *Regina* v. *Odhams Press Ltd.* [1957] 1 QB 73

88 See the dicta of Denning LJ in *Pride of Derby and Derbyshire Angling Association Ltd.* v. *British Celanese Ltd.* [1953] 1 Ch. 149, 192 doubting whether, were a corporation in breach of an injunction, the individual members could be attached. The doubts therein expressed appear, as will be seen, to be ill-founded

89 'The Rules Of The Supreme Court' S.I. 1965/1776

90 *Ronson Products Ltd.* v. *Ronson Furniture Ltd.* [1966] Ch. 603; *Redwing Ltd.* v. *Redwing Forest Products Ltd.* (1947) 177 LT 387

91 *Marengo* v. *Daily Sketch Ltd.* [1948] 1 All ER 406 (HL) per Lord Uthwatt; *Seaward* v. *Paterson* [1897] 1 Ch. 545 (CA)

92 *Ronson Products Ltd.* v. *Ronson Furniture Ltd.* [1966] Ch. 603; overruling *Redwing Ltd.* v. *Redwing Forest Products Ltd.* (1947) 177 LT 387. The distinction between positive and prohibitory orders is well recognised. See also *Lord Wellesley* v. *Earl of Mornington* (1848) 11 Beav. 180; *United Telephone Company* v. *Dale* (1884) 24 Ch. D 778; *In re Tuck, Murch* v. *Loosemore* [1906] 1 Ch. 692. Unfortunately, the *Annual Practice*, in successive editions failed to note that these decisions might be pertinent to corporations and treated *Redwing Ltd.* v. *Redwing Forest Products Ltd.* (1947) 177 LT 387 as the sole authority applicable

93 (1965) LR 5 RP 315 at page 350

94 *Mawji* v. *The Queen* [1957] 2 WLR 277; *Knowbel* v. *The Queen* [1954] SCR 497

95 Dictum of Porter J in *De Jetley Marks* v. *Lord Greenwood* [1936] 1 All ER 863

96 *Rex* v. *Martin* [1933] 1 DLR 434

97 *Goldlawr Inc.* v. *Schubert et al.* 276 F 2d 614 (1960); *Nelson* v. *Motorola Inc.* 200 F 2d 911 (1952)

98 *Reg.* v. *Blamires Transport Services Ltd.* [1963] 3 All ER 170 and see the note by Calvert in (1964) 27 MLR 220

99 *Reg.* v. *Electrical Contractors Association* (1961) 27 DLR (2nd) 193. Cf. *Goldlawr Inc.* v. *Schubert*, 276 F 2d 614 (1960) holding that no conspiracy can be charged in such a situation

100 [1965] 3 WLR 1138

101 [1915] AC 705

102 [1957] 1 QB 159, 172

103 This distinction was explicitly drawn by Nield J, who relied upon *Lee* v. *Lee's Air Farming Ltd.* [1961] AC 12 (PC)
104 (1961) 27 DLR (2d) 193
105 [1965] 3 WLR 1138 at page 1148
106 [1965] 3 WLR 1138 at page 1149 relying on *Rex* v. *Martin* [1932] 3 WWR 1 and Glanville Williams, *Criminal Law; The General Part* (2nd ed. 1961) p 861
107 See Woods, 'Lifting The Corporate Veil In Canada' (1957) 35 Can. Bar Rev. 1176
108 See American cases cited *infra,* and *Regina* v. *Dominion Steel and Coal Company Ltd.* (1956) 116 CCC 117
109 See *Poller* v. *Columbia Broadcasting System Inc. et al.* 284 F 2d 599 (1960) (Corporation cannot conspire with its unincorporated divisions)
110 See Exchange Control Act, 1947 section 30(2); Companies Act, 1948, sections 150-154, and see *Berendsen Ltd.* v. *I.R.C.* [1958] Ch. 1; *Unit Construction Company Ltd.* v. *Bullock* [1960] AC 351; *Caddies* v. *Harold Holdsworth (Wakefield) Ltd.* 1955 SC (HL) 27, but cp. *Firestone Tire and Rubber Company Ltd.* v. *Llewellin* [1957] 1 WLR 464
111 Companies Act, 1948 sections 150-154, and especially section 154, subs. (1) and (2) Companies Act 1967 ss. 16-20 and Schedule 2
112 See e.g. *Minutes of evidence taken before the Company Law Committee,* HMSO 1960-61 at page 1448 (Federation of British Industries)
113 See in general, Berle, 'The Theory Of The Enterprise Entity, 47 Col. L. Rev. 343' (1947)
114 See especially the decision of Judson J in *Regina* v. *Dominion Steel and Coal Company Ltd.* (1956) 116 CCC 117
115 *United States* v. *Yellow Cab Company*, 322 US 221, 227 (1943)
116 *Keefer-Stewart Co.* v. *Seagrams Inc,* 340 US 211 (1951) 95 L. Ed. at page 222 (appellants brief)
117 341 US 593 (1951) 95 L. Ed. 1199
118 95 L. Ed. at page 1210
119 Cp. *Poller* v. *Columbia Broadcasting System Inc.* 284 F 2d 599 (1960)
120 370 US 19 (1960)
121 370 US 19, 29 (1960). The act involved was the *Capper-Volstead Act*, 15 US Code, 17 which provides in part that: 'Nothing contained in the Antitrust law shall be construed to forbid the existence and operation of labor, agricultural or horticultural organizations, instituted for purposes of mutual help . . . or to forbid or restrain individual members of such organizations from lawfully carrying out the legitimate objects thereof; nor shall such organizations, or the members thereof, be held or construed to be illegal combinations or conspiracies in restraint of trade under the Antitrust laws'.
122 Issues of antitrust enforcement fall outside the scope of this thesis. Regard might be had however, to Stengel, 'Intra-Enterprise Conspiracy Under Section 1 Of The Sherman Act' (1963) 35 Miss. L.J. 5
123 In such a situation it would seem preferable to charge the human agents with conspiracy among each other, rather than to charge conspiracies between the several companies. It is difficult to believe that this problem will however, receive any extended discussion by the courts. The reasoning of Judson J in *Regina* v. *Dominion Steel and Coal Company Ltd.* (1956) 116 CCC 117 would probably be followed

124 191 F 2d 313 (1951)

125 [1952] 1 KB 232

126 [1944] KB 551

127 Interpretation Act, 1889, chapter 63, section 2(2)

128 *Rex* v. *Daily Mirror Newspapers Ltd.* [1922] 2 KB 530, and see *Cohen* v. *United States*, 157 Fed. 651 (1907)

129 *Rex* v. *Daily Mirror Newspapers Ltd.* [1922] 2 KB (J) 530

130 *Hart* v. *Hay, Nisbet and Co.* (1900) 2 Fraser (J) 39

131 Most felonies were made finable by the Criminal Justice Act 1948 sec. 13. The distinction between felony and misdemeanour has been abolished by the Criminal Law Act 1967 sec. 1 and all offences save a few such as murder and treason which bear a fixed penalty are now finable

132 *Rex* v. *Ascanio Puck and Co. & Paice* (1912) 76 JP 487

133 *Orpen* v. *Haymarket Capitol Limited* (1931) 145 LT 614; *Green* v. *Kursaal Estates Ltd.* [1937] 1 All ER 732; *Houghton-le-Touzel* v. *Mecca Ltd.* [1950] 2 KB 612; cf. *Hawke* v. *E. Hulton Ltd.* [1909] 2 KB 93; *A.G.* v. *Walkergate Press Ltd.* (1930) 142 LT 408 (*Lotteries Act*, 1823), and see the doubts expressed by Croom-Johnson J in *Goodchild* v. *Welborne* [1941] 2 All ER 449 (*Gaming Act*, 1845)

134 *Mutual Loan Agency* v. *A.G., New South Wales* (1909) 9 CLR 72; *United States* v. *Union Supply Company*, 215 US 50 (1909)

135 *Briggs* v. *Gibsons Bakery Ltd.* [1948] NI 165

136 *Regina* v. *Great North of England Railway Company* (1846) 9 QB 315

137 *Rex* v. *I.C.R. Haulage Ltd.* [1944] KB 551, and see The Times Feb. 5, 1965 'Firm Cleared In Bridge Case' for an account of recent proceedings against the Northern Strip Mining Construction Co. Ltd. for manslaughter at Glamorgan Assizes

138 *Rex* v. *East Crest Oil Co. Ltd.* [1944] 3 DLR 535 (Alberta CA) rev'd on other grounds [1945] 2 DLR 35; *Rex* v. *Bennet & Co. Pty. Ltd.* 1941 TPD 194 (S.Af.)

139 See *Union Colliery Company* v. *The Queen* (1900) 31 Can. SCR 81; *East Crest Oil Company Ltd.* v. *The Queen* [1944] 3 DLR 535

140 See *Rex* v. *Cory Brothers Ltd.* [1927] 1 KB 810

141 As respects murder or battery, the facts in *Denver and Rio Grande Railway* v. *Harris*, 122 US 597 (1887) may give occasion for thought. Respondent, a servant of another railway, was working on a line of its track, when an armed force, led by the appellant's vice-president began a brisk gun battle, in the course of which the respondent was wounded; in such a manner, the report states, that he was unlikely to produce descendants. Appellant was held to exemplary damages, it being held that the actions of its vice-president were personal to it. See for further examples of violent crimes accompanying labour disputes, Mueller, 'Mens Rea And The Corporation' (1957) 19 U.Pitt.L.Rev. 21 at p 23

142 195 NY 102 (1909)

143 360 P 2d 530 (1961)

144 24 & 25 Victoria, chapter 100

145 So argued in *Russell on Crime* (12th ed. edited by Turner, 1964) vol. 1, p 96

146 e.g. Section 20 (inflicting bodily harm upon any other person); section 23 (maliciously administering poison so as to endanger life); section 42 (penalties of fine and imprisonment provided for assault upon 'any other person')

147 *Pharmaceutical Society* v. *London and Provincial Supply Association* (1880) 5 App. Cas. 857

148 *O'Duffy* v. *Jaffe* [1904] 2 Ir. Rep. 27;,*A. G.* v. *George C. Smith Ltd.*
[1909] 2 Ch. 524
149 [1944] KB 551
150 See remarks of Stable J [1944] KB 551 at page 554
151 [1963] 1 All ER 258
152 [1964] 2 All ER 594
153 [1964] 2 All ER 594 at page 598
154 Cross & Jones, *An Introduction To Criminal Law* (5th ed. 1964) at page 101
155 This would follow from the line of cases establishing that a person can aid and
abet an offence for which that person could not be liable as principal in the first
degree at common law. See *Reg.* v. *Ram* (1893) 17 Cox CC 609, and a leading
Canadian decision, *Rex* v. *Hendrie* (1905) 11 OLR 202
156 Perjury Act, 1911 (1 & 2 George V, Chapter 6)
157 [1944] KB 551, 554
158 See Lee, 'Corporate Criminal Liability' (1928) 28 Col. L. Rev. 1
159 *Graff* v. *Evans* (1881) 8 QBD 373; *I. R. C.* v. *Eccentric Club Ltd.* [1924]
1 KB 390 at page 421; *Trebanog Working Mens Club Ltd.* v. *Macdonald* [1940]
1 KB 576
160 [1937] 1 KB 380
161 *Webster* v. *Winnipeg Film Society* (1964) 46 WWR 632 (Can. S.C.). For another
anomalous example see *Reg.* v. *W. MacKenzie Securities Ltd.* (1966) 56 D.L.R. (2d) 56
162 *Denman* v. *City of Idaho Falls* (1931) 4 P 2d 361 (Idaho S.C.)
163 Prevention of Fraud (Investments) Act, 1958, section 2
164 Protection of Depositors Act, 1963, section 5(2)
165 See *Cain* v. *Doyle* (1946) 72 CLR 419; in which the criminal provisions of a
statute which otherwise bound the Crown were held not applicable to it;
Attorney-General of Ontario v. *Canadian Broadcasting Corporation* [1959]
SCR 188 at page 196 per Rand J
166 *Tamlin* v. *Hannaford* [1950] 1 KB 18; *Bank Voor Handel on Scheepvart
N.V.* v. *Administrator of Hungarian Property* [1954] AC 584; *Pfizer* v. *Ministry
of Health* [1963] 3 WLR 999; *British Broadcasting Corporation* v. *Johns* [1964]
2 WLR 1071
167 Friedmann, 'The Legal Status And Organization Of The Public Corporation'
(1951) 16 L & CP 576
168 *British Broadcasting Corporation* v. *Johns* [1964] 2 WLR 1071
169 e.g. Atomic Energy Act, 1954, section 38; Electricity Act, 1957, section 38;
Transport Act, 1962, section 30
170 This is clear on principle, see *United States* v. *Crummer,* 151 F 2d 958 (1945)
171 See *Regina* v. *Howard Smith Paper Mills Ltd.* [1954] OR 543. In the United
States it has been held that under special legislative provisions, prosecutions
pending before an abatement may be preserved. See *United States* v. *Carter et al.*
311 F 2d 934 (1963)
172 For an account of the former procedural inhibitions which culminated in the
procedural provisions of the Criminal Justice Act 1925 see Chapter 2
173 Defined by Criminal Justice Act 1925 sec. 33 (6) to mean a person duly
appointed by the corporation to represent it. Proof of appointment must be in
writing and signed by the managing director or by a person having the management
of the corporation

174 Pursuant to sec. 1 (2) of the Magistrates' Courts Act 1957
175 Magistrates Courts Act 1952 Schedule II, sections 4 and 5
176 Magistrates Courts Act, 1952, section 7
177 [1949] 2 KB 674
178 Administration of Justice (Miscellaneous Provisions) Act, 1933, section 2 (2)
179 Criminal Justice Act 1925 sec. 33 (3)
180 This section incorporates by reference, the provisions of the Administration of Justice (Miscellaneous Provisions) Act, 1933 section 2 (2) Proviso (i)
181 Magistrates Courts Act, 1952 Schedule II, section 7
182 Criminal Justice Act 1967 sec. 10(2) (c)
183 *Ibid.* sec. 10(2) (d)
184 *Ibid.* sec. 10(2) (d)

Chapter 6

The relationship between vicarious liability and corporate criminal liability

Corporations, as has been seen, have long been liable for offences of both strict and vicarious liability. Many of these offences are directed towards the regulation of various aspects of trade and commerce. In practice, they account for the great bulk of corporate convictions. It has been argued that all corporate liability is truly vicarious. Here, however, we are concerned with statutory offences in respect of which employers generally are made liable for the actions of their servants and agents.

No discussion of all the problems posed by strict and vicarious liability is intended. Attention is directed to the particular problems posed by vicarious liability for crimes involving *mens rea* when corporate guilt is in issue. Consequently, the discussion for the most part is directed towards the relationship between corporate liability and vicarious liability. In particular, it demonstrates that, on the tests of corporate liability and vicarious liability as they presently exist, a confusion between the two is virtually inevitable. It also demonstrates that a failure adequately to distinguish between them has been caused by an insufficient appreciation of the function which each is designed to serve. Furthermore, it can be shown that any conceptual difference between corporate liability and vicarious liability is difficult to maintain in practice in the absence of strong policy criteria respecting the impostion of each. This is of course of importance only in respect of the common area in which either vicarious or personal liability may be imposed. It is, however, difficult to define with any precision the permissible ambit of vicarious liability. It is also difficult to determine upon what basis the courts decide which offences are to attract vicarious liability.

In addition, vexed problems arise with respect to defences based upon the exercise of due care and diligence by an employer. It cannot be contended that the courts, when faced with a corporation seeking to avail itself of such a defence, have always characterized the problem correctly, or solved adequately the question who, for the purposes of such defences, shall be said to represent the corporation as such.

It should be added that this discussion is directed towards vicarious

liability for crimes involving criminal intent. Otherwise, there is no need
to distinguish between corporate liability and vicarious liability.
Vicarious liability is directed toward imposing a police function upon
the master in respect of the actions of his servants or agents. Corporations
are in the same position as any other master. Vicarious liability can mean
either of two things. If liability is imposed *respondeat superior,* in the
absence of a requirement of intent, it may mean no more than that a
servant, in performing a routine task has supplied an *actus reus* which
will be imputed to the master as his personal *actus reus.*[1] Alternatively,
if liability is imposed where the servant enjoys a delegated power, the
offence is essentially that of the servant, liability for it being ascribed
to the master. In both cases, the rationale of liability relates to the failure
of an employer adequately to perform a supervisory function.[2] In either
case, because liability is vicarious, it usually matters little whether the
offence is that of the master or of the servant. The same result normally
follows. It may be thought that special problems arise with respect to
corporations because they can act only through their officers, agents
and servants. This however, is not so. The only special problems which do
arise are problems of scale. These have no relevance to the nature of
the entity under consideration. They have however caused difficulty
with respect to defences based upon the exercise of care and diligence
by an employer and are discussed in that connexion. For a discussion
of related problems such as the occasion for imposition of liability,
whether it should be *respondeat superior* or delegation, or the adequacy
of the purported justifications of vicarious liability which fall outside
the scope of this study, reference may be made to a number of general
studies of the topic.[3] Where crimes involving *mens rea* are in issue
however, the problem arises of determining what acts are to be ascribed
as personal to the corporation and which are to be actions for which only
vicarious liability, albeit liability involving intent, is to be ascribed.
In any large business, some functions must of necessity be delegated.
In the case of a corporation however, one must distinguish between
various authorities exercised on its behalf, holding some to be personal
as representing the actions of its government and others to be merely
acts by procuration. In distinguishing between these, the difficulty lies in
determining whose intent shall be ascribed as personal to the corporation.

Tests of vicarious liability

The problem of determining whether any offence carries with it
vicarious liability is essentially a problem of statutory construction.[4]

The accepted test was enunciated by Lord Atkin in *Mousell Brothers Limited* v. *London and North Western Railway Company*.[5] While this test has been discussed in relation to corporate criminal liability earlier in this study, it may be helpful to reiterate that in determining whether an absolute duty has been laid upon a master, regard must be had to[6]:

> . . . the words used, the nature of the duty laid down, the person upon whom it is imposed, the person by whom it would in ordinary circumstances be performed, and the person upon whom the penalty is imposed.

This test represents a synthesis of the desiderata laid down in several earlier decisions. It has been held to be the relevant test both where crimes requiring criminal intent and crimes of strict liability are concerned.[7] Because of the circumstances in which it was enunciated, it has led to a much wider ascription of vicarious liability in crimes of intent than the courts initially envisaged, and it has further resulted in complicating the task of statutory construction. One result has been a fairly widespread ambit of judicial discretion.[8]

Before discussing these developments however, the earlier cases should be examined. In them there is a fairly clear indication under what circumstances the courts were prepared to ascribe vicarious liability. These were forecast in the early smoke nuisance cases, though such offences were cast in terms of strict liability. *Chisholm* v. *Doulton* in 1889 provides an instructive example.[9] The defendant the owner-occupier of certain pottery works, was charged under Sec. 1 (1) of the Smoke Nuisance (Metropolis) Act, 1853, which made it an offence to use a furnace in such a manner that it emitted black smoke. It provided that 'every person so offending, being the owner or occupier of the premises, or other person employed by such owner or occupier . . . ' should be subject to certain penalties on summary conviction. The defendant was free of blame and was acquitted by the magistrates. The Divisional Court dismissed an appeal brought from their decision. The general rule stated by Field and Cave JJ is that a master is not to be made liable for the actions of his servants. The statute in plain terms envisaged the punishment of the actual offender. Field J then delivered an interesting dictum based upon sec. 2 of the same act. That section related to steamers and provided in part that if the engine should be so negligently used as to emit smoke ' . . . the owner or master or other person having charge of such vessel . . . ' should be liable to conviction'. He stated[10]:

From a comparison of the language of those two sections it seems to me that in the one case the intention of the legislature was to strike at the person guilty of the negligence, while in the other owing to the difficulty of finding out who that person was, it struck directly at the owner or person in charge.

The reasoning of Cave J is similar, and it is this type of reasoning which was employed in most of the early decisions imposing vicarious liability for offences involving *mens rea.*

This analysis was, for example, faithfully adhered to in cases arising under the Licensing Acts, the penal provisions of which were, for the most part, directed not to 'any person' or to 'every one', but to 'every holder of a license',[11] or to 'any licensed person'.[12] Accordingly to permit a licensee to delegate management and thus to avoid personal knowledge of the commission of offences upon his premises would have removed them from the control scheme of the act. While judicial statements can be found stating that liability depends on the issuance of license, carrying with it correlative responsibilities,[13] liability really rested on the form of the statutory command.[14] As was said by Lord Reading CJ in *Mellor* v. *Lydiate*[15] : ' . . . the object of the statutory requirement is to make the person who conducts and manages the business there transacted responsible to the licensing justices for its proper and orderly conduct'.

The matter was probably put most clearly by Halse Rogers J in an Australian case, *Alford* v. *Rily Newman Ltd.* when he remarked that[16] :

If the statute is one of the category of statutes regulating trade or business . . . and if also, a liability is thrown on the principal by terms expressly imposing the penalty on him, then he becomes responsible for the knowledge and intent of the servant—his *mens rea.* It is reasonable in such cases that the master on whom responsibility is placed should not be able to avoid that responsibility by putting in his place an agent who will have the *mens rea* which otherwise would be possessed by the master.

This conclusion can be supported by reference to other English and Commonwealth decisions.[17] The same analysis was employed in areas other than liquor licensing.[18] Some early and significant examples occur under the Road Traffic Acts.[19] Essentially, the courts looked to see whether an exclusive duty was imposed in plain terms upon a specified person in the exercise of a given business activity.

In time, however, this analysis was departed from. The cause apparently lay in a failure by the courts to differentiate adequately between crimes of strict liability which could also be committed vicariously, and crimes involving *mens rea* in respect of which vicarious liability was imposed. The tests in respect of the former class of offences in fact permitted a much greater scope to judicial discretion. In order to determine whether commission of a strict liability offence could be ascribed to a master, the courts had regard to the language, and to the scope and object of the statute.[20] Particularly in cases of sale of goods, there was a readiness to find that the act was ' . . . from its very nature, obviously the act of the master'.[21] The language and scope of the section were readily construed to import vicarious liability where the offence was against public order,[22] or was said not to be a crime but an act prohibited under a penalty[23] or 'quasi-criminal'.[24] Furthermore, where the offence was one of strict liability, 'course of employment' and 'delegation' were used indiscriminately as occasions for the imposition of liability.[25] In addition, the justification for such liability was said on occasion to be the same in either class of offence.[26] In such circumstances, it is not surprising that the wider justification of vicarious liability was chosen as applicable to all cases.

That, at any rate, occurred in *Mousell*'s case.[27] The statutory prohibition was laid in neutral terms against any person, owner or otherwise, who should render a false account of goods carried with intent to defraud the railway.[28] It is true that the duty to give a true account of the goods was laid in terms upon 'Every person being the owner or having the care of any carriage or goods passing or being upon the railway',[29] but this was not true of the penalty clause. Seemingly, the wider grounds of justification; that the object of the statute could only be enforced if the master were held liable, and that the acts were such as would be performed by a servant, leading to the inference that it was intended to hold a master liable for his servants acts, were chosen. Thereafter this wider test was employed generally in the field of petty offences.[30] Furthermore, delegation and course of employment competed for favour as occasions for the imposition of liability.[31] Curiously, this gave the licensing cases which proceeded on delegation alone the appearance of anomalies. Yet they alone represented a defensible course of statutory construction, at least in terms of policy. While *Mousell*'s case could be defended in terms of the specific address of the statutory command, if not the prohibition, this was not done. It gave rise to a generally phrased test of wide application.

The extending ambit of liability

As a result of the foregoing developments vicarious liability for offences involving *mens rea* spread from the Licensing Acts and the Factories Acts into the field of road traffic. Today this is probably its most potent, and as respects corporate criminal liability its most troublesome, aspect. The difficulty stems from the fact that the regulations involved frequently employ a disjunctive wording the intended effect of which may be very far from clear. It is for example an offence to use or cause or permit a vehicle to be used contrary to the Construction and Use regulations. It is also an offence to fail to keep or cause to be kept certain information relating to specified classes of motor vehicle. On one view this can result in a wide measure of personal as well as vicarious liability, and at one and the same time for *mens rea* and strict liability offences embedded in the same clause of a particular regulation. Thus in *James & Son Ltd.* v. *Smee*,[32] a decision which illustrates some of the problems in this area the court held that a corporation could only be convicted of permitting user of a motor vehicle contrary to the Construction and Use regulations where some responsible officer had knowingly permitted such user. In accordance with earlier authority[33] it also held that a corporation could be held liable vicariously for simple user. The apparent absurdity of the result was percieved by Lord Goddard CJ.[34] It may well be that for the sake of completeness of coverage the occasional difficulty of this sort must be tolerated, though persons who advocate negligence as the lowest common denominator of liability are unlikely to be convinced. At all events, the decision may be supported by reasoning which is not wholly unattractive. The concept of user may well be wider than the mere physical act of driving. Relying upon this consideration, Australian courts have consistently held that it is only the master who uses the vehicle on the highway and not the servant.[35] The statutory duty and the prohibition thus lies upon the person undertaking the activity. Conceivably, simple user was the offence intended primarily to be laid against the undertaker, and permitting and causing, though in many cases applicable to him, were included because of their possible application to other persons.[36]

Fortunately, after some considerable wavering, it has now been recognised that permitting user of a vehicle in contravention of the regulations is an offence of purely personal liability in respect of which a corporation can be convicted only for the knowledge and acts of a responsible officer.[37] But however satisfactory the situation may be with respect to 'permitting' user, the word 'causing' is still so construed as to import vicarious and indeed strict liability. The danger is that 'causing' will be interpreted in this fashion whatever the context; in other words, that it will be treated as having one fixed meaning. In some cases, given the tendency in the English courts to refuse to recognise negligence as a proper basis of liability, this is perhaps inevitable. The Divisional Court early held that where a duty was cast in terms which required a licensee to keep or cause a true record to be kept liability was absolute in either case.[38] Despite a persuasive dissent by Lord Moncrieff in the Scottish case of *Mitchell* v. *Morrison*[39] where he sought to demonstrate that liability for failing to cause was based on personal negligence in the performance of supervisory functions regarding record-keeping, the English rule probably represents the preferable construction. Adoption of the minority view in the Scottish case would have resulted in an alteration of the basis of liability to the licensee's benefit in cases where the physical keeping of the record had been delegated. It is unlikely that the regulations could be said to evince any such intention. The particular phrase does not necessarily become otiose in its relation to the licensee because the task of record-keeping could, for example, be performed by an independant contractor. In other contexts 'causes' may be susceptible of an interpretation requiring full *mens rea* thus re-opening the argument concerning vicarious liability for offences involving criminal intent. Thus before a vehicle superintendant can be convicted of causing a vehicle to be used on the road in a dangerous condition, he must be aware of the dangerous condition.[40] On the other hand it has been held that a company whose vehicle is on the road in a dangerous condition causes it to be used in contravention of the regulations notwithstanding that the defect is latent and unknown.[41] In the former case the driver was not the employee of the accused and so there could be no question of vicarious liability whereas in the latter case he was. Even so, vicarious liability affords no sufficient explanation for the disparity in result because in the latter case the servant was unaware of the defect and therefore had no knowledge which could be imputed to the accused. The cases thus appear to be irreconcilable. The context in which the word is used should influence the result and one would expect the Divisional Court to insist on knowledge here, just as it does in cases of permitting user in contravention of the regulations. Furthermore, by parity of reasoning the offence of causing a vehicle to be used in contravention of the regulations should also be an offence to which vicarious liability does not apply. Unfortunately, it is unwise to be unduly sanguine regarding the probable course of events in the Divisional court, and in *Wurzal* v. *Wilson* the Divisional court seems to

suggest that negligence, in taking precautions[42] may found the offence.
Permitting and perhaps causing user contrary to the Motor Vehicle
(Construction and Use) Regulations apart, the ambit of vicarious liability
for offences involving intent is still unclear. It includes certain offences
under the Licensing Acts, the Factories Acts, and possibly under certain
miscellaneous legislation.There are few firm principles by reference to
which one can state when a statutory duty will be declared to be absolute
in this sense. The rough guidance afforded by *Mousell*'s case is not a
substitute for precise statutory constructions. It is no doubt true, as Lord
Cooper stated in *Duguid* v. *Fraser*, that the question is whether on a sound
construction of the statute[43]:

> ... the obligation imposed by statute is of such a character that an
> offence can be committed by, and a prosecution taken against the person
> carrying on the business even although the act which is the subject of the
> prosecution may have been committed by some subordinate in his
> employment acting within the scope of his employment.

It is equally true that the cases afford little assistance in answering it. It
is not helpful to state that such liability exists only with respect to 'public
welfare offences'. It is impossible to differentiate between these and other
offences either in terms of the moral quality of the act, or according to the
gravity of the offence. One could say that such offences are minor and
directed primarily to regulating the social order rather than ensuring
punishment and correction. Here the difficulty arises in the composition of
the list. Two such offences mentioned by Sayre, [44] narcotics offences[45]
and some traffic offences, might well be regarded as deserving of punishment
and the offenders as requiring correction.[46] Similarly, to describe public
welfare offences as adaptations to an impersonal economy and directed
primarily to the conduct of a particular activity is to afford only a very
rough guide.[47] Virtually the sole exclusionary rule enunciated has been
that vicarious liability may not be ascribed where imprisonment is the
primary punishment for the offence.[48]

Even the status of this principle is in doubt. In *Warner* v. *Metropolitan
Police Commissioner*[49] Lord Reid was prepared to impose strict liability
only where the offence was of a minor character. Lord Pearce by contrast
would have treated the existence of a minimum penalty as a strong
argument in favour of the offence not being absolute. There are however
few such penalties in English Criminal Law.

The decision of the House of Lords in *Vane* v. *Yiannopoullos* holds

out some hope for the future.[50] Lord Evershed clearly adverted to the
exclusive address of the statutory command there in issue as founding a
vicarious liability construction. Lord Reid was prepared to adhere to the
liquor licensing cases only because of their longevity. He was inclined to
think that where a statutory offence is cast in terms clearly requiring
mens rea, personal liability alone is intended. Lords Morris and Donovan
employed the latter proposition exclusively as the foundation of their
judgment, while Lord Hodson found it unnecessary to decide the issue.
It is possible therefore that with strong judgments in the House of Lords
enunciating the doctrine that *mens rea* offences cannot normally give
rise to vicarious liability, many of the problems considered herein will
someday cease to exist. The lower courts have however taken the view
that the liquor licence cases have not been overruled and in England have
continued to apply the vicarious liability doctrine.[51] While vicarious
liability for *mens rea* offences imposed on the principle of delegation
continues to exist, a very real possibility of a blurring of concepts will
continue.[52] Delegation and course of employment are both employed as
bases upon which vicarious liability may be imposed, and it has indeed
been suggested that delegation is the proper footing for all such liability.[53]

It must be stressed that 'delegation' and 'course'of employment' are
not synonymous terms. Delegation involves a power to control certain
aspects of a business enterprise and a discretion in the manner of its
exercise.[54] The conclusion to which the cases dealing with vicarious
liability for *mens rea* offences leads is that, in those areas of the law where
vicarious liability is admitted, a corporation may be held liable where a
person enjoying a delegated authority over an aspect of the corporation's
business commits an offence. In such cases the corporation is made
criminally liable in respect of his knowledge and actions.

The primary difficulty is that a similar analysis is employed with
respect to criminal liability. In both cases the acts or omissions of an
individual are imputed to the corporation. No doubt in some cases the
persons involved will be different and will enjoy a different authority.
In some cases they may well be identical. It may be difficult to distinguish
between the different authorities and different liabilities involved. It is
said that personal libility depends upon the doctrine of identification.
This doctrine presumably operates only where the actor is a high
managerial officer. This however does not necessarily afford a clear guide
because the officer, while occupying a position of importance within the
corporate structure, may yet enjoy only a delegated authority. Within the
scope of delegated authority, substantial questions of degree, particularly

in the independence with which an authority is exercised, may arise. The distinction between primary and vicarious corporate criminal liability is largely a matter of degree. As yet there has been no judicial indication of the underlying policy bases requiring a distinction between the two modes of liability. All this makes for uncertainty.

Difficulty will most readily arise when an officer or agent does enjoy an extensive delegated authority. Conceptually, the tests employed are little different. The result is a statement such as that in *Reg.* v. *Stanley Haulage Ltd.*,[55] an inquiry not into corporate policy, but into the extent of a given officer's authority. When to this is married an uncertainty whether or not vicarious liability is to be ascribed in respect of an offence, it may become difficult to draw a meaningful conceptual or functional distinction between vicarious and corporate personal liability. This difficulty is enhanced because in fact the bulk of corporate criminal liability involves violations of regulatory legislation. There is a very natural inclination to deny the existence of any meaningful distinction between the two, and to hold simply that a corporation is always liable for the acts of its officers, agents, and servants.[56] One might well ask what relevance such a distinction has.

An example may perhaps clarify the issue. In *James & Son Ltd.* v. *Smee*[57] the court did not impose liability because it was not shown that any responsible officer of the corporation permitted the offence. It seems a fair inference that had the corporation's transport officer permitted the offence, the corporation would have been held liable. Provided that he had exclusive control over that aspect of corporate business he might well have been 'identified' with the corporation.[58] Were vicarious liability in issue the actions of the same officer might well be taken as the foundation of liability. In either event the same enquiry would be conducted. It would have to be shown that he permitted the offence and that he enjoyed an authority over the area in question. In the former case one might strive more vigorously to show that the transport manager enjoyed greater autonomy, but such a distinction would basically be meaningless. In either case liability is predicated simply upon the exercise of a delagated authority.

This analysis, if valid, is probably viable throughout much of the area of corporate criminal liability. Because most charges against corporations are charges of conspiracy, a crime to which vicarious liability has no application, the difficulties have not been squarely faced. The conspiracies charged have generally directed towards breaches of regulatory offences. When the substantive offences themselves arise for consideration a body of case law could grow up confounding the two. That, as will be seen, happened in the United States. The seeds of a similar development have been sown in England although recent decisions on the doctrine of identification could avert this result.

Due care and diligence: the third-party defences

Judicial adoption of doctrines of strict liability effectively foreclosed common law defences based on an absence of negligence. This is so whether or not the offence was also treated as attracting vicarious liability. Personal liability for negligence would at some stage permit an inquiry into corporate policy in an endeavour to determine whether all possible care had been taken.[59] Strict liability with or without vicarious liability as its concomitant effectively forecloses such an inquiry, lending an added harshness to an unattractive area of criminal law.[60] This inflexibility has been carried over into the realm of statutory defences, wherein a failure to distinguish between acts ascribed personally to a corporation and acts ascribed by procuration has emasculated statutory defences based on due care and diligence.

Such defences are now commonly provided by much regulatory legislation.[61] Broadly speaking, they take either of two forms. In the one, the legislation provides that the actual offender may be brought before the court. If his guilt be proven, and if in addition the master proves that he used due care and diligence to prevent commission of the offence, and that it was committed without his knowledge, consent or connivance, the master may be exempted from penalty. Another variant enables the person to whom the act or default is due, to be brought before the court. The contravention is first proved. If the accused can prove that the contravention was due to the act or default of the actual offender, and can further show that he used all due diligence to secure compliance with the statutory provisions, he may himself be acquitted. The necessity for such provisions is clearly apparent. There is otherwise a real possibility that a careful employer may be convicted in respect of an isolated wilful or negligent act of an employee.

The issues are rather similar to those discussed above. Because exculpation is based on the personal due care and diligence of an employer, the enquiry is concerned not only with his policies but also with the steps taken to effectuate them. The enquiry should be directed towards determining whether a given system of supervision is consonant with the due care and diligence requirement. Again the salient problems relate, not to the mode of business organization employed, but to the scale of the

operations conducted. Only in the smallest sole proprietorships will the
actual proprietor be able to exercise a personal supervision. Otherwise he
can reasonably be expected to impose an adequate supervisory system,
and so far as is possible, to ensure that it functions adequately. A
corporation may do this by some person in its structure, possibly the
managing director, who deputes the task of ensuring the adequate working
of the system. Personal due care and diligence should ideally be shown by
proving the system and submitting its adequacy and efficiency of operation
to the court. In early decisions under mining legislation this was the
analysis adopted by the court. While some decisions seem in the result
clearly indefensible, largely because the standard of due care and diligence
imposed was low, the mode of analysis was proper.[62] Admittedly, a
stricter standard is applied in charterparty cases where due diligence in the
work itself is required, the carrier only being exculpated in the case of
defects not discoverable by inspection. This rule however, ameliorates
a harsher common-law rule. Such a construction in criminal cases would
not confer any benefit on an employer.[62a]

Unfortunately, this analysis has not always been employed. In cases
arising under the now repealed Merchandise Marks Act problems have
substantially been avoided by refusing to recognise their existence.[63]
Under other statutes, even where the problem was recognised, the results
have occasionally been unhappy. *R. C. Hammett Ltd.* v. *Beldam* is an
early example, involving a due diligence defence under the Weights and
Measures Act, 1926. The appellant, a multiple butcher, was convicted of
the offence of delivering meat to a purchaser without providing a legible
statement of the net weight upon which the purchase price was based.
The statute provided a due diligence defence. The corporation charged
its branch manager as the actual offender. He was aware of the regulations.
It was the corporation's policy to ensure that its managers were aware of
and adhered to them. To ensure this, its superintendent visited the shops
regularly. In a short judgment Lord Hewart CJ held that whether or not
there had been due diligence was a question of fact. He found that, on
the facts, the corporation had exercised due diligence.

In a subsequent case, *R. C. Hammett Ltd.* v. *London County Council*[65]
the corporation, charged with the identical offence, was less fortunate.
Once again the fault was essentially that of a servant. On the facts the
company had clearly taken extensive precautions to ensure compliance
with the regulations. All this notwithstanding, the corporation was
convicted. Liability was imposed for the manager's inattention. *Beldam's*
case was distinguished on the somewhat unreal basis that there alone due

diligence had been shown. The court overlooked entirely the primary enquiry, which should have been into the efficacy of a system and the reasonableness of the means adopted to enforce it. Provided that the corporation (or any employer) devises an adequate system and employs reasonable and systematic means of enforcement, the defence should be made out.

There is little sign of an improvement in the situation. In *Melias Ltd.* v. *Preston,*[66] the Court was prepared to treat the manager of a shop as the person in possession for sale and not the company for the purpose of a due diligence defence to a charge of having improperly packed goods in possession for the purpose of sale.[67] In *Series* v. *Poole,*[68] the Divisional Court reverted to a misapplication of the doctrine of indentification which could cause difficulty in company cases. The accused was charged with failing to ensure that a current driving record was kept in connection with one of his vehicles. He had in fact delegated the physical task of record-keeping to a secretary and could well have been denied the defence because, despite a finding of fact to the contrary, he had not employed due diligence in supervising her work. The Court however, held that the obligation to keep records was absolute, that it was not enough to prove that the licence-holder had set up an adequate record-keeping system, and that the due diligence defence only applied where some person such as the vehicle driver had so acted as to make it impossible for the licence-holder to ensure the accuracy of the records by personally checking them. Seemingly, where a subordinate errs or is negligent, in the performance of his duties the master must always be liable notwithstanding the fact that he may have taken extensive precautions. All this is most unfortunate.

It is to be hoped that more enlightened constructions will be followed in the future. Generally, in relation to these defences, there is a tendency to seize upon the actions of some person in authority and to refuse the defence to the corporation because of his lack of due care and diligence. In the search for a more satisfactory construction of such provisions, regard ought to be had to Scottish and Commonwealth authority. In *Dumfries and Maxwelltown Co-operative Society* v. *Williamson*[69] the High Court of Justiciary held that a corporation had employed due diligence in ensuring that its branch managers were aware of statutory provisions applicable to its business, and of the necessity to abide by them. It was said to be wrong automatically to identify the corporation with its branch manager, and to equate his fault with a lack of due diligence on the part of the corporation.

The clearest authority is an Australian decision, *Freeman* v. *C. T. Warne*

Pty. Ltd.[70] There a due diligence defence was raised to a charge of selling foodstuffs at a price greater than that permitted by price-fixing legislation. Herring CJ approached the issue in impeccable fashion. The question had to be answered in the light of the company's organization. Where the corporation could show that it exercised all due diligence, it would succeed. In this respect it was not conclusively to be identified with the actions of any particular officer. It is to be hoped that the more extended inquiry envisaged by these decisions will ultimately commend itself to the English courts.

The conclusion to be drawn from this aspect of the study can be summed up quite briefly. At present there is a possibility that as regards certain offences, their precise ambit being uncertain, both personal and vicarious liability involving intent can exist. In the light of existing tests for determining when an employer shall be personally liable there is, where the accused is a corporation, ample room for confusion. The dilemma can only be solved (within the framework of existing law) by adopting different criteria of liability referable to clearly discernible policy considerations. 'Identification' is as such no more than a catch-word, and points to no real difference in analysis between the two concepts.

Where due diligence defences are provided, 'identification' is largely inappropriate. It may serve to assist in raising a *prima facie* case against a corporation, or indeed any mode of business organisation. As an end to the enquiry however, it ignores its factual basis; the quantitative questions of the system employed and the effectiveness of its enforcement. It is therefore capable of doing injustice. Here, as in the entire field of corporate criminal liability, justice will best be done not by automatic processes of identification based on abstract rules substantially divorced from the actual workings of the individual corporation, but from the more mundane task of examining the facts.

1   Glanville Williams, *Criminal Law: The General Part* (2nd ed. 1961) pp 273-284
2   *Griffiths* v. *Studebakers Ltd.* [1924] 1 KB 102; *Reynolds* v. *G. H. Austin & Sons Ltd.* [1951] 2 KB 135
3   Glanville Williams, *Criminal Law: The General Part* (2nd ed. 1961) pp 266-286; Hall, *General Principles Of Criminal Law* (2nd ed. 1960) pp 330-336; Edwards, *Mens Rea In Statutory Offences,* Chapter 9; Baty, *Vicarious Liability* (1916); Sayre, 'Criminal Responsibility For The Acts Of Another' (1930) 43 Harv. L. Rev. 689; Devlin, Lord, *Samples Of Law-Making, Statutory Offences* (1962); Howard, *Strict Liability* (1963); Sayre, 'Public welfare offences' (1933) 33 Col. L. Rev. 55
4   See especially per Lord Cooper in *Duguid* v. *Fraser* 1942 JC 1

5 [1917] 2 KB 836
6 [1917] 2 KB 836, 845 per Atkin LJ (as he then was)
7 See for example the discussion in Hanbury, *Principles Of Agency* (2nd ed. 1960) pp 209-217; *Star Cinema (Shepherds Bush) Ltd.* v. *Baker* (1921) 86 JP 47
8 Devlin (Lord) *Samples Of Law-Making, Statutory Offences* (1962) pp 70-72
9 (1889) 22 QBD 736
10 (1889) 22 QBD 736 at page 740
11 Liquor Licensing Act, 1872, sec. 7 (sale of spirits to children)
12 Liquor Licensing Act, 1872, sec. 10 (illicit storing of liquor); sec. 13 (permitting drunkenness); sec. 14 (keeping disorderly house); sec. 15 (permitting premises to be used as a brothel); sec. 16 (harbouring a constable); sec. 17 (permitting gaming); sec. 20 (possession of adulterated liquor)
13 *Massey* v. *Morris* [1894] 1 QB 412 at page 414 per Cave J
14 *Allen* v. *Lumb* (1893) 57 JP 377; *Boyle* v. *Smith* [1906] KB 432
15 [1914] 3 KB 1141
16 (1934) 34 SR (NSW) 261
17 *Nicholls* v. *Hall* (1873) LR 8 CP 322 per Honyman J; *The King* v. *Australasian Film Limited* (1921) 29 CLR 195; *Emary* v. *Nolloth* [1903] 2 KB 264; *Redgate* v. *Haynes* (1876) 1 QBD 89; *Bond* v. *Evans* (1881) 21 QBD 249; *Commissioners of Police* v. *Cartman* [1896] 1 QB 655; *Somerset* v. *Hart* (1889) 12 QBD 360
18 *Crabtree* v. *Fern Spinning Co. Ltd.* (1902) 85 LT 549; *Dept. of Agriculture* v. *Burke* [1915] 2 IR 128 and the licensee cases under sec. 44 of the Metropolitan Police Act, 1839. See *Allen* v. *Whitehead* [1930] 1 KB 211; *Linnett* v. *Commissioner of Police* [1946] 1 KB 290; *Armitage Ltd.* v. *Nicholson* (1913) 108 LT 983
19 *Griffith* v. *Studebakers Ltd.* [1924] 1 KB 102
20 *Coppen* v. *Moore*(2) [1898] 2 QB 306; *Davies* v. *Harvey* (1874) LR 9 QB 439
21 *Roberts* v. *Woodward* (1890) 25 QBD 412, 415 per Pollock B. *Brown* v. *Foot* (1892) 61 LJ (MC) 110
22 *Mullins* v. *Collins* (1874) LR 9 QB 292 (a licensing case)
23 *Davies* v. *Harvey* (1874) LR 9 QB 439
24 *Collman* v. *Mills* [1897] 1 QB 396
25 e.g. *Coppen* v. *Moore* (2) [1898] 2 QB 306 (delegation); *Strutt* v. *Clift* [1911] 1 KB 1 (delegation); *Brown* v. *Foot* (1892) 61 LJ (m.c.) 110 (course of employment); *Kearly* v. *Tylor* (1891) 57 JP 421 (course of employment); *Parker* v. *Alder* [1899] 1 QB 20 (actions of stranger)
26 *Mullins* v. *Collins* (1874) LR 9 QB 292; *Sherras* v. *De Rutzen* [1895] 1 QB 918
27 [1917] 2 KB 836
28 Railway Clauses Consolidation Act, 1845 sec. 98
29 Railway Clauses Consolidation Act, 1845 sec. 99
30 e.g. *Griffiths* v. *Studebakers Limited* [1924] 1 KB 102; *Star Cinema (Shepherds Bush) Ltd.* v. *Baker* (1921) 86 JP 47; *Brentnall and Cleland Ltd.* v. *London County Council* [1944] KB 115
31 Edwards, *Mens Rea In Statutory Offences* (1955) chapter 9
32 [1955] 1 QB 78
33 *Sidcup Estates Ltd.* v. *Sidery* (1940) 24 R & TC 164
34 [1955] 1 QB 78 at p 83
35 The development begins with *Pioneer Express Pty. Ltd.* v. *Hotchkiss* (1958)

101 CLR 536 where the applicable statute defined 'operate' in a much wider sense than 'drive'. In *Jackson* v. *Horne* (1965) 114 CLR 82 and *Winston Transport Pty. Ltd.* v. *Horne* (1965) 115 CLR 322, the Court treats the concept of user as wider than mere driving

36 Thus in *Windle* v. *Dunning & Son Ltd.* [1968] Crim. LR 337 it is held that the defendants who hired lorries which were driven and operated by the hire firm did not itself use the lorries, but might be said to 'cause' the lorries to be used

37 *Magna Plant Ltd.* v. *Mitchell* [1966] Crim. LR 395; *Grays Haulage Ltd.* v. *Arnold* [1966] 1 WLR 534; *Evans* v. *Dell* [1937] 1 All ER 349. cf. *Sidcup Estates Ltd.* v. *Sidery* (1940) 24 R & TC 164 and *Forsyth* v. *Phillips* (1964) 108 Sol. J. 36 where the Court held that the offence was one which attracted vicarious liability.

38 *Cox and Sons Ltd.* v. *Sidery* (1935) 24 R & TC 69

39 1938 JC 64

40 *Rushton* v. *Martin* [1952] WN 258

41 *F. Austin (Leyton) Ltd.* v. *East* [1961] Crim. LR 119

42 [1965] 1 WLR 285

43 *Duguid* v. *Fraser* 1942 JC 1, 7

44 Sayre, 'Public Welfare Offences' (1933) 33 Col. L. Rev. 55

45 The situation in narcotics cases is chaotic. In *Beaver* v. *The Queen* [1957] SCR 531 the Supreme Court of Canada held possession of narcotics to be a serious offence requiring full *mens rea*. In *Lockyer* v. *Gibb* [1967] 2 QB 243 the Court held that a person could be guilty of unauthorised possession of dangerous drugs where he knew that he had an article but was ignorant of its nature. In *Warner* v. *Metropolitan Police Commissioner* [1968] 2 All ER 356 the House of Lords reached no concluded view on the meaning of possession in this context. In *Yeandel* v. *Fisher* [1965] 3 WLR 1002 a draconian view regarding the mental element in and the ambit of the offence of being concerned in the management of premises which were used for the smoking of cannabis was taken. But in *Sweet* v. *Parsley* rev'd [1969] 1 All ER 347 the House of Lords held that the offence required knowledge that cannabis was being smoked on the premises and strongly restricted the normal presumption of *mens rea* in statutory offences. On the whole, the presence of narcotics offences in Professor Sayre's list appears to be dubious

46 Willett, *Criminal on the road* (1964) chapter 2 found that a significant proportion of offenders found guilty of major offences under the Road Traffic Act had convictions for other serious offences. In respect of some motoring offences, deterrence and rehabilitation seem respectable ends of punishment

47 Hall, *General Principles Of Criminal Law* (2nd ed. 1960) pp 330-331

48 *Srinivas Mall Bairoliya* v. *King-Emperor* ILR 1947 Patna 460 (PC)

49 [1968] 2 All ER 356

50 [1965] AC 486

51 See *Ross* v. *Moss* [1965] 3 All ER 145; *Reg.* v. *Winson* [1968] 2 All ER 113, In Scotland, the doctrine has now been jettisoned. See *Noble* v. *Heatley* [1967] Crim. LR 423

52 See for example, the discussion in Fisse, 'The Distinction Between Primary and Vicarious Corporate Criminal Liability' (1967) 41 ALJ 203 at pp 209-210, and the discussion in chapter 8 at pp

53 See Edwards, *Mens Rea In Statutory Offences* (1955) at pp 221-238. I have

D

ventured to question this in 'Statutory Offences and Vicarious Criminal Liability', (1964) 27 MLR 98. The subject is not of great relevance to the present argument and so has not been pursued farther herein

54 *Gallagher* v. *Dorman Long & Co. Ltd.* (1947) 2 All ER 35, 41

55 [1964] Crim. LR 224

56 See Slade J (dissenting) in *James & Son Ltd.* v. *Smee* [1955] 1 QB 78

57 [1955] 1 QB 78

58 See i.e. *Reg.* v. *Stanley Haulage Ltd.* [1964] Crim. LR 224; *Reg.* v. *H. J. O'Connell Ltd.* [1962] Quebec QB 666 and see Burrows, 'The Responsibility Of Corporations Under Criminal Law' (1948) 1 Jo. Crim. Sc. 1, 9-11; 17-19

59 See for example the investigation into corporate policy and its enforcement conducted in *Holland Furnace Co.* v. *United States* 158 F 2d 2 (1946)

60 For a trenchant criticism of these developments, see Howard, *Strict Responsibility* (1963) pp 72-73

61 For example, Shops Act 1950 sec. 71; Food and Drugs Act 1955 sec. 112; Road Traffic Act 1962 sec. 20; Weights and Measures Act 1963 secs. 25, 26, 27; Offices, Shops and Railway Premises Act 1963 sec. 67; Agriculture and Horiculture Act 1964 sec. 18; Agriculture Act 1967 sec. 6(5); Farm and Garden Chemicals Act 1967 sec. 3. As to subordinate legislation see Food Standards (General Provisions) Order 1944, art. 4(1); Labelling of Food Order 1953, art. 13. This list does not purport to be exhaustive

62 *Watkins* v. *Naval Colliery Co. Ltd.* [1912] AC 693, 705 per Lord Atkinson; remarks of Buckley LJ in *David* v. *Britannic Merthyr Coal Company* [1909] 2 KB 146, 167-8, decision affirmed, sub. nom. *Britannic Merthyr Coal Company* v. *David* [1914] AC 74 without discussion of this point. See Coal Mines Regulation Act, 1887 sec. 50; *Baker* v. *Carter* (1878) 3 Ex. D. 132; *Stokes* v. *Mitcheson* [1902] KB 857, 864; *Bell* v. *Bruce* (1891) 55 JP 535 the decision in which case is questionable

62a See *Riverstone Meat Co. Pty. Ltd.* v. *Lancashire Shipping Co. Ltd.* [1961] AC 807

63 Particularly by holding that sec. 2(2) of the Act was not intended to afford a due diligence defence to an employer. *Allard* v. *Selfridge & Company Limited* [1925] 1 KB 129; *Slatcher* v. *George Mence Smith Ltd.* [1951] 2 KB 631; *Re Application of Vitamins Ltd.* [1955] 3 All ER 827 (Ch.D.); and see Edwards, *Mens Rea In Statutory Offences* (1955) p 173; Glanville Williams, 'Merchandise Marks Act, Intent To Defraud' (1952) 15 MLR 77. See now Trade Description Act (1968) sec. 24

64 (1931) 95 JP 180

65 (1933) 97 JP 105

66 [1957] 2 QB 380

67 Overruling *R. Walkling Ltd.* v. *Robinson* (1931) 94 JP 73 which was decided *per incuriam, Hotchin* v. *Hindmarsh* [1891] 2 QB 191 not having been cited to the Court. See also *Hart* v. *Hudson Bros.* [1928] 2 KB 629

68 [1967] 3 All ER 849

69 1950 JC 76

70 [1947] VLR 279

Chapter 7

The doctrine of identification and corporate representation

In the English courts, corporate criminal liability has been imposed in respect of acts performed or commanded by persons of high standing in the corporate hierarchy. It has been asserted that the corporation may be identified with such persons; that they represent its *alter ego*, and that their activities are, by direct attribution, those of the corporation. This in turn reflects a conceptual bias to the problem. As has been seen, civilly and in the realm of public welfare offences, it had been conceded that a corporation could have a mind and that that mind could entertain an improper motive or intention. No wider principle was deduced from the cases. Mr. Winn concluded that[1]:

> It was not possible on the view which the English Courts took of the directors of a corporation as being the *agents* of the corporation to impose criminal liability for their acts upon the corporation.

The existing rule of liability was still that corporate liability was vicarious liability. Consequently, before criminal liability could be imposed upon corporations, some method had to be found for ascribing liability personally to the body corporate. The *alter ego* theory has been said to provide the necessary device.

In this chapter, it is proposed to discuss the *alter ego* theory, its development, its present status, and its context in the existing body of English case law relating to corporate representation. In a further chapter, its strengths and weaknesses as a basis of corporate criminal liability will be discussed, as will be the solution reached in the American Federal Courts and in the *Model Penal Code*.

The *alter ego* theory of corporate representation

In *Lennards Carrying Company Limited* v. *Asiatic Petroleum Co. Ltd.*[2] the view was advanced that liability personal to a corporation could be predicated on the actions of certain officers who might be said to be the *alter ego* of the corporation. It has been said that this development took place without regard to a line of decisions establishing the Board of Directors as the governing constitutional organ of the corporation.[3] This may overstate the matter. The view propounded in *Lennards* case may well depend in part upon a line of nineteenth and early twentieth century decisions in which the position and functions of the Board of Directors, single directors, and the general meeting, were defined. In the process, Blackstone's 'little republic' was seen to be a managerial oligarchy.[4]

The position of the board of directors defined

Under the Companies Act, 1862, corporations were governed by a Board of Directors elected by the body of shareholders in general meeting.[5] The board was thereby invested with the executive government of the corporation. The courts soon recognised that the functions vested in the board could not aptly be subsumed under the concept of agency, or the concept of trusteeship.[6] It is true that early decisions such as *Ferguson* v. *Wilson*[7] characterized the Board of Directors as agents of the company. In these cases however, the courts were striving to show that liabilities entered into on behalf of the company by the board were liabilities of the company and not of its Board of Directors,[8] or of individual directors who negotiated the transactions.[9] The courts also sought to assert that the Board of Directors could have no greater powers than those conferred upon the corporation itself, and resorted to the concept of agency to achieve this result.[10] The impropriety of explaining the board's position by reference to the concepts of agency and trusteeship, was clearly put by Jessel MR in *In re Forest of Dean Coal Mining Company*. He there stated[11]:

Directors have sometimes been called trustees, or commercial trustees, and sometimes they have been called managing partners, it does not matter what you call them so long as you understand what their true position is, which is that they are really commercial men managing a trading concern for the benefit of themselves and of all the other shareholders in it.

Thereafter the courts searched for a new and more precise analogy. The board was said to be analogous in position to the managing agent of a mercantile house to whom the control if its property and extensive powers of management have been confided.[12] In *Imperial Hydropathic Hotel Company, Blackpool* v. *Hampson* the directors were said by Bowen LJ to be neither servants, trustees, nor managing partners, but rather 'persons invested with strictly defined powers of management under the articles of association of a statutory corporation'.[13] The board while owing duties of care, skill and good faith to the company, was neither its agent nor trustee of its assets.[14]

Early twentieth century cases made the matter even clearer. In *Gluckstein* v. *Barnes*[15] Lord Robertson referred to the directors of a company as its executive organ, a neutral term used to describe a relationship unique in private law. The analogy employed was that of a body politic. In *The Gramaphone and Typewriter Limited* v. *Stanley*[16] the Court of Appeal held that the Board of Directors was not the agent of a person who owned all the shares in a company. Buckley LJ stated[17]:

> The directors are not servants to obey directions given by the shareholders as individuals; they are not agents appointed by and bound to serve the shareholders as their principals. They are persons who may by the regulations be entrusted with the control of the business, and if so entrusted they can be dispossessed from that control only by the statutory majority which can alter the articles.

The independant position of the board as the governing executive organ of the corporation was further confirmed by the Court of Appeal in *Automatic Self-Cleansing Filter Syndicate Company* v. *Cuninghame.*[18] A controlling shareholder desired that the assets and undertaking of the company be sold and arranged a sale. At a general meeting, a resolution favouring sale was passed. The directors were of opinion that the sale would not be in the company's interests and refused to carry it out. By the articles, the directors were accorded a general and complete power of management including power to sell the company's property. That article could only be altered by special resolution. The Court of Appeal, affirming a judgment of Warrington J held that the Board of Directors could not be controlled in the exercise of their executive discretion by a simple majority of shareholders at a general meeting. Under the articles of association an extraordinary resolution was required in order to limit their general authority. The Court of Appeal explicitly held that the Board of Directors was not the agent of the majority shareholders, but was rather in the position of manager. The decision of the House of Lords in *Quin & Axtens Limited* v. *Salmon*[19] further strengthened the independant position of the Board of Directors. Article 75 of the company's articles of association provided that the directors were to manage the business. They might exercise all the powers of the company, 'subject to such regulations (being not inconsistent with the provisions of the articles) as may be prescribed by the company in general meeting'. By Article 80 no resolution of a meeting of the directors relating to the acquisition or letting of premises should be valid unless notice should have been given to each of two managing directors and neither of them should have dissented therefrom. The directors passed resolutions with the object of acquiring and letting premises. One of the managing directors dissented. Resolutions to the same effect were then passed at an extraordinary general meeting of the shareholders by a simple majority.

The company contended that the directors were enitled to proceed upon the resolutions passed in general meeting. Lord Loreburn LC however, held that the directors were bound by the articles. The resolutions were inconsistent with the articles which delimited the directors powers, and were therefore ineffective. The power to manage the company was vested in the directors, and not the general meeting, and the company in general meeting could not therefore exercise powers of management. Both the board and the general meeting exercised powers conferred by, and subject to, the articles of association.

While the powers of the Board of Directors over the general management of the company have received subsequent judicial amplification,[20] the position of the board as an independant governing organ of the corporation was, by 1915, clearly established. That the general meeting was also an organ of the corporation was equally clear.[21]

The position of individual directors

During this period, the courts were also clarifying the status of individual directors. Here a difficulty was that a director might act in several capacities. As an individual member of the Board of Directors his office is that of a manager of the company.[22] He owes duties of care and good faith to the company in respect of his managerial obligations.[23] *Qua* director, he is not required to give his full time to the company and will generally do so only when he holds some full time office in the company additional to his directorship.[24]

The individual director may also however be an agent of his company. This implies that he has been given authority from the board (or perhaps the managing director) to enter into transactions as agent of the company. That the status of an individual director, acting on behalf of the company is generally that of agent was well-established during the nineteenth century. Certain cases arising under the rule in *Royal British Bank* v. *Turquand*[25] dealt with the agency powers of directors or managing directors.[26] The rule in *Turquand*'s case is not however restricted to powers of agency asserted by directors. It is of more general application.

The most significant line of authority deals with cases where a common director purports to act on behalf of two companies in a common transaction. The question could then arise whether both companies were bound by his knowledge. If the director were more than an agent, the answer seemingly would be in the affirmative.

In fact the courts have consistently held that the personal knowledge of a common officer does not in all circumstance affect each of the boards upon which he acts, with knowledge of the affairs of the other company. In *In re Hampshire Land Company*[27] Vaughan Williams J held that the personal knowledge of a common officer will only bind both companies where he is under a duty to communicate the knowledge to both. In *In re David Payne & Co. Limited*[28] the position of common directors was again considered. It was there held that a single member of the board of dirctors is an agent whose knowledge, where there is a conflict of interest between two companies of which he is a board member, is not to be imputed to each where he had an interest which would lead him not to disclose to one company information which he had obtained in his capacity as a member of the board of the other. In *In re Fenwick, Stobart & Co. Ltd.*[29] the same principles were applied to the knowledge of a common officer, in this case the secretary. Before knowledge could be imputed to the second company, it must be shown that the officer acquired the knowledge under circumstances which required him to communicate it to the other company.[30]

This is not to say that similar principles were not applied in cases where companies had common boards. In *Lagunas Nitrate Company* v. *Lagunas Syndicate*[31] the Court of Appeal had held that the knowledge possessed by members of common boards could not be imputed to both companies unless a duty of communication existed and unless there were no conflict of duty and interest which would conduce to non-disclosure. What is significant is first, that whereas the courts attempted to show that the board was not merely an agent of the company, in the case of individual directors they were content to characterize their functions in terms of agency, and secondly, that they saw no need for any other analogy. Until 1915 it had not been suggested that individual directors could occupy any status other than that of servant, or agent.

The position of the managing director

The managing director, however, could occupy a fundamentally different position to that of individual directors; a position analogous to that of the board as a whole. Table A to the Companies Act, 1862, envisaged

management by the Board of Directors as a whole. It contained no
provision analogous to Article 107 of Table A to the Companies Act, 1948
enabling the board to appoint a managing director to whom, by Article 109,
the directors powers could be entrusted either collaterally with or to the
exclusion of their own powers. Table A to the 1862 Act contains only a
power of delegation from the board to committees of one or more members
of the board, subject to regulations made by the board.[32]

Individual companies however, did not always follow the pattern of
articles found in Table A. In some companies, the articles did confer power
upon the directors to delegate some or all of their functions to a managing
director. An example is the articles discussed in a case under the *Turquand*
rule, *Biggerstaff* v. *Rowatt's Wharf Ltd.*[33] Article 81 of the Wharf
Companies articles provided:

> 81. The directors may from time to time appoint a managing director,
> and when they they think fit remove any managing director so appointed,
> and they may from time to time entrust to and confer upon any such
> managing director such of the powers, authorities, and discretions
> exercisable under these presents by the directors as they may think fit,
> other than the drawing, accepting, or indorsing of bills of exchange or
> promissory notes, and may confer such powers for such time and to be
> exercised for such objects and purposes and upon such terms and conditions
> and with such restrictions as they think expedient, and may from time to
> time revoke, withdraw, alter or vary all or any such powers . . .

The existence of such powers did not lead the courts to characterize the
managing director as other than an agent for his company. There is
nineteenth century authority dealing with the position of the managing
director. For most purposes agency was a convenient category.
Nonetheless, the scope of authority which might be conferred on such an
official was wide.[34] As Blackburn LJ said in *Gibson* v. *Barton*,[35] the
manager of a company is a delegate having control of all the affairs of the
company. The wide ostensible authority of managing directors was
recognised in several cases under the rule in *Turquand*'s case. The power to
delegate directoral powers to committees contained in Table A articles, and
the ostensible exercise of agency powers by managing directors sufficed to
found liability in the company, in the absence of any indication in its
public documents that no delegation has been made, or that delegated
powers had been circumscribed.[36] In short, wide powers of agency on the
part of a managing director were assumed in the absence of an indication
to the contrary in the public documents. His status as a controlling figure

was widely recognised. The manager of a company was one who managed its affairs as a whole.[37] His position was recognised to be quite different to that of one who was but an agent of the company.[38] He was clearly envisaged as performing functions which might otherwise be performed by the board as a whole.[39]

Even though the managing director was clearly regarded as a central figure in corporate management, the English courts did not accord to him a formal status greater than that of agent. *Hirst* v. *West Riding Union Banking Company, Limited*, illustrates the point.[40] To an action for misrepresentation brought against the bank in respect of a letter signed by one of the defendant's branch managers, the defendant set up Section 6 of the Statute of Frauds (Amendment) Act, 1829, which provided that no action should be brought to charge any person upon a representation concerning the character, credit, ability, trade or dealings of another person unless it were signed personally by the party. The Court of Appeal held that the bank was a person within the meaning of the section, and that it could not be held liable in respect of a representation signed by its officers. It is clear that the court was not prepared to identify any person by whom the bank acted as the bank for this purpose.[41]

The development of the *alter ego* theory

The *alter ego* theory may well have developed in part from the line of decisions clarifying the nature of the board, and from those decisions which stressed the independant authority of the managing director. If this be denied, the *alter ego* idea is bound to appear anomalous. In part however, it derived from these decisions and was a response to a particular situation. It had long been accepted that civil responsibility could in general be imposed *respondeat superior*. The courts were thereby absolved from solving the problem how an entity, ' . . . invisible, intangible, and existing only in contemplation of law'[42] could itself act wrongfully or negligently. Continental lawyers, lacking this easy solution, took refuge in metaphysical constructions of the nature of the corporate entity and its relationship to the humans who acted on its behalf. From the concepts so created practical solutions, albeit couched in a language foreign to the common lawyer, were formulated and applied.[43] To the great Victorian, Lord Lindley, such concepts represented ' . . . metaphysical subtleties, both needless and fallacious'.[44] An intelligible body of company law had grown up without resort to them. The law of agency and of vicarious liability had served to place corporations firmly within the ambit of civil liability.[45]

Vicarious liability could not provide an adequate solution where

D*

personal fault alone was an ingredient in liability. A rare example of such a formulation occurs in the Merchant Shipping Act, 1894. It was in this context that the *alter ego* idea was first formulated by the House of Lords in *Lennards Carrying Company Limited* v. *Asiatic Petroleum Co. Ltd.*[46] The respondent company claimed damages from the appellant company in respect of the fire loss of a cargo of benzine carried by the appellant for the respondent by sea. The appellant pleaded Section 502 of the Merchant Shipping Act, 1894, which provides that the owner of a British ship shall not be liable to make good claims for fire loss ' . . . happening without his actual fault or privity.' The problem posed for the House was unique in this respect; that if the company were to be found liable at all, a distinction between its personal acts and the acts of its agents had necessarily to be drawn.

In the instant case the greater part of the company's affairs were carried on by J. M. Lennard as managing director. The board as such, had no knowledge of the unseaworthiness of the carrying vessel. Rejecting an argument that only the Board of Directors who have the general management and control of the company could be taken to act as the company, Viscount Haldane LC states[47]:

My Lords, a corporation is an abstraction. It has no mind of its own any more than it has a body of its own; its active and directing will must consequently be sought in the person of somebody who for some purposes may be called an agent, but who is really the directing mind and will of the corporation, the very ego and centre of the personality of the corporation. That person may be under the direction of the shareholders in general meeting, that person may be the board of directors itself, or it may be, and in some companies it is so, that that person has an authority co-ordinate with the board of directors given to him under the articles of association, and is appointed by the general meeting of the company, and can only be removed by the general meeting of the company.

With this view may be compared that of Lord Dunedin, who, stating that a company can be guilty of actual fault or privity even though the fault be not that of the Board of Directors, stated[48]:

I can quite conceive that a company may be entrusting its business to one director be as truly represented by that one director, as in ordinary cases it is represented by the whole board. I am quite sure that you cannot at least put as a general proposition in law that it is true that nothing will ever be the actual fault or privity of an incorporated company unless it is the fault of the whole board of directors.

The House of Lords were thus examining the control structure of a limited company in order to determine how a statutory provision which spoke in terms of personal liability could be applied to it. The search essentially was to determine who initiated policy within the corporation; for the person or persons in this case who could decide whether or not the company's ship was to be maintained in a seaworthy condition. The ambit of inquiry was largely conventional. A company is generally governed by its Board of Directors. It could in some cases be as fully represented by its managing director, whose powers might be quite as ample. The House of Lords did not say that a company was personally liable in respect of the acts of single directors. It did not say that a corporation would always be personally liable for the actions of its managing director. It did not in fact say that a corporation would, in general, in future be capable of personal liability. It said, in the context of the Merchant Shipping Act, 1894, and with respect to the appellant company, that the managing director exercised the functions which might otherwise be performed by the board. It further said that where personal liability was required it might be ascribed in respect of the actions of such a person.

It could be said however, that no matter for whose actions the company was held liable, liability was still vicarious. This contention was answered by Viscount Haldane LC. Eschewing the language of ascription, he propounded the relevant creed. Liability must be founded upon the fault or privity of someone[49] :

. . . who is not merely a servant or agent for whom a company is liable on the footing respondeat superior, but somebody for whom the company is liable because his action is the very action of the company itself.

This latter statement has given rise to difficulty. It has been called a fiction, and its precise formulation may have been due to Lord Haldane's acquaintance with the German realist school.[50] It is perhaps the language of a conclusion reached for a particular purpose.[51] It may be that Lord Haldane, aware of the uses of the concept in German law (and surely not unaware of the tendency of the English cases) intended to import the *alter ego* doctrine into English law, leaving future courts to make of it what they would. That he did not indicate that *alter ego* was a doctrine of limited application would tend to support the inference. What was decided was that where personal liability must be ascribed to a corporation, it is proper to ascribe it in respect of the acts or omissions

of those persons who govern it. The acts and omissions of such persons
must be distinguished from the acts or omissions of persons who, in
relation to the company, occupy the position of servant or agent. Lord
Dunedin seemingly intended to go no farther for in *Houghton and
Company* v. *Nothard, Lowe and Wills Limited*[52] we find him holding
that there are exceptions to the rule that a company knows what a
director knows or ought to know, one of which occurs where the director
is acting in breach of his duty to the company. The distinction appears in
the extract from the speech of Lord Dunedin reproduced above. The
appellant company was held liable for the fault of J. M. Lennard because,
for all that appeared, he managed the company. So viewed, the concept
of personal responsibility, or *alter ego*; the search for the directing mind
and will of the company, seems not unduly obscure.

Difficulties in relation to the *alter ego* Notion

The *alter ego* concept has certainly caused difficulties. In speaking of
its application to the field of corporate criminal liability, the Law Journal
has editorially castigated the term as 'a glib facade of learning to hide the
obscurity of the law on this topic'.[53] Certainly confusion has arisen in the
criminal cases. The Law Journal is probably correct in saying that the
alter ego doctrine ' . . . expresses the idea that in certain circumstances
which the phrase does nothing to define, an individual's act or mental
state or both, will by law be imputed to a corporation'.[54] The confusion
is perhaps unnecessary. In *Lennard*'s case, in determining whether personal
fault could be ascribed to a corporation, Lord Haldane and Lord Dunedin
both drew attention to questions of position and function; was the officer
concerned vested with and exercising primary managerial functions.

Subsequent development of the *alter ego* doctrine

The *alter ego* doctrine has been applied with varying degrees of fidelity
in the fields of merchant shipping, criminal law, tort, and perhaps taxation.
In some respects, its formulation has tended to differ depending upon the
branch of law in which it was employed. It has received most careful
consideration in cases arising under the Merchant Shipping Act, and it is
with these that it is proposed to commence.

The *alter ego* doctrine under the Merchant Shipping Act

Until recently, at any rate, the *alter ego* doctrine received a very strict
interpretation in cases arising under the Merchant Shipping Act. It was
generally denied that an employee exercising a merely delegated authority

could be considered the *alter ego* of a company. Accordingly, while a managing director has been held to be the *alter ego* of a company,[55] this status has been denied to a ships captain,[56] an Assistant Marine Superintendent[57] or a dispatcher.[58] The courts restricted the application of the term to persons enjoying a primary authority, at least over the subject matter concerned.[59] There was a tendency to remove discretionary elements from the search. Certain writers advocated what was essentially a formal constitutionalism.[60] The actions of those persons who, by the fundamental documents of the company were vested with its management and control, could be said to be personal to the corporation. Even in the case of the managing director, this was not always convincing.[61]

So rigid a position could be supported by certain of the decisions under the Merchant Shipping Act, *The Truculent* provides a good example.[62] H.M.S. Truculent, a submarine owned by the Crown was in collision with another vessel due to a failure to carry adequate navigational lights. The Crown, sued under the provisions of the Crown Proceedings Act, 1947 pleaded section 5 (1) thereof which made section 503 (1) of the Merchant Shipping Act, 1894, apply to claims against the Crown. Wilmer J, holding that the expression 'Her Majesty' was used in a corporate sense, found that the Admiralty was in the position of owner of the vessel. Adequate navigational lights were not prescribed by the Admiralty due to peculiarities in submarine construction. The fault lay in not notifying mariners of this fact. It was held that the Admiralty was therefore at fault. The board had delegated its functions over the whole area of design, construction, and maintenance of ships to the Third Sea Lord. He was thus authorised to act in the name of the board. On these facts his fault was held to be the fault of the Board of Admiralty; the personal fault of of the owners. It is noteworthy that the Court explicitly declined to hold the Crown liable for the acts and omissions of such important subordinate officers as the ship's Captain and the Commander in Chief, Nore.

Personal fault was not attributed to the Crown simply because the Third Sea Lord was an important official acting in the scope of a delegated authority. Were that so, fault on the part of the Commander-in-Chief, Nore, could also have been ascribed personally to the Crown. The dispositive factor was the primary authority over the subject matter of design construction and maintenance of ships vested in the Third Sea Lord.

A similar strictness is evident in later decisions under the Merchant Shipping Act, notably *Beauchamp* v. *Turrell*[63] and *The Anonity*.[64] In the former case, the test propounded in *Lennard's* case was accepted. In *The Anonity*, the suggested *alter ego* was the chairman of the plaintiff company who conducted the management of its affairs. Holroyd Pearce LJ expresses the test thus[65] :

> In considering whether there has been actual fault or privity on the part of a limited company, the Court considers the conduct of the person who, by reason of his position, can be said to be the *alter ego* of the company.

The *alter ego* theory then, as it developed in cases under the Merchant Shipping Act enabled the courts to ascribe personal liability to bodies corporate. The conditions for such ascription were strict. Liability was ascribed in respect of the acts or omissions of some person or persons exercising primary authority over the corporation's affairs in virtue of their positions as a primary governmental organ. In order to be personal, the fault had to be that of a person or persons who, in a primary sense, managed the company's affairs. The issue then, was whether a prudent owner would have foreseen a risk and whether it was reasonable to expect the owner personally to take steps respecting it. If however, the owner foresaw an urgent danger, and gave adequate warning and instructions regarding it to his servants, he could not be said to be personally at fault for damage resulting from the danger though he might well be vicariously liable for the negligence of his servants in dealing with the matter.[66]

In other areas of the law, the relevant considerations were enunciated with less precision. The relevant issues were not always the same. The *alter ego* doctrine was enunciated because, in order to enforce the limitation of liability provisions of the Merchant Shipping Act, some basis had to be found for imputing personal liability to bodies corporate. A cognate problem arose under section 29 (1) of the Workmen's Compensation Act, 1925 which provided:

> When the injury was caused by the personal negligence or wilful act of the employer or of some person for whose act or default the employer is responsible, nothing in this Act shall affect any civil liability of the employer . . .
> . . . but the employer . . . shall not be liable to any proceedings independantly of this Act, except in case of such personal negligence or wilful act as aforesaid.

The *alter ego* idea could be relevant to the construction of this provision. In *Rudd* v. *Elder Dempster and Company Limited*,[67] The Court of Appeal held that the principles enunciated in *Lennard*'s case applied. An employer would be liable independantly of the act only for his (or its) own personal act or negligence. Such negligence could be proven by showing that the injury was caused by the negligence of some person other than a fellow workman of the plaintiff, such as the managing director or the general manager, or some other person having authority from the board of directors to conduct the company's business.[68] The application of the *alter ego* doctrine to this field was however foreclosed by the decision of the House of Lords in *Lochgelly Iron and Coal Company* v. *McMullen*[69] holding that an employer could be 'personally liable' within the meaning of section 29 (1) where a servant to whom he had delegated performance of a duty personal to himself had been negligent in its performance. Where a duty had been imposed on an employer at common law or by statute, a failure to perform it by the owner acting personally or through the instrumentality of a delegate rendered him liable, and to this situation the doctrine of common employment had no application.[70]

The *alter ego* doctrine has been mentioned in the context of trade disputes. In *Thomson* v. *Deakin*,[71] the Court of Appeal dealing with the tort of interfering with contracts stated that if a person approaches a servant of the company, the intervener will only be liable if the act which he procures the servant to do is either a breach of contract towards the servant's master or is otherwise tortious in itself. However[72]:

In the case of a company, the approach to or the persuasion of a managing director, or of some person having like authority, may be regarded as being in all respects equivalent to the direct approach of the individual contractor . . .

It has also made an appearance in the law of landlord and tenant. In *H. L. Bolton (Engineering) Co. Ltd.* v. *T. J. Graham & Sons Ltd.*[73] Denning LJ in an expressive dictum stated:

A company may in many ways be likened to a human body. It has a brain and nerve centre which controls what it does. It also has hands which hold the tools and act in accordance with directions from the centre. Some of the people in the company are mere servants and agents who are nothing more than hands to do the work and cannot be said to represent the mind or will. Others are directors and managers who represent the directing mind and will of the company, and control what it does. The state of mind of these managers is the state of mind of the company and is treated by the law as such. So you will find in cases where the law requires personal fault as a condition of liability in tort, the fault of the manager will be the personal fault of the company . . .[74]

The *alter ego* theory in the criminal cases

Much has already been said of the *alter ego* theory in relation to corporate criminal liability.[75] The extent to which the *alter ego* theory has been consciously applied in criminal cases by the courts is an open question.[76] Certainly, recent decisions, and in particular *John Henshall (Quarries) Ltd.* v. *Harvey* and *Regina* v. *McDonnell*[77] accept statements such as that of Denning LJ in the *Bolton* case as the basis for imputing criminal liability to corporations.

It is interesting to note the inversion which has occurred in the criminal cases. In the English cases at least, it has never explicitly been stated that criminal statutes had necessarily to apply to corporations. It has rather been held that, as a corporation has a mind (that of the board or of a 'responsible officer') it can therefore entertain a criminal intent. The conclusion then follows; that the corporation is a criminally responsible entity. In other words, there has been a shift of meaning from ascription to immanence.

Finally, the *alter ego* doctrine appears to mean different things in the criminal law than it does in, for example, cases arising under the Merchant Shipping Act. Until recently at least, the courts were careful, in shipping cases, to draw a precise line between liability ascribed to the corporation as personal liability and vicarious liability. This line was not drawn with the like precision in the criminal cases. As a result, it was occasionally difficult to distinguish between personal and vicarious liability in the case of corporations.[78] The criminal cases, for the most part[79] deal not with primary authority but with delegated authority.[80] It is only in the recent cases that the courts have begun to inquire whether the officer concerned exercised in fact a primary authority over some aspect at least of the corporations affairs.[81] Even this solution might be a departure from the *alter ego* doctrine as enunciated in shipping cases.[82] There the courts tended to speak of fault on the part of the board or the managing director. In the criminal cases, the same emphasis was not evident. In *Rex* v. *I. C. R. Haulage Ltd.* the corporation was convicted because ' . . . we were satisfied . . . that the facts proved were amply sufficient to justify a finding that the acts of the managing director were the acts of the company . . .', but the issue of identification was not always so clearly put.[83]

Recent developments in the *alter ego* doctrine

It would now appear however, that the formulation of the *alter ego* doctrine in the merchant shipping field is undergoing modification. The effect of this modification is to bring the doctrine as it has been applied in that field closer to the doctrine as it exists in the criminal law, and perhaps to clarify its meaning in both fields. The decision in question is that of the Court of Appeal in *The Lady Gwendolen*.[84] The plaintiff company, Arthur Guinness Son & Co. (Dublin) Ltd. sought, under section 503 of the Merchant Shipping Act, 1894 (as amended) to limit their liability in respect of a collision in fog between their vessel, *The Lady Gwendolen,* and another ship, *The Freshfield.* In 1953, Guinness ships were fitted with radar. The captain had no previous experience of radar, but later undertook a course of instruction. The captain, as was well known, habitually navigated in fog at excessive speeds. It was found that he was not under adequate supervision. Furthermore, no action was taken to acquaint the captain with, or to emphasise the importance of, a Ministry of Transport notice regarding navigation in fog. The Court of Appeal, affirming a decision of Hewson J, found that the proper use of radar in fog was of such importance as to merit the personal attention of the owners. It was their duty to ensure that it was properly employed.

The crucial issue was whether the failure adequately to supervise and warn was personal to the corporation. The company was actively managed by a joint managing director assisted by three assistant managing directors who were also members of the board. Williams, one of the assistant managing directors had, as one of his duties, supervision over shipping. He had however, as he admitted, no day-to-day interest in that department and left its detailed running to a traffic manager and a marine superintendent. The assistant managing director was not specifically authorised by any resolution to act in the name of the board. In fact, however, he had ultimate duty of supervision over the traffic department. The traffic manager never sought to interfere with, or display any interest in, navigational problems. The marine superintendent, though he had the opportunity for doing so, did not discover that the vessel was habitually negotiated in fog at excessive speeds. On these facts the Court of Appeal was able to find the company guilty of personal fault.

The Court of Appeal found that the assistant managing director in charge of shipping was a person in respect of whose acts or omissions the corporation could be held personally liable. This stemmed from his position as having, in fact, the ultimate duty of supervision over the traffic department. Sellers LJ characterised him as the person who was in charge of, and responsible in the capacity of owner, for the running of ships. His failure to consider the problems of radar navigation in fog was the personal fault of the owners.

Willmer and Winn LJJ were prepared to go further. They indicated that the person whose fault is to be the actual fault of the corporation need not necessarily be a director.

Winn LJ put the matter thus:

. . . wherever the fault either occurs in a function or sphere of action which the owner has retained for himself or is that of a manager independant of the owner to whom the owner had surrendered all relevant powers of control, it is actual fault of the owner within the meaning of the section.[85]

On this analysis a corporation could be held personally liable for the fault of a departmental manager provided that primary control in fact was placed in his hands.

The decision in *The Lady Gwendolen* represents a very welcome development. Its chief value lies in the pragmatic approach of the court to the problem. There is no hint in the judgments of any metaphysical relationship of a corporate officer to the corporation for which he acts. There is no hint of abstract constitutionalism in the courts approach. Rather, there was a careful factual analysis of the workings of the management of the plaintiff company. This is, it is submitted, commendably sound. By declining to fasten constitutional shackles to personal corporate liability it will be possible to fit corporations with complex, decentralized modes of organization into a meaningful framework of liability. Corporations, seemingly, will be held personally liable for the acts and omissions of top management, but the issue of who ought for these purposes to be identified with the company will be decided by the careful investigation and analysis of particular corporate organizations in relation to the facts of particular cases.

There is an element of discretion in determining in respect of whose actions the corporation is to be personally liable. There is no clear analytical distinction in kind between personal and vicarious corporate liability. The doctrine of identification can play a useful part in determining under what conditions liability is to be ascribed as personal. There are dangers of which Winn LJ in *The Lady Gwendolen* was well aware. He states:

The present case is one where such management of the ships as there was was carried out by employees of the owners. I appreciate that in such situations it is as essential as it may be difficult not to allow a *respondeat superior* responsibility to assume the guise of a retained responsiblity for a transferred function of management.[86]

The Court of Appeal has enunciated the conditions necessary for the ascription of persoanl liability; namely, that the function be a managerial function and that the person in respect of whose actions liability is to be ascribed be either the owner or some person to whom the owner has transferred all relevant powers of control. This could affect the formulation of the *alter ego* doctrine in relation to the criminal law, and is apparently the direction in which the criminal courts have been moving.[87] It is now possible that the criminal courts will ascribe liability, not largely because the official concerned is important,[88] or because he was a 'responsible' officer,[89] but because he was vested whether formally or informally with primary powers of control over all or a relevant part of the companies activities.

The *alter ego* and corporate representation generally

Finally, it should be noted that the *alter ego* doctrine has not supplanted the earlier body of learning which decides that an individual director is an officer, and may possess agency powers. He is not for all purposes to be identified with the company for which he acts.[90] It has for example been held that a company director can be convicted of fraudulent conversion from his company even though the other directors and the shareholders know of and consent to his actions.[91] In addition, it may be noted that the *alter ego* doctrine is not always employed, even in situations to which it might clearly seem to be relevant.[92] And, though the doctrine allows knowledge to be imputed to a corporation, it is not clear that it works in reverse so as to enable a corporation to cease to have knowledge of an event, or if it so operates, to what situations it will be applied. While it has been said that the knowledge of the company can only be the knowledge of persons who are entitled to represent the company it is by no means clear that a company can be permitted to say that it has forgotten an event once a record of it has been entered in the minute book. The point arose in *Bates* v. *Stone Parish Council*[93] where an infant was injured in an accident of a type which had occurred in the same playground twenty years before and in respect of which precautions against recurrence had then been taken. Birkett LJ treated the defendant as having knowledge of the event via the minute book. Somervell and Romer LJJ were inclined not to impute present knowledge of the dangerous condition on this ground alone. In fact the problem was less acute than it might have been since two persons who were members of the Council on the previous occasion were still members when the cause of action arose. As Lord Sumner recognised in a previous case,[94] it would be unsatisfactory to hold dogmatically that in all cases a company must be deemed to have knowledge of every event of which a record has been entered in the minute book. Equally, it can hardly be satisfactory to hold that a company no longer knows of an event when all the officers and directors who were then active have left the company's service.

The doctrine of identification seems to have little useful part to play in this area, and questions of the character considered by the court in the *Bates* case can best be answered by reference to the magnitude of the occurrence and whether a reasonable time has elapsed since. Furthermore, the contents of the minute book might have to be conclusive in property and contract matters, but not necessarily in tort and crime.

There is then, no single coherent theory of corporate representation in English law. The board, it is true, is treated as the governing organ of the corporation. Directors, and even the managing director, may act in several capacities. They may act as the government of the corporation. They may act as agents for the board in carrying out certain transactions. Under certain circumstances, the managing director may act as agent for the body of shareholders as a whole, as for example where he is appointed to negotiate the sale of their shares to some person wishing to take over the company.[95] He may, as *Lee* v. *Lee's Air Farming Ltd.*[96] shows, be at once the principal shareholder, managing director, and employee of the company. Yet he is not to be identified as the company.[97] The *alter ego* theory means rather that the actions, of an important officer of company, exercising primary managerial functions over the company's affairs as a whole, or over some aspect of its affairs, may be taken, where this is required, to be actions personal to the company. Personal liability is not immanent; it is ascribed. It is only seldom necessary that such liability be ascribed to a corporation, and the *alter ego* notion is the device which has been adopted for this purpose. It is a useful device, but it has pretensions to no greater status.

1   Winn, 'The Criminal Responsibility Of Corporations' (1927) 3 Camb. LJ 398
2   1915 AC 705

3   Gower, *Modern Company Law* (2nd ed. 1957) p 134
4   Blackstone, *Commentaries,* Book 1, p 476
5   Companies Act, 1862, Schedule 1, Article 55
6   Early cases spoke of directors as being agents or trustees. See *Pickering* v.
Stephenson (1872) LR 14 Eq. 322; *Beatty* v. *Ebury* (1872) 7 Ch. App. 777, 792
n; *In re Exchange Banking Company, Flitcroft's Case* (1882) 21 Ch.D. 519 per
Bacon VC at p 525, 'That the relationship of trustee and *cestui que trust* subsists
between the directors of joint stock companies and the shareholders I do not
entertain the slightest doubt.' But note also the cautious statement of Jessell MR on
appeal, stating that directors are quasi-trustees, and the statement by Brett LJ that
directors are not trustees for the shareholders
7   (1866) LR 2 Ch. App. 77
8   *Wilson* v. *Lord Bury* (1880) 5 QBD 518 (CA); *Ferguson* v. *Wilson* (1866)
LR 2 Ch. App. 77
9   *In re European Bank, ex.p. Oriental Commercial Bank* (1870) LR 5 Ch. App. 358;
Ramskill v. *Edwards* (1885) 31 Ch.D. 100
10   *In re Kingston Cotton Mill Company Limited*(2) [1896] 1 Ch. 331; *In re
Sharpe* [1892] 1 Ch. 154; *In re London, Hamburg, and Continental Exchange Bank,
Zulueta's Claim* (1870) 5 Ch. App. 444; *Chapleo* v. *The Brunswick Permanent
Building Society and Others* (1881) 6 QBD 696; *In re West of England Bank*
(1880) 14 Ch.D. 317
11   (1878) 10 Ch.D. 450
12   *In re Faure Electric Accumulator Company* (1889) 40 Ch.D. 141, 151 per
Kay J
13   (1883) 23 Ch.D. 1, 12-13 per Bowen LJ
14   *Smith* v. *Anderson* (1880) 15 Ch.D. 247, 275-6 per James LJ
15   [1900] AC 240, 259
16   [1908] 2 KB 89
17   [1908] 2 KB 89 at pages 105-6
18   [1906] 2 Ch. 34
19   [1909] AC 442
20   *Shaw and Sons (Salford) Ltd.* v. *Shaw* [1935] 2 KB 113
21   *Peel* v. *London and North Western Railway* [1907] 1 Ch. 5 at page 18 per
Buckley LJ
22   *Smith* v. *Anderson* (1880) 15 Ch.D. 247
23   *In re Kingston Cotton Mills Limited*(2) [1896] 1 Ch. 331
24   *London and Mashonaland Exploration Company Limited* v. *New Mashonaland
Exploration Company Limited* [1891] WN 165; *Re City Equitable Fire Insurance
Company* [1925] Ch. 407
25   (1856) 6 E & B 327. Gower, *Modern Company Law* (2nd ed. 1961) chapter 8
contains a valuable discussion of the rule which, briefly stated, provides that where
a company is incorporated under the Companies Acts, persons dealing with the
company are bound to ensure that the proposed dealings are not inconsistent with
the provisions of the registered documents of the company, i.e. that the company has
power to undertake then, and that for example, it has power to appoint an agent to
act in the premises, but the outsider is not bound to do more, and need not inquire
into the regularity of the internal proceedings of the company

26 *Mahoney* v. *East Holyford Mining Company* (1875) LR 7 HL 869; *Biggerstaff* v. *Rowatt's Wharf Ltd.* [1896] 2 Ch. 93

27 [1896] 2Ch. 743

28 [1904] 2 Ch. 608

29 [1902] 1 Ch. 507

30 See also as to directors and officers, *In re Marseilles Extension Railway Company, ex parte Credit Foncier and Mobilier of England,* (1871) LR 7 Ch. App. 161, and from a later period, *Houghton & Co.* v. *Nothard, Lowe and Wills,* [1928] AC 1 at p 15 per Viscount Dunedin

31 [1899] 2 Ch. 392

32 Companies Act, 1862 Schedule 1, Article 68

33 *Biggerstaff* v. *Rowatt's Wharf Ltd.* [1896] 2 Ch. 93

34 But not necessarily unlimited, see *In re Bread Supply Association* [1890] WN 210

35 (1875) LR 10 QB 329, 344

36 Compare e.g. *Biggerstaff* v. *Rowatt's Wharf Ltd.* [1896] 2 Ch. 93 with *Kreditbank Cassel g.m.b.h.* v. *Schenkers* [1927] 1 KB 826

37 *Rex* v. *Lawson* [1905] 1 KB 541

38 See dicta in *Dovey* v. *Corey* [1901] AC 477

39 See *Gibson* v. *Barton* (1875) LR 10 QB 329

40 [1901] 2 KB 560 (CA)

41 The corporate seal would have to be affixed to the document. See *Bishop* v. *Balkis Consolidated Co.* (1890) 25 QBD 512. Curiously, the Ontario Court of Common Pleas held, in *Bank of Toronto* v. *MacDougall* (1865) 15 UCCP 475 that a bank could sign a declaration to a chattel mortgage personally by its managing director, but the correctness of this decision was doubted by the Ontario Court of Appeal in *Craig & Co.* v. *Gillespie* (1920) 47 OLR 529

42 per Marshall CJ in *Trustees of Dartmouth College* v. *Woodward* (1819) 4 Wheat. 636 at page 659

43 Hallis, *Corporate Personality* (1930) p 152 and see Maitland, *Introduction* to Gierke, *Political Theories Of The Middle Age* (1902) at page xl

44 In *Citizens Life Insurance Company* v. *Brown* [1904] AC 423 at page 428

45 See Fifoot, *Judge And Jurist In The Reign Of Victoria* (1959) Chapter 3

46 [1915] AC 705

47 [1915] AC 705 at page 713

48 [1915] AC 705 at page 715

49 [1915] AC 705 at page 714

50 See Gower, *Modern Company Law* (2nd ed. 1957) p 135

51 No such formulation occurs in other of Lord Haldane's judgments on company law. See especially his treatment of companies incorporated under provincial statutes in *Bonanza Creek Gold Mining Company* v. *The King* (1916) 1 AC 566. There are some irritatingly allusive remarks in *Sinclair* v. *Brougham* [1914] AC 398

52 [1928] AC 1

53 (1964) 114 L.Jo. 17

54 (1964) 114 L.Jo. 17

55 *Royal Exchange Assurance Company* v. *Kingsley Navigation Company* [1923] AC 235

56 *Robin Hood Mills Limited* v. *Paterson Steamships Limited* [1937] 3 DLR 1

57 *Leval & Co.* v. *Colonial Steamships Limited* (1961) 26 DLR (2d) 574

58 *Maxwell Equipment Co.* v. *Vancouver Tug Boat Company* (1961) 26 DLR (2d) 80

59 See *The Truculent* [1952] P 1

60 See Gower, *Modern Company Law* (2nd ed. 1957) p 131

61 If, as has been contended, the corporation ought to be personally liable only for the actions of its primary representatives, then surely the managing director cannot be said to occupy this position. Table A, art. 107 gives the directors broad powers of delegation to one of their number, either concurrently with or to the exclusion of their own powers. The managing directors powers, while recognized by the articles, derive from a power of delegation from the primary organ, the board of directors

62 [1952] P 1 at p 12

63 [1952] 1 Lloyds Rep. 266

64 [1961] 2 Lloyds Rep. 117

65 [1961] 2 Lloyds Rep. 117 at p 120

66 *Beauchamp* v. *Turrell* [1961] 2 Lloyds Rep. 120

67 [1933] 1 KB 566

68 [1933] 1 KB 566 at page 576 per Scrutton LJ

69 [1934] AC 1

70 This defence was abolished by the Law Reform (Personal Injuries) Act, 1948

71 [1952] Ch. 646

72 [1952] Ch. 646 at page 682 per Evershed MR

73 [1957] 1 QB 159

74 [1957] 1 QB 159 at page 172

75 See the discussion in chapters 4 and 6

76 See chapter 4, and chapter 5 dealing with the relationship between corporate liability and vicarious liability

77 *John Henshall (Quarries) Ltd.* v. *Harvey* [1965] 1 All ER 725; *Regina* v. *McDonnell* [1965] 3 WLR 1138

78 See the discussion in chapter 5, and the judgment of Slade J dissenting in *James and Son Ltd.* v. *Smee* [1955] 1 QB 78, and the decision in *National Coal Board* v. *Gamble* [1959] 1 QB 11

79 *Rex* v. *I. C. R. Haulage Ltd.* [1944] KB 551, and *John Henshall (Quarries) Ltd.* v. *Harvey* [1965] 1 All ER 725 are notable exceptions. In Canada where the same principles apply, the *alter ego* idea has been strictly construed for the most part. See *Rex* v. *Fane Robinson Ltd.* [1941] 3 DLR 409; *Rex* v. *Ash Temple Co. Ltd.* [1949] OR 315; *Regina* v. *Electrical Contractors Ltd.* (1961) 27 DLR (2d) 193, but cf, *Regina* v. *H. J. O'Connell Ltd.* [1962] Que. QB 666

80 See *Moore* v. *I. Bresler Ltd.* [1944] 2 All ER 515; *National Coal Board* v. *Gamble* [1959] 1 QB 11, *D. P. P.* v. *Kent and Sussex Contractors* [1944] KB 146, and a helpful note by Downey in (1959) 22 MLR 91

81 *John Henshall (Quarries) Ltd.* v. *Harvey* [1965] 1 All ER 725 and possibly *Regina* v. *Stanley Haulage Ltd.* (1964) 114 L. Jo. 25

82 But in *The Truculent* [1952] P 1, liability was imposed in respect of the omission of a person having primary authority over only a part of the Admiralty's affairs.

83 [1944] KB 551, 554 per Stable J

84 [1965] 2 All ER 283 (CA) affirming [1964] 3 All ER 447 (PD & A)

85 [1965] 2 All ER 283 at page 302

86 [1965] 2 All ER 283 at page 302

87 *John Henshall (Quarries) Ltd.* v. *Harvey* [1965] 1 All ER 725; *Regina* v. *Stanley Haulage Ltd.* (1964) 114 L. Jo. 25

88 *Moore* v. *I. Bresler Ltd.* [1944] 2 All ER 515; *D. P. P.* v. *Kent and Sussex Contractors Ltd.* [1944] KB 146

89 *James and Son Ltd.* v. *Smee* [1955] 1 QB 78

90 See *Freeman and Lockyer* v. *Buckhurst Park Properties Ltd.* [1964] 1 All ER 630, a recent decision on the rule in *Royal British Bank* v. *Turquand* (1856) 6 E & B 327; *Wheeler* v. *New Merton Board Mills* [1933] 2 KB 669 at page 678 per Talbot J

91 *Reg.* v. *Arthur* [1967] Crim. LR 298. Similarly, there is no doubt that a director can conspire to defraud the company. *Reg.* v. *Sinclair* [1968] 3 All ER 241

92 e.g. *In re Fazal Ilahi and Razim Khan* [1957] 2 Lloyds Rep. 517 where it could have been argued that an arrest made by a corporate owner's agents was made personally by the owner within the meaning of sec. 221(1) of the Merchant Shipping Act 1894

93 [1954] 3 All ER 38

94 In *Houghton & Co.* v. *Nothard, Lowe and Wills* [1928] AC 1 at p 18

95 *Briess* v. *Wooley* [1954] AC 333

96 [1961] AC 12

97 *Tunstall* v. *Steigmann* [1962] 2 WLR 1045; *Regina* v. *McDonnell* [1965] 3 WLR 1138

Chapter 8

The bases upon which corporate criminal liability is imposed

In the previous chapter, an examination of the *alter ego* notion of corporate representation was undertaken. It is now intended to examine the *alter ego* theory and other bases upon which corporate criminal liability is imposed, principally the bases employed by the United States Federal Courts, and in the *Model Penal Code*.

The choice of a basis upon which corporate criminal liability may be imposed must inevitably reflect the view taken of the policy underlying the imposition of corporate liability. In one view, corporate criminal liability serves the same function as vicarious liability; that is, the function of inducing management to police the observance of legislation on its own part and on the part of its employees. In the alternative, corporate criminal libility may be viewed as a form of liability intended primarily to deter management itself from utilising corporate forms and assets in the commisssion of offences. The formulation of the bases for imposing liability will differ in either case.

In England and under the *Model Penal Code* the underlying assumption apparently is that corporate criminal liability is designed to deter managerial criminality. As much for this, as for conceptual reasons, a basis of liability has been chosen in order to ensure, as far as possible, that corporations will be penalised only for the policy decisions of managerial personnel.[1] In the United States Federal Courts the underlying assumption is, at least in part, that corporate criminal liability is primarily designed to secure compliance with certain regulatory legislation, although liability in theory at least is not so restricted. Hence principles generally applicable to offences in respect of which vicarious liability has long been recognised are imposed. In the American Federal Courts there has, as a result, been no effort to search for bases of imposition which will clearly differentiate corporate criminal liability from vicarious liability.

This chapter seeks to examine and evaluate the various bases of liability mentioned, and finally to suggest a basis which will take account of certain shortcomings of each. It should be said that, for the purposes of this part of the study, the desirability of corporate criminal liability is assumed. It is proposed first to deal with the solution adopted in the American Federal Courts, secondly with the *alter ego* doctrine, and then with the solution propounded in the *Model Penal Code.*

Liability in the American Federal Courts

In the Federal Courts, assumptions which elsewhere appear to have governed the course of liability have not operated. In general, the Federal Courts have assumed that no meaningful distinction can be drawn between vicarious liability and corporate criminal liability. The object of the Federal Courts has been to ensure compliance with regulatory legislation much of which affects the operation of large loosely-organized corporations engaged in interstate commerce. The courts, while suspecting that the highest rank of corporate officers may well have been implicated in the commission of offences, have not assumed that these necessarily originate in the formal atmosphere of the board room. Liability has been imposed in respect of the conduct of the middle-range of corporate officials, such as area and branch managers. It has been imposed regardless of whether the offence reflected the policy of the corporation as seen by the highest echelons of management. Furthermore, it has been recognised that, were the prosecution under an obligation to prove complicity on the part of the highest range of managerial official, it would frequently prove impossible to convict the corporation. Accordingly, the basis of liability adopted is not essentially different from vicarious liability.

The basis of liability was not precisely defined in the early Federal cases. Some courts spoke of the action of officers as the basis of liability.[2] The analogy here, as Judge Hough stated in *United States* v. *New York Herald Co.*,[3] was to the punitive damage rule in torts as applied to corporations. In other cases the courts merely spoke, in imposing liability, of the action of corporate officers and agents.[4] The trend towards overt vicarious liability began with *New York Central and Hudson Rail Road Company* v. *United States.*[5] This case involved the constitutional validity of the Elkins Act which prohibited the giving of rebates by common carriers in interstate commerce.[6] Its object was to ensure common treatment to shippers. The Act provided that in construing and enforcing the charging section, the acts, omissions or failure of an agent or officer employed by a common carrier and acting within the scope of his employment should also be deemed to be the act failure or omission of the carrier. Objection was taken to the section on the ground, *inter alia,* that such vicarious liability was unconstitutional as denying to the accused the benefit of the basic presumption of innocence.

The court conceded that there were offences of which a corporation could not be convicted. It found however, that liability could be imposed where the gravamen of the offence consisted in the doing of an act prohibited by statute.[7] Finding that liability had to be imposed in the public interest, the court met the railroad's constitutional argument with scant sympathy. It stated that corporations can only act through their officers, agents, and servants, and therefore concluded that no question of vicarious liability arose. It was unable to see why, in law, the corporation could not be held liable for the actions of its officers, agents or servants.

In the Federal Courts this approach to the problem became dominant. No attempt was made to distinguish between regulatory legislation and the more traditional forms of crime. Judge Learned Hand, in *United States* v. *Nearing,*[8] a charge of conspiracy to print seditious publications contrary to the *Espionage Act,*[9] held that no distinction could be drawn between the civil and the criminal liability of corporations. Each, he said, ' . . . is merely an imputation to the corporation of the mental condition of its agents.'[10] The criminal liability of a corporation is to be determined ' . . . by the kinship of the act to the powers of the officals who commit it'.[11]

Followed in most cases, whether involving *mens rea* or not,[12] the *respondeat superior* rule was clearly articulated in *Egan* v. *United States.*[13] The appellant, an officer of an electrical company, the company, and others, were charged with making political contributions contrary to statute. The corporation, in its defence, argued that the acts of its agents in making the alleged contributions were in excess of their authority. It was urged that before their actions could be said to be the company's actions, the sanction of the board was necessary. The court, reiterating the vicarious liability test, held that no essential distinction between corporate civil and criminal liability existed. The test of liability enunciated by the court is whether the officer or agent, in doing the acts complained of, was engaged in exercising corporate powers for the benefit of the corporation while acting in the scope of his employment.

This test is now generally employed. It has been applied to cases of conspiracy where the conspirator was a plant or branch manager.[14] It has been applied generally in the field of regulatory legislation enacted by Congress under the commerce power.[15] In general the fact that an action has been performed contrary to corporate policy has not been permitted to influence the result. There seems a distinct strain of judicial scepticism inherent in the conclusion that a corporation ' . . . cannot divorce itself

from its responsible agent to insulate itself from criminal prosecution'.[16]
In only one case has a corporation been exonerated after showing that
it issued positive instructions to its agents to refrain from a given sort of
illegal practice.[17] That decision has not been followed.[18] It has been
adversely criticised as tending to render enforcement of the legislation
nugatory, a dismal proposition with whch, in the realm of public welfare
offences, one cannot but be familiar.[19] The rule seemed at one time to
be so far reaching that an intention to benefit the corporation had no
part to play in determining whether liability would be imposed or not.
Whether or not the human actor intended to benefit the corporation,
liability was imposed.[20]

The present rule, despite some judicial wavering,[21] is that liability
will be imposed whenever an officer or agent in doing the acts complained
of, was engaged in exercising corporate powers and acting within the
course and scope of his employment, provided that he intended thereby
to benefit the corporation.[22] In theory, the status of such an agent or
officer is unimportant. The primary question is whether he has been
invested with the performance of functions in the area to which the acts
which he has performed relate. It has been said that the corporation might
well be liable for the acts of menial servants,[23] but in practice, liability
is imposed in respect of the actions of middle range managerial personnel.
In *Steere Tank Lines Inc.* v. *United States*[24] it is held that where the
evidence discloses that inferior personnel might have acted to benefit
themselves, superior personnel must know of their activities before a
conviction will be allowed.

Reasons underlying the federal rule of liability

One factor underlying the choice of rule in the Federal Courts was the
type of legislation with which the courts were primarily concerned. The
legislation, comparatively modern in terms of subject matter, was designed
to regulate matters such as the conduct of business, examples being afforded
by the antitrust laws, standards legislation, wartime profiteering laws,
and the like. Very few decisions concern traditional criminal offences.[25]
The courts did not distinguish between commission of the substantive
offences and conspiracy to commit them. There may have seemed little
distinction to be drawn between failing to make certain statutory returns,[26]
'knowingly and wilfully' confining cattle in cars in excess of the time
permitted by statute,[27] the sale of foodstuffs at prices in excess of those
permitted by wartime legislation,[28] and conspiracy to fix prices in
violation of anti-trust legislation.[29] Such offences were, in some measure,

regarded as less than criminal. Some courts took a lenient view of
offending businessmen. Furthermore, penal statutes were not always
systematically enforced by criminal sanctions. This was found to be
true of certain wartime price control violations. Only recently have the
serious penal provisions of the Sherman Anti-Trust Act been systematically
enforced through the criminal courts. Heavy fines and prison sentences
meted out in recent cases have come as a distinct, and perhaps salutary,
shock.[30] However, insofar as these offences were regarded as less than
truly criminal the test used in imposing liability cannot be seen as
particularly surprising.

Problems of proof owing to the complexities of large scale organisation
and the attendant difficulty of proving complicity on the part of the
highest echelons of management conduced to the same result. In *Egan*
v. *United States*[31] the court carefully excluded from the ambit of inquiry
questions whether the criminal act had been authorised by the board.
In several cases, American courts have upheld convictions made against
a corporation in circumstances where the jury convicted the corporation,
but acquitted officers charged with it and on whose actions corporate
guilt was said to depend.[32] In *United States* v. *General Motors
Corporation*[33] the court, drawing attention to the indictment which
charged the corporation with conspiring with the named accused and
other persons unknown, rationalised the result by holding that the
acquittal of the named officers did not exhaust the list of persons with
whom the corporation might have conspired. One may also draw attention
to the remarks of Chief Judge Ganey in a celebrated recent anti-trust
prosecution involving General Electric Corporation and others.[34] The
corporation was charged with price-fixing in violation of the Sherman
Act. The actors involved were secondary officers in the corporate
structure. It could not be shown that either the president of the
corporation or the chairman of the board were implicated in price fixing,
and these officers consistently denied complicity on their part.[35] In
sentencing the corporation, the Chief Judge observed[36]:

> While the Department of Justice has acknowledged that they were
> unable to uncover probative evidence which could secure convictions
> beyond a reasonable doubt, of those in the highest echelons of the
> corporations here involved, in a broader sense they bear a grave
> responsibility for the present situation, for one would be most naive
> indeed to believe that these violations of the law, so long persisted in,
> affecting so large a segment of the industry and finally, involving so
> many millions upon millions of dollars, were facts unknown to those

responsible for the conduct of the corporations and accordingly, under their various pleas, heavy fines will be imposed.

It is suggested that a belief that management was frequently implicated in the commission of offences influenced the Federal Courts in the choice of a test.

Disadvantages of the federal courts rule

Respondeat superior cannot be considered to be a satisfactory general basis of liability, however valuable it may be in the enforcement of certain legislation. Several objections to its employment may be urged.

It is discriminatory in application. A single proprietor is not held liable for all offences committed by his employees. His liability is restricted to a roughly circumscribed area in which vicarious liability is generally admitted. The same observations apply to partnerships. In even the largest partnerships partners are not made personally liable for all criminal offences committed by their employees.[37] Unless some differentiating principle can be found, it is anomalous to place corporations in a unique position. It is true that the corporation can only think and act as its officers, agents and servants think and act. Not all these classes of personnel perform the directive function that would be performed by the entrepreneur and the partners. One can take account of the differentiation of functions within the entity and hold the corporation liable only for the actions of its directive personnel. Nothing compels a different result.

The factor upon which reliance is generally placed is one of scale, a factor which, while obviously relevant to the large corporation, is by no means unique to it. Scale has a two-fold relevance. First it is contended that the size of the corporation gives to those in control of it a unique potential for harm. This has apparently been felt in the field of anti-trust.[38] Secondly, it is often argued that the large scale of corporate enterprise with resulting wide lower echelon responsibility makes it difficult to prove that the commission of an offence originated in policies adopted at the highest levels of corporate management. It could also be argued that where a wide delegation over aspects of a corporation's business affairs has been made the power to commit offences which thus passes into the hands of persons enjoying delegated responsibilities requires the imposition of a supervisory duty upon management.[39]

Even if the validity of these consideration be granted, it can still be argued that *respondeat superior* is inadmissible as a general basis of liability. The second argument advanced above; that the corporation has a great potential for harm which can be realised by the formulation of policies which contravene the law, does not justify the *respondeat superior* test. In effect, this basis of liability excludes any investigation into company policy and its enforcement. Liability is imposed without reference to the actual course of conduct desired by those who control the corporation. So extreme a solution can hardly be justified by evidentiary factors alone. Liability is thereby imposed upon a corporation for serious offences at a point at which an investigation into the affairs of a different form of business organisation might be commenced.[40]

The argument that delegated power over a corporation's affairs is likely, in the absence of the imposition of corporate liability, to render enforcement of criminal legislation nugatory is also open to objection. It may be that difficulties are experienced in enforcing certain types of legislation. It may be difficult to show that breaches of the legislation occurred as a result of managerial complicity. One problem however, that of scale, can be advanced in favour of the imposition of such liability upon all forms of business enterprise. The argument may in fact be compelling as respects all business enterprises in respect of some criminal offences, but it can hardly be justified as applicable to one form of business enterprise in respect of all offences. There is, for example, little indication of any particular enforcement problems, attributable to corporations in respect of the traditional criminal offences. Yet the test is, in the Federal Courts, made to cover the whole ground.[41]

Furthermore, the imposition of liability *respondeat superior,* achieves one of its desired results only coincidentally. In part it seeks to ensure that corporations will comply with the law and force their employees to do the same. The present test of liability however, gives rise to an obvious risk that corporations will be penalised in respect of actions by their agents which have been performed in violation of company policy.[42] In addition, a possible oblique result of an extended rule of vicarious liability in company cases may be the subsequent imposition of a wider rule of vicarious liability on non-corporate employees.[43] It is then, in theory, an unsatisfactory general basis of liability.

Liability in England, Canada, and under the model penal code
In England and Canada, and under the *Model Penal Code*, the formulation of bases of liability reflects a desire to differentiate between

corporate criminal liability and vicarious liability. A search has taken place to ascertain a basis upon which a corporation can be held liable only for the policies which those in control of it adopt. The search essentially, has been to locate those persons in the corporate structure who can be said to represent the mind and will of the corporation. In part this reflects a desire to construct a personal liability on the part of bodies corporate; in part it reflects a desire to impose liability in respect of policies adopted by the corporation.

The English courts presently impose liability on corporations for the actions of high managerial officers. These include not only the Board of Directors, but the managing director and other high officers as well. The essential prerequisite to corporate guilt is apparently, that the officer in respect of whose actions liability is ascribed to the corporation, must be of sufficient status that he can be presumed to be performing directive functions. As has been indicated, the courts, in the criminal cases at least, have to some extent begged the questions of the meaning of corporate policy and control. It is of course possible to have distinct levels of each. An example may clarify what is meant. Assume that company X carries on a road haulage business through a number of widely dispersed branches. Each branch manager may have daily control over the routine activities of his branch. He can direct company employees where to drive, what loads to carry, and to what destinations. In this sense he wields control, and were he to conspire with the corporation's drivers to cause them to drive longer hours than are permitted by road traffic regulations, under the present law the corporation might well be convicted of 'causing' a breach of the regulations or of conspiring to commit an offence contrary to them.[44] Those in ultimate control of the corporation might well desire that the law be strictly observed. Their control is an ultimate control. The branch manager wields his power as their delegate, and within a broad framework of policy the considerations of which are determined or determinable by the highest echelons of management. In a sense, the manager is a directive employee; at another level, an executive. To impose liability for his actions, without more, is to impose a vicarious liability upon the corporation. The English courts could be taken to imply that a single officer enjoying a delegated authority can be treated for this reason alone as wielding primary authority within a corporation.

It has been urged that corporate criminal liability should only be imposed in respect of the actions of those who, by direct attribution, wield corporate powers.[45] This is not the present law in England. As has been shown, the courts are essentially looking into the question of *de facto* exercise of primary authority. It is probable that to base liability only on the actions of primary representatives would be insufficiently inclusive. In modern large corporations the board may exercise what is essentially an approval function. Initiation of policy may come from the executive; the corporation's civil service. Departmental heads may well be left with virtually autonomous powers, exercised largely without immediate supervision.[46] A corporation's business may be organised into several departments, each dealing basically with a different business, and over which directoral control may be of the loosest character. The task of policy implementation will certainly come at this level. A rule of liability which excludes corporate responsibility for the actions of these officers may be open to attack as laying undue stress on form rather than function. It may represent a survival of an outmoded concept of corporate organisation. R. A. Gordon concludes that[47]:

. . . decisions of considerable significance for the firm as a whole may be at least initiated, and sometimes approved by department heads and other subordinate officials.

The notion of the board as a tightly constituted mind of the corporation seems, in many cases, outdated.[48]

Canadian experience in the anti-trust field would seem to support this contention. Liability in Canada has explicitly been stated to proceed on the footing of *Lennard*'s case[49] and this has been adhered to with some consistency.[50] It has been said that a corporation is not liable for actions performed in its name by controlling shareholders where these are not its officers.[51] It has also been said that where control of the corporation passed to bondholders, the corporation, because it is no longer in control of its activities, cannot be criminally liable for their activities.[52] While some cases appear simply to hold corporations liable for the actions of their officers,[53] those in which the bases of liability are discussed stress the strict *alter ego* theory. An essential factor stressed by Canadian courts, has been that the human actor must have had authority from the company to perform the prohibited act.[54] The courts have held that before a corporation could be convicted of a criminal offence, there must be evidence that the governing members were implicated in its commission.

This comparatively rigid test was found to be inhibiting in Canadian anti-trust prosecutions. The effects of problems of scale and concomitant difficulties of proof arose in *Rex* v. *Ash Temple Co. Ltd.*[55] In that case,

E

eighteen corporations were charged with conspiracy to unduly prevent
or lessen competition in trade in certain items of dental equipment. The
Crown at trial sought to introduce a large number of documents in
evidence as proof of the conspiracy. The documents came from the files
of an alleged conspirator company. It was held that this was not enough.
It had to be shown that the company, by the board or by an officer to
whom pricing was delegated, had knowledge of the existence and contents
of the documents.

It would obviously be impossible in many cases to identify a person
as having the requisite knowledge with sufficient precision. In the result,
the Canadian Combines Investigation Act (the Canadian anti-trust statute)
was amended.[56] It now provides that anything done by an agent of a
participant[57] should, *prima facie*, be deemed to be done with the
participant's assent. Any document, received or written by a participant's
agent or in the possession of a participant or agent is *prima facie*
brought home to the participant as evidence against it. Problems of
proof of complicity by the governing members of a corporation have
thus been alleviated in anti-trust prosecutions.

Liability under the Model Penal Code

The formulation adopted by the *Model Penal Code* reflects an
assumption that an overt act, committed by some person of high standing
in the management of the corporation, is sufficiently indicative of
corporate policy to warrant the imposition of liability. Section 2.07
provides[58] :

> A corporation may be convicted of the commission of an offence
> if and only if: . . .
> (c) the commission of the offence was authorised, requested, commanded,
> performed or recklessly tolerated by the board of directors, or by a high
> managerial agent acting in behalf of the corporation within the scope of
> his office or employment.

Section 2.07 (2) (c) defines high managerial agent to mean an officer of
a corporation, or any other agent of a corporation, ' . . . having duties of
such responsibility that his conduct may fairly be assumed to represent
the policy of the corporation or association'.

The aim of the American Law Institute in adopting this formulation
in the *Model Penal Code* was to ensure that liability for serious offences
would not be imposed on a general footing of *respondeat superior*. In
their notes to the section, the rapporteurs state[59] :

. . . corporate liability is confined to situations in which the criminal
conduct is performed or participated in by the board of directors or
by corporate officers and agents sufficiently high in the hierarchy to
make it reasonable to assume that their acts are in some substantial
sense reflective of corporate policy.

To this end, an earlier draft of section 2.07 (1) (c) which included in
the definition of high managerial officer persons having supervisory
responsibility over the subject matter of the offence was changed to
its present form.[60] The practical effect of the draft is said to be that
liability will result from the conduct of a corporation's president or
general manager, ' . . . but not for the conduct of a foreman in a
large plant or of an insignificant branch manager in the absence of
participation at higher levels of corporate authority'.[61] This obviously
leaves a wide area to judicial discretion. The justification for so limiting
liability is that it should only be imposed in cases where shareholders
are most likely to bring pressure to bear to prevent corporate crime.[62]

The *Model Penal Code* formulation is, in terms of existing American
case law, restrictive. It represents an improvement over existing case law,
at least in that it seeks to articulate a rationale of corporate criminal
liability. Whether in practice the incidence of corporate convictions
would be much reduced is problematical. Liability is now imposed in
respect of the actions of at least important officials, although its
theoretical ambit is wider.[63] Furthermore, it is open to criticism in
two respects.

Criticisms of the Model Penal Code formulation

The first criticism which may be made of the Code is that it seeks
to elevate a proposition of evidence into a rule of substantive law. It
assumes that the actions of certain high managerial officers are
sufficiently indicative of corporate policy to warrant a finding of
guilt. It is probably true that in many cases this assumption is warranted.
Nonetheless, there may be important corporate officials who do not
share in the primary function of policy making. Professor Mueller
argues that liability should be imposed in respect of the actions of
officers, whether elected or appointed, ' . . . who direct, supervise
and manage the corporation within its business sphere and policy-wise
the inner circle'.[64] It is at this point that one encounters difficulty.
There is no indication what criteria are to be employed in order to
determine who falls within the inner circle. The composition of the

policy making organs of a corporation will necessarily vary from
corporation to corporation.[65] One could have several 'inner circles'
with the board exercising simply an approval function.[66] The managing
director of a corporation is the key figure in its management, but it
cannot be said with certainty that department and branch managers
necessarily occupy the like position.[67] Shortly stated, the formulation
adopted in the *Model Penal Code* reflects a tautology. It is an attempt
to arrive at a rule which will punish the corporation only in respect of
policies adopted by those who control it. The attempt cannot be entirely
successful. The idea of an 'inner circle' is a dangerous inexactitude. It is
inexact because there is no abstract manner of determining what officers
within any given company necessarily take a part in the formulation of
policy. It is dangerous, because, by its superficial attractiveness, it tends
to preclude further examination. By relying upon the actions of high
managerial officers as sufficiently indicative of corporate policy to warrant
the conviction of a corporation, it fails to quantify the issues adequately.
The conclusion which can be derived from the formulation is that a
corporation will be liable whenever an important corporate official
commits an offence in some way related to the corporation's business
activities. Once the basic assumption has been made that the person whose
acts it is desired to ascribe to the corporation falls within the definition
of high managerial officer, liability follows. It is necessary to realise that
the basic assumption may well be no more than that.

A suggested improvement in the formulation of bases

It is necessary that the various problems in issue be identified. It is
reasonably clear that the various tests suggested are prompted largely
by evidentiary factors. To these, much of the shape of the present law
and the formulation adopted in the *Model Penal Code* are attributable.
The search is for a basis of liability which will ensure that corporations
are held liable only in respect of the policies adopted on their behalf
by management at the highest levels. The course of this development
can be seen quite clearly in some American decisions.

It is not desired to affirm that there cannot be persons whose actions
represent corporate policy in the widest sense. What is urged is that it
is impossible in the abstract to posit any individual or group, save perhaps
the Board of Directors, whose actions taken singly will infallibly reflect
corporate policy. At most, actions of single directors and officers can
serve to raise a plausible inference that a given policy was formulated.

These factors appear in certain American decisions. Reference has

already been made to the effect of these considerations in the Federal
courts. In *People* v. *Canadian Fur Trappers Corporation* the court,
declaring that corporate liability for crimes would be imposed only
where the criminal intent was that of the corporation, stated[68] :

How this intent may be proved or in what cases it becomes evident
depends entirely on the circumstances of each case. Probably, no general
rule applicable to all situations could be stated.

The court tacitly approved statements in earlier cases that repeated
wrongful acts done by the corporation's servants might be sufficient
to raise an inference that the acts were authorised by the corporation's
governing officers.[69] The problem was primarily evidentiary.

The evidentiary aspects are occasionally blurred in later cases, so
that an evidentiary proposition wears the guise of a proposition of
substantive law. *People* v. *Raphael* provides an example.[70] A property
company was charged with unlawfully receiving rent in excess of that
permitted by rent control legislation. The actions were performed by a
superintendent without the knowledge of any of the officers of the
landlord corporation. The corporation was acquitted. Magistrate Ploscowe
in his discussion of the law enunciated the following instances in which
a corporation might properly be convicted of a criminal offence.
Something more must be shown than agency or employment. He states[71] :

A corporation is chargeable with the crime of an agent or employee,
acting in the scope of his employment when (1) the corporation has
benefited or profited from the crime, or (2) its officers participated
in the crime, or (3) its officers authorised, sanctioned or acquiesced
in the commission of the crime by the agent or employee, or (4) it had
knowledge of the crime, or (5) it was chargeable with negligence in not
obtaining knowledge through reasonable inquiry.

This statement derives from an examination of several American cases.[72]
In three at least, some of the propositions advanced in *People* v. *Raphael*
under the guise of substantive law appear as evidentiary considerations.[73]
As a predicate of liability corporate benefit, for example, appears entirely
out of place. Surely it is not desired to punish someone merely because
he (or it) has derived a coincidental benefit from the commission of an
offence. Nor surely ought liability to be predicated on mere knowledge
by some officer of the corporation. Even were one to grant the existence
of a general duty on the part of corporations to police the activities of

their employees, one can urge that liability ought only to depend on foreknowledge of the intended commission of a specific criminal act. The notion of ratification, for example, has no application as such to the foundation of criminal liability.[74] On the other hand, that benefit accrued to the corporation, or that it acted subsequently with knowledge that a crime had been committed might, under certain circumstances, help to establish a *prima facie* case that the persons in control of the corporation commanded or authorised the commission of the offence. Here again the search is for factors which may legitimately give rise to an inference that the commission of an offence reflects an underlying corporate policy.

A suggested solution: quantifying the issues

None of the tests advanced above can afford an entirely satisfactory basis for the imposition of corporate criminal liability. A criticism of the *respondeat superior* rule has already been ventured. To base liability on the actions of the corporation's primary organs is to invite needless difficulty, especially in cases where authority has been widely delegated. The test may not be sufficiently inclusive. It invites a descent into an essentially sterile constitutionalism in which questions of form rather than substance predominate. Furthermore, difficulties in proving complicity in the commission of an offence by the Board of Directors or managing director, likely to be felt in the case of a large corporation, may give rise to an essentially fictional ascription of liability. There is an obvious risk that liability will be imposed even where the acts complained of are in fact performed contrary to express company policy. Even on the high managerial agent formulation this difficulty cannot be said to have been eliminated.

It is submitted that, within the framework of the present law, liability for major crimes should only be ascribed to the corporation in respect of acts performed pursuant to corporate policy. This however, is the sole legal constant in issue. Whether a criminal offence is to be imputed to a corporation should depend not upon the status of the actor performing it, but on whether the crime represents a policy decision on the part of those in control of the corporation.[75]

Secondly, separate attention should be devoted to the evidentiary issues involved. This is clearly necessary in the light of difficulties in proving directly that high management was implicated in commission of the offence. It would be preferable to adopt as a drafting model the formulation employed in the Canadian Combines Investigation Act[76] and to deem certain matters if proven sufficient to afford a *prima facie* case against a corporation. Among such matters could be the actions of high managerial officials, repeated violations of a given provision by employees of whatever rank, or more questionably perhaps and certainly not taken alone, a failure by the corporation when informed of the commission of an offence by its employees to take disciplinary action against the employee or employees involved. The prosecution obviously cannot as a practical matter, be expected in the first instance to conduct a minute investigation into the organisational structure of a given company.

At the same time, these matters should be relevant to the defence. Proof, for example, that a high managerial officer committed or caused an offence to be committed should be recognised as the possible beginning and not the infallible end of judicial inquiry. Such a suggestion requires a modification of the existing law, but one which could be achieved judicially. Equally, the change could be brought about by statute. The Canadian legislation referred to has proven workable and there is no reason to suppose that a statute of more general application would not prove satisfactory.[77]

In effect the formulation advanced above will provide a manner whereby the prosecution can advance a *prima facie* case. The burden of proof throughout will remain on the prosecution. The corporation will not however, be denied an effective opportunity of making a defence. Its ability to do so would be much enhanced. Furthermore, if, as the American Law Institute contends, liability should only be imposed in circumstances where the shareholders can bring pressure to bear, the suggested test should certainly assist the process. By its adoption, not only corporate policy, but also the efficacy of the means adopted in its enforcement, will be capable of receiving a public appraisal.[78]

1   *Rex* v. *I. C. R. Haulage Co. Ltd.* [1944] KB 551, 559 per Stable J; *Model Penal Code* TD 4, Notes at page 151
2   *American Socialist Society* v. *United States* 266 Fed. 212 (1920); *Mininsohn* v. *United States* 101 F 2d 477 (1939); *United States* v. *New York Herald Co.* 159 Fed. 296 (1907)
3   159 Fed. 296 (1907). On the punitive damages rule in torts as applied to corporations, see Hildebrand, 'Corporate Liability For Torts And Crimes' (1935) 13 Tex. L. Rev. 253
4   *United States* v. *Wilson* 59 F 2d 97 (1932); *Zito et al.* v. *United States* 64 F 2d 772 (1933)
5   212 US 481 (1909)

6   Now *United States Code* Title 49, S 41(2)

7   212 US 481, 494

8   252 Fed. 223 (1918)

9   The text of the Act is reproduced in 266 Fed. 212 (1920) and is cast in terms requiring *mens rea*

10   252 Fed. 223, 231 (1918)

11   252 Fed. 223, 231 (1918)

12   e.g. *United States* v. *Union Supply Company* 215 US 50 (1909); *United States* v. *Illinois Central R.R. Co.* 303 US (1937); see Egerton 'Corporate Criminal Responsibility' (1926) 36 Yale LJ 827. Note, 'Corporate Criminal Liability In New York' (1948) 48 Col. L. Rev. 794; Mullen, *Development And Rationale Of Corporate Criminal Liability* pp 114 *et seq.* (unpublished thesis, 1951 NYU)

13   137 F 2d. 369 (1943) cert. den. 320 US 788 (1943)

14   *United States* v. *Armour & Co.* 168 F 2d 342 (1948); *Continental Baking Company* v. *United States* 281 F 2d 137 (1960)

15   Which includes such matters as labour regulation, interstate commerce, commodity standards and public health legislation

16   *Continental Baking Company* v. *United States* 281 F 2d 137, 150 (1960) per Weick J., Cecil and Kent JJ concurring

17   *Holland Furnace Company* v. *United States* 158 F 2d 2 (1946)

18   Not followed in *United States* v. *Armour & Co.* 168 F 2d 342 (1948)

19   Note, 19 U. Pa. L. Rev. 557 (1947)

20   *Old Monastery Company* v. *United States* 147 F 2d 905 (1945)

21   *United States* v. *Thompson-Powell Drilling Company* 196 F Supp. 571 (1961), reversed *sub. nom. Standard Oil Company of Texas* v. *United States* 307 F 2d 120 (1963) in which Judge Dooley, at trial, stated that 'It may be that the assent of some agent in supervisory or executive authority would be necessary to commit a corporation to conspiracy'.

22   *Standard Oil Company of Texas* v. *United States* 307 F 2d 120 (1963); *United States* v. *Carter et al.* 311 F 2d 934 (1963)

23   per Brown J in *Standard Oil Company of Texas* v. *United States* 307 F 2d 120 (1963) at page 127

24   330 F 2d 719 (1964). See also *United States* v. *Johns-Manville Corporation* 231 F Supp. 690 (1964); *Continental Baking Corporation* v. *United States* 281 F 2d 137 (1960); *C. I. T. Corporation* v. *United States* 150 F 2d 85 (1945); *United States* v. *Armour & Co.* 168 F 2d 342 (1948)

25   *Model Penal Code* TD 4 Notes at page 150, but cf. *Magnolia Motor Company* v. *United States* 264 F 2d 950 (1959) (larceny); *United States* v. *Nearing* 252 Fed. 223 (1918)

26   *United States* v. *Union Supply Co.* 215 US 50 (1909)

27   *United States* v. *Illinois Central R.R. Co.* 303 US 239 (1937)

28   *United States* v. *Armour & Co.* 168 F 2d 342 (1948)

29   *American Medical Association* v. *United States* 130 F 2d 233 (1942) and see *Model Penal Code* TD 4, Notes at page 149

30   See the discussion in chapter 9

31   137 F 2d 369 (1943)

32   *United States* v. *Dotterweich* 320 US 277 (1943); *United States* v. *Austin-*

Bagley Corporation 31 F 2d 229 (1928); *United States* v. *General Motors Corporation* 121 F 2d 376 (1941)

33 121 F 2d 376 (1941)

34 The relevant extracts are contained in Donnelly, Goldstein & Schwartz, *Criminal Law* (1962) pp 1087-88

35 See the statement by General Electric Company, reproduced in Donnelly, Goldstein & Schwartz, *Criminal Law* (1962) pp 1088-89

36 Donnelly, Goldstein & Schwartz, *Criminal Law* (1962) p 1087

37 See *Johnson* v. *Youden* [1950] 1 KB 544

38 See Baldwin, *Antitrust And The Changing Corporation* (1961) pp 238-240

39 See the discussion in chapter 9

40 See Dolan & Rebeck, 'Corporate Criminal Liability For Acts In Violation Of Company Policy' (1962) 50 Geo. LJ 547

41 Model Penal Code, TD 4, Notes at page 151; *Magnolia Motor Company* v. *United States* 264 F 2d 950 (1959) (larceny) *United States* v. *Nearing* 252 Fed. 223 (1918)

42 Dolan & Rebeck 'Corporate Criminal Liability For Acts In Violation Of Company Policy' (1962) 50 Geo. LJ 547 and see *Standard Oil Company* v. *State* 100 SW 705 (1907)

43 See Fisse 'The Distinction Between Primary And Vicarious Corporate Criminal Liability' (1967) 41 ALJ 203 at p 206

44 See *Regina* v. *Stanley Haulage Ltd.* (1964) 114 L. Jo. 25

45 Winn 'The Criminal Responsibility Of Corporations' (1927) 3 Camb. LJ 398; Welsh 'The Criminal Liability Of Corporations' (1946) 62 LQR 345

46 Gordon, *Business Leadership In The Large Corporation* (1944) p 114; Florence, *Ownership, Control And Success Of Large Companies* (1961) pp 80-82

47 Gordon, *Business Leadership In The Large Corporation* (1944) p 114

48 See Timberg 'Corporate Facts And Fictions: Logical, Social And International Implications' (1946) 46 Col. L. Rev. 533

49 *Rex* v. *Fane Robinson Ltd.* [1941] 3 DLR 409; *Rex* v. *Ash Temple Co. Ltd.* [1949] OR 315; *Regina* v. *Electrical Contractors Ltd.* (1961) 27 DLR (2d) 193

50 Cf. *Regina* v. *H. J. O'Connell Ltd.* [1962] Que. QB 666 in which it was said that liability could be predicated on the acts of an agent, provided that he enjoyed a sufficiently ample authority. The decision has been persuasively criticised by Yarofsky 'The Criminal Liability Of Corporations' (1964) 10 McGill LJ 142

51 *Regina* v. *Canadian Western Trampolines Ltd.* (1962 Alberta App. Div. unrep.) I am indebted to H. W. Schwab of the Alberta Bar for permission to peruse the Appeal Book and transcript of the judgment

52 *Lake St. John Power Company* v. *Otis* (1942) 79 CCC 398

53 See e.g. *Rex* v. *McGavin Bakeries Ltd.*(6) (1951) 101 CCC 22; *Regina* v. *Howard Smith Paper Mills Ltd.* [1954] OR 543; *Regina* v. *Northern Electric Co. Ltd.*

54 In *Reg.* v. *J. J. Beamish Construction Co. Ltd.* (1966) 59 DLR (2d) 6, aff'd. (1967) 65 DLR (2d) 260 the trial judge appears to have been prepared to extend the *alter ego* doctrine to the activities of a single director having authority over the relevant area of corporate activity. A majority in the Court of Appeal appear to have had doubts concerning any such extension

55 [1949] OR 315

56 13 Geo. vi (2nd Session) Chapter 12 (Canada)

57 See Combines Investigation Act RSC 1952, Chapter 314, section 41

58 *Model Penal Code* TD 4 at page 22

59 *Model Penal Code* TD 4 notes at page 151

60 American Law Institute, *Proceedings,* 1956, pp 170-171

61 *Model Penal Code* TD 4, Notes at page 151

62 *Model Penal Code* TD 4, Notes at page 151

63 See per Brown J in *Standard Oil Company of Texas* v. *United States* 307 F 2d 120 (1963)

64 Mueller 'Mens Rea And The Corporation' (1957) 19 U. Pitt L. Rev. 21

65 For example, the American General Electric Company is organised into over 100 autonomous, profit-seeking units, the managers of each of which enjoy a substantial measure of autonomy in the organisation and management of their departments. General Electric Company, *Share Owners Quarterly* (Jan. 25, 1961), cited in Donnelly, Goldstein & Schwartz, *Criminal Law* (1962) p 1086

66 See Gordon, *Business Leadership In The Large Corporation* (1944) p 114

67 See Florence, *Ownership, Control And Success Of Large Companies* (1961) pp 80-82

68 248 NY 159, 161 NE 455 at page 456

69 161 NE 455 at page 456

70 72 NYS (2d) 748 (1947)

71 72 NYS (2d) 748 (1947) at page 750

72 *New York Central and Hudson R.R. Co.* v. *United States* 212 US 481 (1909); *People* v. *Hudson Valley Construction Co.* 217 NY 172 (1916); *People* v. *Dunbar Contracting Co.* 151 NYS 164 (1914); *Mininsohn* v. *United States* 101 F 2d 477 (1939); *People* v. *Sheffield Farms* 225 NY 25 (1918); *People* v. *Canadian Fur Trappers Corporation* 248 NY 159, 161 NE 455 (1928)

73 *People* v. *Canadian Fur Trappers Corporation* 248 NY 159, 161 NE 455 (1928); *People* v. *Hudson Valley Construction Co.* 217 NY 172 (1916); *People* v. *Sheffield Farms* 225 NY 25 (1918)

74 Even those former offences nearest the idea of ratification, i.e. misprision of felony, and accessory after the fact, require knowledge of the commission of an offence and some further action, whether to shield the offender, or a failure to notify the authorities. See *Sykes* v. *D. P. P.* [1962] AC 528; *Rex* v. *Jones* [1948] 2 All ER 964. The new offences of impeding the apprehension and prosecution of offenders and concealing offenders require that the accused know or believe that an arrestable offence has been committed. See Criminal Law Act, secs. 4, 5

75 Most of the English decisions, except *Moore* v. *I. Bresler Ltd.* [1944] 2 All ER 515, are consistent with this approach

76 RSC 1952 Ch. 314, section 41 (Can.) The formulation of attempt adopted by the *Model Penal Code,* section 5.01 employs a similar idea in ascertaining what is a proximate act

77 On the effect of the Canadian legislation see *Eddy Match Company* v. *The Queen* (1955) 18 CR 357, 366 and on evidential difficulties surmounted thereby, see Goldenberg (1949) 27 Can. Bar Rev. 461

78 See, for example, the decision of Dunphy J in *Australian Stevedoring Industry Authority* v. *Oversea and General Stevedoring Co. Pty. Ltd.* [1959] 1 FLR 298

Chapter 9

The social policy of corporate criminal liability

This chapter seeks to examine what social policy may be said to underlie the reception of corporate criminal liability as a general principle of English criminal law. The policy issues involved have seldom been the subject of judicial discussion.[1] They have received substantial attention in only one English work, Professor Glanville Williams' *Criminal Law; The General Part*[2] The major English periodical account dealing with policy issues is Winn's 'The Criminal Responsibility of Corporations,' now forty years old.[3] Most accounts, in England[4] and the Commonwealth,[5] are analytical. As a result, issues such as the reality of the corporate mind and the distinction between corporate liability and vicarious liability dominate the discussions. Much attention has been devoted to policy issues by American writers. The relevance and desirability of corporate criminal liability to English conditions remain largely unexplored. One is met by statements of faith favouring or opposing such liability.[6]

In part, this situation is probably due to a dearth of information regarding business crimes in Britain. The process of exploration into the field of white collar crime in the United States began a quarter century ago. In England with the exception of tentative studies by Backman in 1943 and by Hadden into company fraud it has scarcely begun.[7] It seems fair to say that there is no general awareness in Britain of special problems in the field of offences which American scholars such as Hartung define as ' . . . a violation of law regulating business, which is committed for a firm or its agents in the conduct of its business'.[8]

This is not to say that English law has failed to provide a sufficient framework of deterrence in this area. It can mean simply that corporate criminal liability has been imposed generally, in the absence of any clear policy. Mr. Turner in the latest edition of Russell on Crime states[9]:

The modern tendency of the courts however, has been widening the scope within which criminal proceedings can be brought against institutions which have become so prominent a feature of everyday affairs, and the point is being reached where what is called for is a

comprehensive statement of principles formulated to meet the needs
of modern life in granting the fullest possible protection of criminal
law to persons exposed to the action of the many powerful associations
which surround them.

This chapter endeavours to provide a tentative framework within which
such a statement of principles can be formulated; such a framework
cannot be other than tentative at the present time. In the absence of
relevant criminological research one cannot indicate with confidence
what the character of the problem is. Mr. Turner's statement, noted above,
seems to indicate that the major problem may lie with respect to
oppressive practices by large institutions. But this, however true of the
United States, seems to be an assumption for which there is little evidence
in England. It may well be that the problem lies elsewhere than in the
field of the traditional criminal offences.

Corporate criminal liability has been elevated to the status of a general
principle of English criminal law, and it must be judged as such. A finding
that its claim to that status cannot be substantiated on policy grounds
need not foreclose the inquiry. There may well be circumstances in which
such liability is desirable and necessary and in respect of which provision
should be made. The proper limits of corporate criminal liabillty may be
neither as broad nor as narrow as has sometimes been suggested.

The problems involved are complex. Several separate issues must be
identified and considered. One must inquire what social policy corporate
criminal liability seeks to serve. Here the primary need is to identify, with
some accuracy, the specific problems which we face in the field of law
enforcement which cannot presumably be met adequately by traditional
techniques. Another issue relates to the methodology employed. One
must consider the characteristics of the method. One must consider the
justifications advanced in its favour, and also its shortcomings. The
application of the method; essentially a study of the sanctions which
can be employed in its application offers a further field of inquiry. Finally
no study could be complete without considering whether in fact better
methods cannot be devised in the interests of social control. We are not
only concerned with the question whether there is a social need to which
corporate criminal liability is responsive, but also whether such liability
is the best available response to the need. At that point, one can hope to
make at least a tentative value judgment.

Identifying the problems

Corporate criminal liability is a response to problems created by the business activities of the large corporation. The problems, and the rationale of the response, are basically to be found in American literature. To a large extent they reflect the impact of the anti-trust laws.[10] These seek to restrain combinations in restraint of trade by the use of criminal sanctions. Although criminal sanctions are in fact used in a minority of cases, there can be no doubt that the famous Sherman Anti-Trust Act is criminal in form.[11] Furthermore, the Sherman Act did not stand alone. Other business practices were also struck at by the use of the criminal sanction.[12] The era of capitalist ruthlessness gave rise to a judicial and legislative response exhibiting at least nominally many of the same tendencies.[13] The law was brought into collision in a direct and immediate way with the interests of the capitalist system. That system, reflecting deeply held beliefs about the proper role of business and government, tended to react unfavourably to regulation.[14] Government and business were thus in a state of tension. Furthermore, sustained efforts to foster a state of competition were bound to result in tension within industry and particular corporations.[15] Widespread infractions of penal legislation were perhaps to be expected. In turn this phenomenon was bound to attract wide attention and afforded an obvious field of investigation for the criminologist.

Research into corporate criminality in Britain

By contrast, the problems giving rise at a much later date to the like response in Britain are more difficult to trace. For when corporate criminal liability was imposed in Britain, the worst aspects of the industrial revolution were past. Predatory practices by large corporations to whatever extent they existed, lacked the intensity shown in America in its age of industrial expansion. Furthermore, regulation in Britain, for the most part, tended to be peripheral. Restraint of trade on the part of corporations, or industries was tolerated at common law.[16] Public utility regulation was an accepted phenomenon. This is not to suggest that regulation in Britain was not inhibiting. In many respects it clearly was so. But Parliament tended towards specific regulation of discrete subjects, in the interest of matters such as health, industrial safety, highway safety and welfare.[17] In respect of these matters a common consensus existed, at least by 1940.[18] In many respects regulatory legislation was drafted on the assumption that the real need was not to punish managerial criminality, but rather to ensure managerial policing of a business enterprise. The spate of inhibiting regulatory legislation embodied in the Defence Regulations was clearly necessary to the efficient prosecution of the war. The fact of war, its effects, and the possible consequences of losing it were felt more vividly here than in America. These factors presumably conduced to its observance. And, it should be noticed, the regulations incorporated provisions designed to ensure effective personal liability as well as corporate liability.

In Britain, three company law amendment committees have found that corporations are generally governed honestly.[19] The same point has been made by authorities of repute, particularly during the debates on company law amendment in 1947.[20] A committee which dealt with the problems of fraudulent share-pushing seems to reveal in its conclusions that the major problem arose, not from the conduct of institutions, but from the conduct of a number of marginal operators.[21] There seems no reason to suppose that Mr. C. A. R. Crosland is incorrect in concluding that business in Britain is honestly run, that it is sensitive to public opinion, and in its dealings shows little sign of capitalist ruthlessness.[22]

The existence of business criminality in Britain

This general impression however, ought not to lead to the conclusion that the business activities of corporations, or of any other mode of business organisation, are never so conducted as to fall within the ambit of the criminal law. The whole area of economic regulatory offences has never been made a subject of detailed criminological investigation.[23] Several observations might here be ventured. It is the practice to charge the commission of major offences to the human actors concerned. This is particularly noticeable in certain of the major fraud cases.[24] In America, there is a greater propensity to charge the corporation as well. Secondly, little publicity is given to economic crimes. The Board of Trade for example, enforces the penal provisions of the Hire Purchase Acts and Regulations.[25] Contravention of these provisions is not uncommon, yet I have been able to find only one reported case dealing with the matter.[26] In addition, two other cases have gone before the superior courts and are therefore accessible.[27] Contraventions of the Road Traffic Act provisions relating to the operation of commercial vehicles are again not uncommon. Here, reports of proceedings are more common, but it is only recently that public concern has been aroused. In these circumstances the dimensions of such enforcement problems as exist are virtually unknown and the same might be said of their character. Furthermore, we know little of the institutions in whose name these offences were committed. Yet this can be of distinct importance. If there be a problem with respect to the large institution, the character of the sanction required may be far different from that required where the accused is a close corporation, analogous in structure to the partnership or sole proprietorship. In the present state of criminological research we know enough to be sure that much further research is required. We do not know what number of offences are committed in the name of corporations. We do not know whether the large corporation is primarily responsible or whether difficulties arise primarily with respect to smaller firms, or whether there is any distinction worth drawing. We do not know whether violations represent corporate policy, and if so, why such policies are adopted. We do not know whether the problem lies primarily in deterring wilful infractions, or whether the nub of the problem is managerial negligence.

American research into business crimes

American research has given rise to some interesting speculation. Three original studies deserve mention. The first of these is Sutherland's work on white collar crimes, first published in periodical form in 1940.[28] In this pioneer work, Sutherland analysed data relating to seventy large corporations. His tripartite definition of white collar crime deserves to be recalled. It is '. . . a violation of criminal law by a person of the upper socioeconomic class in the course of his occupational activities'.[29] Sutherland found the conduct of the seventy large corporations in question to be persistently criminal; that in essence those who managed large corporations conducted corporate affairs in a manner which directly contravened the criminal law. It was a dramatic revelation. The key to differential treatment favouring the businessman which Sutherland found was the use under the Sherman Anti-Trust Act of non-criminal sanctions. This enable businessmen to escape the stigma of criminality. As Sutherland states, speaking of crimes dealt with in later Federal statutes pertaining to anti-trust and similar regulatory legislation[30]:

The violations of these laws are crimes . . . but they are treated as though they were not crimes, with the effect and probably the intention of eliminating the stigma of crimes.

Furthermore no consistent policy was adopted with respect to the manner of proceeding against anti-trust violators.[31]

This part of Sutherland's work can readily be corroborated. Although the Sherman Act is a criminal statute, its provisions have only infrequently been enforced by criminal sanctions. The content of this statute is notoriously vague. In only a minority of cases, where clarity had been achieved by judicial decision, was the apt remedy thought to lie in prosecution.[32] It is encouraging to note that the English courts seem prepared to adopt a stern attitude to violations of this type. In *In re Galvanised Tank Manufacturers Agreement*[33] Megaw J indicated that violations of undertakings not to enforce restrictive trade agreements would be visited not only with fines against the errant corporations, but with attachment and possible imprisonment of corporate officers. It is interesting also to note that American courts are now proceeding directly against the officers concerned in the case of clear anti-trust violations.

Sutherland's work has been criticised. On occasion he departed from his own definition to discuss matters which, while not criminal, were in his opinion so closely allied to criminal behaviour as to be proper subjects for inclusion in his study. This may have led to distortion.[34] Some examples of business conduct which appeared to Sutherland to be typical of the large corporation were probably questionable in their attribution.[35] The study is perhaps too loosely drawn to be entirely satisfactory for analytical purposes. It would however, be wrong to deny its merits. It did show that business practices were being pursued which brought corporations into conflict with the criminal law. It notes the ambivalence with which offenders were regarded by the courts and the public. It stresses the enforcement problems which arise when the enforcement policy itself is ambivalent. It draws attention to a major law enforcement problem in this area: the difficulty of attributing the offence to high managerial officials of corporations with sufficient precision to enable them to be prosecuted. This theme appears throughout other studies as well.

Recent studies by Clinard[36] and Lane[37] also indicate that there is a problem with respect to legislation which inhibits or prohibits certain formerly accepted business practices. Clinard undertook a study in the wartime black market operating in the United States. Offences were widespread. Again, as Clinard pointed out, the causes of violations were complex. That large corporations were involved was clear. An assumption that large institutions were less likely than the small enterprise to violate the law was subjected to examination by Clinard and found to be unfounded. Many violations were thought to be wilful, but in only a minority of cases was evidence sufficient to lead to a criminal conviction found. In most cases *mens rea* could not be proved, and the cases were not disposed of by prosecution.[38] Lane found that violations fell into three categories of which the first and last were the most important; these were: wilful violations, violations resulting from ignorance of the law, and violations resulting from inadvertent misapplication of legal provisions. Recidivism was found to be infrequent.

Criminological investigations in the United States thus establishes that violation of regulatory legislation by corporations is not uncommon. The technical difficulties to which reference is made relate to problems of proof. There is an assumption that many offences involve complicity, in some measure at least, by top management. It is generally conceded that evidence against the highest rank of managerial officials is hard to obtain. In addition, when such evidence was obtained, managerial officials were often either acquitted or subjected to penalties which were felt to be inadequate. Clinard sums up the matter thus[39]:

> There are . . . obvious legal difficulties in bringing a criminal action against a corporation, since all that may possibly be achieved, after a long drawn out suit with many technical difficulties, is a moderate fine for the corporation or a short jail sentence for an officer of the company.

One result has been the use by some American administrative agencies of informal settlements, reserving the use of the criminal sanction for hard-core offences only.[40]

Problems of enforcement

It is clear that in the United States substantial problems of enforcement of regulatory legislation have arisen. One may at least attempt to identify some of the causal factors. There is, first, an ambivalence in public and judicial attitudes to certain offences. Why this should be so is not entirely clear. In part it is no doubt due to the lack of a coherent systematically applied enforcement policy.[41] In part it is due to the novelty of the regulations involved. In part it is due to the difficulty of obtaining evidence sufficient to prosecute corporate officers personally. It has been noted that the sanction most feared by businessmen was imprisonment, but this sanction was rarely employed. In the absence of personal responsibility, enforcement became ineffective.[42] The primary problem with which we are here concerned lies in obtaining evidence sufficient to convict those persons who occupy high managerial office in the endocratic corporation.[43]

The assumption of managerial criminality

The identification of the problem so made involves an assumption that many offences are commanded, or at least encouraged, by high managerial officials. It is clear also that at another level, with which we are not concerned at the moment, there is a problem also with violations of public welfare legislation in respect of which strict and vicarious liability may be imposed.

The validity of the assumption that high managerial officials commonly share complicity for wilful violations of penal provisions applying to the conduct of their business is clearly crucial. Unless this can be shown to be a valid general assumption, there is a possibility that corporations will be held liable for offences which management not only did not encourage but actively tried to prevent. This was clearly recognised in early American decisions.[44] It is a matter to which recent studies have again drawn attention. The strict view taken in the United States Federal courts reflects the assumption that, operating behind the facade of multiple responsibility, corporate management has encouraged wilful violations where such violations would appear to benefit the corporation and, indirectly, themselves. In the absence of corporate liability imposed essentially in respect of acts delegated by the highest levels of management to middle range personnel, the corporation, and hence high management could immunize itself from liability.[45]

The difficulty here, as stated, is that the incidence of punishment may fall capriciously upon the innocent and the guilty alike. Corporate criminal liability in its present form fails to provide a defence to the corporation the governing officers of which in no sense desired the commission of criminal offences.[46] Essentially, the corporation is made liable for a failure to police the activities of its servants, agents and officers. This result may be appropriate where the legislation is cast in terms which indicate that such a duty is intended to be imposed. Any broader application is at least questionable.

The responsible officers in the corporate structure: the middle range official

It is clear that in some cases at least and perhaps in many cases, the commission of criminal offences is not resolved upon in the boardroom. It was thought at one time that the typical case which the criminal law had to meet was a case of deliberate infraction of the criminal law by the governing members of the corporation, acting as such. Thus Mr. Winn, writing in the Cambridge Law Journal, and relying on realist notions of corporate personality asserted that the governing members of corporations were likely, unless stringently supervised, to employ corporate assets and forms for unlawful purposes. He asserted that corporations have, because of their magnitude, a unique potential for harm. He argued that directors wield their powers not as private men, but as a group exercising corporate powers by direct attribution. Regarding the consensus of directors as reflecting a group will in action, and fearing that directors would influence one another in the adoption of policies which, singly and in private each would repudiate,[47] he felt the need for an additional sanction. The purpose of the sanction, corporate criminal liability, was to compel shareholders to exercise care in the selection of directors and to ensure shareholder supervision of their policies.

Criminal conduct of such intensity on the part of top management is probably very rare.[48] Most reported cases deal with the activities of the middle range of managerial officer.[49] The reported cases provide little evidence of group passion in operation. Even in the leading American anti-trust cases, price-fixing agreements were not uncommonly arrived at by important, but basically subordinate figures.[50]

This is not to argue that top management is never implicated in the commission of criminal offences. It is perhaps enough to say that the common assumption that offences are usually directed by top management using the corporation as a cloak for their activities is not the only situation involved, and perhaps, not even the most common situation.[51] Increasing diversification of corporate activities and decentralisation of management functions in the large corporation may enable management to use corporate activities as a cloak for crime. It also renders control over and supervision of corporate activities by the Board of Directors and the managing director less immediate.[52] Inevitably, functions must be delegated and their exercise once delegated must involve a substantial measure of autonomy. This in turn means that violations may take place as the result of the activities of an official to whom managerial functions have been delegated. The reasons underlying the commission of offences by such personnel may well be various and may bear little resemblance to the true interests of the corporation, at least as seen by the highest echelons of management.[53]

How necessary is the assumption of managerial criminality?

It may be that whether or not the assumption is generally sound is a matter of little importance. In respect of much legislation, the courts, if not the legislature, have assumed that the true function of such legislation is to impose the duty upon corporations of ensuring its enforcement throughout all levels of corporate activity. If this be the legislative purpose and the response be adequate, it is of little importance who in the corporate structure actually bears the responsibility for infractions. If a police function is to be imposed upon corporate management, it would be unrealistic to restrict liability to acts commanded or knowingly tolerated by top management. The consequence however, of accepting and adopting corporate criminal libility as a general principle of criminal law, is to admit it to the function also of serving as a sanction for serious offences of which *mens rea* on the part of the offender is a necessary ingredient. Traditionally such liability has been personal. The emphasis has not been simply on ensuring the due performance of a police function, but on individual punishment and deterrence. Hence it is necessary to ascertain whether corporate criminal liability adequately fulfills these functions. It is also necessary to determine whether the result of its applications is likely to prove just.

Relevant characteristics of corporate criminal liability

The most striking feature of corporate criminal liability is its indirect character. Corporate criminal liability is a proposition relating to both the substantive law of criminal responsibility and also to the law of sanctions. As a sanction corporate criminal liability is an indirect method of deterrence or control. Nominally the sanction is imposed directly upon a responsible legal person, the corporation. At another level the sanction is aimed at the actions of natural persons. In any case a circuity of sanctions involving a form of legal shorthand is involved. The corporation acts by its officers, agents and servants. It is their acts or omissions to which the sanction is really directed. The cumulative character of corporate criminal liability really illustrates this point. At common law, both the corporation, and any of its officers against whom sufficient evidence can be found, are dealt with as principals.[54] It is clear that both may be convicted in respect of the same offence. Offences may be charged as corporate crimes, as individual crimes, or as both. In the war crimes trials against various German industrialists the accused persons were charged with the commission of war crimes acting through the instrumentality of their corporations.[55] At common law the corporations as well could have been charged.

Vicarious liability offences, where the corporation is charged as master, involve a similar circuity. 'Corporate' negligence in the performance of a policing function is really negligence in the performance of supervisory functions by some person occupying a position of managerial responsibility. The same comment may be made of strict liability offences. The *actus reus* attributed to the corporation is the act of a natural person whether the offence consists of a prohibited act or of an omission to perform a legal duty.

The means by which the corporate sanction is enforced, the fine or the injunction, again are indirect in effect. The entity is formally punished. The impact of penalty, in any real sense, is felt elsewhere. It may not be felt in any meaningful sense by those whose acts or omissions are involved.[56] It may be felt only by a substantially helpless body of shareholders.[57] If it is desired to single out some person for punishment, essentially to punish personal fault, corporate criminal liability may well be an inefficient method. Its operation is indirect. It is essentially a blunt instrument, employed in circumstances where a scalpel might rather be required.

Because it is an oblique method of achieving the highly personal aims of sanctions imposed at least in respect of serious offences, the penalty, in order to achieve the desired purpose of individual deterrence and punishment, may require to be substantially more drastic than would be thought appropriate were the individual concerned singled out for punishment. This may in turn prove detrimental to the interests of persons in no way implicated.

Because corporate criminal liability is an indirect sanction it can serve as a cloak for the activities of those natural persons to whom it is essentially directed. No element of stigma will attach to them, at least outside the confines of the corporation for which they act. Provided that the sanction does not result in the imperilling of their personal position they may well be prepared to repeat the offence. They may hope that the repetition will not be detected; they will have little to fear if it is.

A final point may be taken. In those offences in respect of which it is desired to impose personal liability the corporate sanction is employed largely because it has not proven possible to amass evidence sufficient to convict those managerial officials who are assumed to be implicated in the commission of the offence. It is clear, from this, that the incidence of punishment may well fall capriciously upon the innocent and guilty alike.[58]

All these factors, which run counter to the accepted tradition of insisting upon personal liability in criminal law, at any rate as respects most serious offences, indicate that corporate criminal liability is to be regarded with caution. Essentially, as has been shown, the inquiry is into the permissible bounds of vicarious criminal liability.[59] At the least a very clear and cogent set of justifications is required in order to support the imposition of such liability. In the light of these considerations the field can further be explored.

Justification for corporate criminal liability: the difficulty of identifying the actual offender

The most important justification for corporate criminal liability has already been referred to: the difficulty in implicating high managerial officials. It has indeed, been said to be its sole justification.[60] The argument, as has been indicated, is that the complex structure of many large corporations makes it virtually impossible to detect the persons who are generally responsible for the commission of the offence. This consideration is stressed by criminologists and in the *Model Penal Code*.[61]

Here the problem arises on two levels. In order to sustain a conviction against a corporation an actual offender must be identified, and he must occupy a position of considerable authority. It is presumably not suggested that this essential prerequisite to corporate conviction should be dispensed with. The problem is the further one of penalising top management for an assumed fault. This assumes what, *ex hypothesi*, cannot be proved; that the highest range of management in the corporation was in fact responsible. Granting the validity of the assumption however, it is argued that the deterrent to top management is provided by punishing the corporation.

This solution poses two problems. The first, which will be discussed at length in connection with sanctions, is that such persons may not feel the sanction. Secondly, suspicion is not proof and by whatever adjective it may be dignified, may be in substance unfounded. An example of such a suspicion at work is to be found in the remarks of the trial judge delivered when sentencing the American General Electric Company and certain of its officers for widespread violations of the anti-trust laws.[62] It will be recalled that Chief Judge Ganey, in sentencing the corporation, imposed a very substantial fine upon it. He assumed that while complicity in the offences could not be proven against the highest echelon of corporate management, they were not ignorant of the actions of their subordinates. A recent article suggests that the president of that corporation may well only have been guilty of a managerial failure to exercise adequate supervision of subordinates occupying responsible positions.[63] Subordinates responded to business pressures by entering into price-fixing arrangements with competitors. It has been argued that the response was not that which top management desired. The amount of the fine was conditioned by a hypothesis which may have been invalid.

One cannot overlook the possibility that top management may be implicated in the commission of offences. For various reasons, evidence against such personnel may not be forthcoming. A guilty subordinate may be unwilling to testify against his superior for fear of imperilling his own position. The prosecution may not have available to it documents secreted in the corporation's files. Assertions that corporate criminal liability is a necessary way of dealing with the problem are unimaginative. The problem of anonymity might be tackled either by evidentiary reform in the shape of extended powers of search and seizure where an offence has been committed under the cloak of a corporation, or by legislation making directors *prima facie* liable for such offences. Such a deterrent, because direct in character, seems likely to have a greater personal impact.[64]

Jury reluctance to convict business offenders

Another justification advanced for liability is that juries are said to be reluctant to convict persons whose actions are basically responsive to intra-corporate pressures, or pressures felt generally throughout an industry.[65] Much of the discussion reflects difficulties felt in the United States with respect to anti-trust violations. In a number of cases corporations have been convicted while officers, charged with the same offences have been acquitted. This has occurred where the acts sought to be ascribed to the corporation were the acts of those officers whose personal guilt was denied by the jury. There has been a distinct reluctance to convict otherwise reputable persons whose offences lack the immediate impact of traditional crimes.[66]

The situation is clearly one of some difficulty. The assumption regarding jury conduct affords no reason for removing individuals from the ambit of liability and substituting corporations in their place. This could be the effective result of corporate criminal liability. Its very existence may conduce to erratic jury behaviour. The effect may be to afford a substantial immunity to corporate officers. Any such exemption would appear to be ill-founded. The law neither has, nor should have, exempted the organisation man from responsibility. If management sets standards of conduct to which the individual cannot lawfully conform it is his duty to decline to abide by them, and if necessary to resign.

Compensation for unjust enrichment

It has also been said that a fine may be levied upon a corporation as a form of exacting compensation from a criminal who has been enriched by the commission of an offence for the benefit of society at large.[67] The argument is not attractive. The corporation and its shareholders cannot be regarded as guilty parties even though the shareholders may have in fact benefited. Only seldom will they have assented to the commisssion of the offence. In this situation, it is questionable whether the end of compensation ought to be enforced by criminal proceedings. In addition, there are practical factors militating against such a justification. With rare exceptions, the quantum of benefit can only be determined by using a complex costing analysis. Any rougher method of solution, while perhaps justified if the end of punishment be deterrence, is not justified if the end be compensation.[68] Inquiries as to the amount of benefit obtained are not really suited to the summary procedures of a criminal trial. Furthermore, the end of criminal punishment is not monetary compensation and there is no reason to permit an exception in the field of corporate crime. To admit the exception in the case of corporations is to leave the field open for its relation back in other areas to ordinary individuals. To admit monetary compensation to society as a general justification for criminal liability would be a radical and unwelcome departure.[69]

Convenience and fairness

Certain other justifications have also been advanced. Corporate liability has been justified on the basis of convenience. It has been argued that it is easier to apprehend and prosecute one corporation than a number of individuals.[70] This could hardly serve as a justification for imposing liability in respect of major offences. There is also an argument based on notions of fairness. It is contended that it is unfair to penalise a servant for conduct for which management is really responsible. As Professor Laski put it, it is unfair to penalise the mere agent of a mindless entity.[71] This again can hardly serve as a justification for individual exemption in the case of serious crime.

The appeal to experience: judicial sources

To all these arguments are added arguments born of experience.[72] Corporate criminal liability, and the host of regulatory provisions penalising corporations, are seen as reflecting a practical experience that corporate liability is necessary to deter corporations from violations of legislation affecting their business practices.

Experience however, affords no very certain guide. Criminological studies and judicial statements can be prayed in aid of the argument. Judicial experience however, really reflects little more than a particular judge's view of the matter. It rarely depends upon empirical data. A good example of this is afforded by *New York Central and Hudson Railroad* v. *United States*.[73] A prosecution was brought against the railroad, a common carrier, for the offence of unlawfully giving rebates in interstate commerce contrary to the Elkins Act. The problem of rebates had been acute both from the point of view of the railroads and the public. The railroads had been losing revenue because of the unconscionable tactics employed by the large trusts in exacting special favours from the carriers. The Act, designed to prohibit this, was, as Mr. Sharfman the historian of the Interstate Commerce Commission makes clear, '. . . a truce of the pirates to abolish piracy'.[74] In the course of his judgment in the Supreme Court, Day J stated[75] :

It is part of the public history of the times that statutes against rebates could not be effectually enforced so long as individuals only were subject to punishment for violation of the law, when the rebates or concessions enured to the benefit of the corporations of which the individuals were but the instrument. This situation, developed in more than one report of the Interstate Commerce Commission, was no doubt influential in bringing about the enactment of the Elkins law, making corporations criminally liable.

And he went on to say[76] :

We see no reason in law and every reason in public policy, why the corporation which profits by the transaction and can only act through its agents and officers, shall be held punishable by fine because of the knowledge and intent of its agents to whom it has entrusted authority to act in the subject matter of making and fixing rates of transportation, and whose knowledge and purpose may well be attributed to the corporation for which the agents act.

Corporate liability was '. . . the only means of effectually controlling the subject-matter and correcting the abuses aimed at'.[77]

Seemingly, Justice Day's view of the history of the measure was unduly simplistic. Mr. Sharfman states that while the Elkins Act had a salutary effect, it was the Hepburn Act of 1916, giving the Interstate Commerce Commission the power to determine and prescribe rates, which remedied abuses and put rates on an equitable footing. The remedy lay, not exclusively in the imposition of corporate criminal liability, but in the development of a genuine system of administrative control to which corporate criminal liability was an adjunct though no doubt essential.

One wishing to balance judicial statements could cite the view expressed by Riddell JA in a Canadian case, *Rex* v. *Michigan Central Railroad Company*, to the effect that corporate criminal liability probably

produces no great effect on the human actors involved.[78] In *Rex* v.
McGavin Bakeries Limited, Boyd McBride JA took a similar pessimistic
view of its utility.[79] Judge Learned Hand's mordant statement in *United
States* v. *Cotter* might also be cited. The corporation and two of its officers
were found guilty at trial of using the mails in the fraudulent sale of
mining stocks. The officers sold stocks to the company which were then
resold to the public under certain false pretences one of which was that
the officers were deriving no personal benefit from the sale. The
corporation was fined at trial. In the Circuit Court of Appeals, Judge
Learned Hand stated[80]:

> The company protests against the fine levied against it. It argues that
> this merely takes from the victims of the fraud, assuming that there was
> a fraud, part of the little that was left them. We agree. Why it should
> promote observance of the law to put into the treasury money of which
> innocent persons have been robbed, is not apparent. But it is a matter with
> which we have nothing to do; the company was a juristic person to which,
> by a fiction, criminal responsibility is imputed. It could commit a crime
> and be punished in the only way it could be made to suffer. Where the
> burden falls, the trial judge must consider; we have no power to change his
> decision.

As he makes clear, Judge Learned Hand at least doubted the advisability
of imposing a substantial fine upon an insolvent company. Seemingly,
although he himself had contributed much to the acceptance of corporate
criminal liability in the United States, he was not altogether convinced of
its efficacy in promoting observance of the law.

Such a balancing of judicial views is however, of little value. It is
preferable to admit at the outset that little evidence in support of
corporate criminal liability is likely to come from judicial sources.

The appeal to experience: legislative policy

What regard is to be paid to legislative policy? One can assume that the
shape of legislation is likely to be determined by the practical problems of
law enforcement. The situation is equivocal. In England, corporations
have not been made specially liable by statute. Prosecutions have
proceeded upon the basis that their liability is assured by reason of the
Interpretation Act, 1889. There is not even a general statutory provision
respecting vicarious liability although certain statutes probably owe their
form to an observed judicial propensity for introducing vicarious liability
into the interpretation of cognate enactments. On the other hand, there

has been a spate of legislation incorporating directors liability clauses.[81] The practical exigencies giving rise to such clauses have never really been discussed. For this purpose, Parliamentary debates have proven to be a singularly barren field in which to plough.[82] On the other hand, the powers given to the Board of Trade to request the suspension of a convicted director from managing a company have been used extensively.[83]

American experience similarly affords no very clear guide. Throughout the United States Code there exist provisions specifically rendering corporations liable to conviction. Generally, these relate to regulatory offences. These seemingly include the anti-trust laws in spite of the severity of possible punishment for violations of their provisions. These provisions, however, do not represent the whole story. The anti-trust laws have, for example, been re-inforced specifically with directors liability clauses.[84] Lee, in a 1928 article in the Columbia Law Review, drew attention to strong congressional views favouring the institution of criminal proceedings against officers for failure to ensure that corporate employees conducted corporate affairs in accordance with the provisions of regulatory legislation. One such report bluntly stated that that was the only way of ensuring effective control.[85] Similar suggestions have been made recently in the wake of the General Electric Company anti-trust case. In particular, the late Senator Kefauver advocated a clause to be added to the existing Clayton Anti-Trust Act,[86] the present provisions of which go no farther than the ordinary personal liability at common law.[87]

Seemingly therefore, the most that one can say is that legislative experience is equivocal. As respects much crime and in particular regulatory offences, we are still groping for an answer and a method.

The experience of enforcement

Enforcement experience also has varied. Personal liability is regarded as the most effective deterrent. Professor Dession, relying on the Office of Price Administration Manual, states that corporate liability is generally ineffective unless the human actor concerned is also made liable.[88] On the other hand, as Professor Kadish points out, the general policy until recently in prosecuting anti-trust violations was to proceed against the corporation alone.[89] In any event, as we have seen, criminal sanctions were used but rarely. Apparently there has been a change of policy. There has been a recent emphasis on prosecuting the officers concerned.[90] This, so far as one can judge, seems to be successful.[91]

In Britain, as respects wilful infractions of such legislation, the accent appears to be on personal responsibility. In most common types of commercial fraud, officers rather than their corporations, were charged.[92] This practice is not universal.[93] The general policy of the Board of Trade is, however, to reserve prosecutions against corporations to certain well-defined areas. Hire-purchase offences fall within this category, but the responsible officers are also charged. Another category concerns offences in respect of which the statute directs that the malefactor be deprived of any profit. Again, in certain cases where the corporation is the entity primarily subject to a statutory duty it will be charged with the breach thereof.[93a] Usually the corporation has made the profit. It is therefore charged. One would expect prosecutions against corporations for conspiracy under the Prevention of Frauds (Investments) Act, 1958. Section 13 however, the major offence section, aimed at preventing persons from fraudulently inducing others to invest money, provides both for the substantive offence and for conspiracies to commit it a term of imprisonment not exceeding seven years. Presumably therefore, the Act is intended primarily to apply to natural persons. But in *Reg.* v. *MacKinnon*[93b] a charge of conspiracy under the like provision of a former statute was brought against both the natural persons involved and two limited companies, one of which was fined £300. In general however the Board of Trade adheres markedly to the rule of personal responsibility.

Adherence to the traditional view exists also in the United States. There is evidence to suggest that primarily, liability is imposed upon individuals. Where the corporation is merely used as a cloak for the fraud of some individual, the corporation is usually not made liable.[94]

In practice then, there is some warrant for concluding that corporations are not generally made liable for traditional criminal offences. The practical ambit of liability, conceding the exception of the American anti-trust laws, is really restricted to various forms of regulatory offences.[95] Studies of white collar crime as we have seen indicate that corporate contact with the criminal law generally occurs in this area. Clearly these offences cannot all be termed minor, but even allowing for this, where moral turpitude is in issue personal responsibility remains the general, although certainly not the invariable, rule.[96] Experience affords no clear guide. Various experiments have been attempted. One cannot draw any clear set of conclusions from them. One cannot say that experience justifies the general imposition of corporate criminal liability.

The enforcement of regulatory legislation

The justifications advanced favouring corporate criminal liability are more compelling when viewed as general justifications for the imposition of strict and vicarious liability. In this area they are not unique to corporations. They are valid, if at all, with respect to all forms of business organisation. Furthermore, they are valid only in relation to public welfare or regulatory offences in respect of which strict and vicarious liability are commonly applied. The end served by such legislation is the efficient supervision of legislative requirements by those in control of business organisations operating within the industry concerned.[97] In the case of these minor offences, expediency demands a less cumbersome and more rapid means of ensuring enforcement than an extended inquiry into the actions of high managerial personnel will permit. Two considerations govern the efficacy of the sanction here. An honest but negligent management may well, from a feeling of loyalty to the corporation, be readily amenable to pressure to enforce statutory standards governing the conduct of its business.[98] Furthermore the fine serves to minimize the cost of compliance with the regulations as a factor conducing to their non-observance. Other factors are also relevant. So far as regulatory legislation is cast in very general terms it is unfair to single out some person for punishment.[99] In the abstract it is no doubt equally unfair so to penalise shareholders, but it must be remembered that the cost to them individually is slight, and no stigma generally falls upon them. Furthermore, to fine the corporation presumably affords a demonstration to the industry and the public that a particular standard of care is applicable. In the case, for example, of food and drug legislation the public, if aware that standards have been violated, may cease to purchase from the manufacturers concerned.

Similarly, the argument that it is unfair to penalise employees in respect of the commission of regulatory offences may well have a bearing here. The case of the minor servant is frequently the clearest. Though his be the *actus reus*, he may well be unaware of the surrounding circumstances rendering himself liable to conviction in respect of it. Furthermore, he may well have no control over that aspect of affairs to which the statutory provision primarily relates.[100] In such circumstances, his conviction would serve no useful purpose. In addition, standards of care might be better enforced throughout the organisation by penalising the corporation. Its officers will then have an incentive for bringing a general pressure to bear throughout the organisation.

The primary concern of the legislature in respect of public welfare offences is not with intentional crime. Essentially such legislation is intended to enforce standards of care. Violations may be negligent or, while wilful, may be less indicative of determined criminality than of a propensity to gamble. In such cases a fine which deprives the corporation of any commercial benefit from the infraction, may conduce to observance of the legislation. One can expect that the normal factors which serve to weld the corporation together, such as loyalty to the entity, and a desire to protect its good name, will operate.[101] One need subscribe to no theory of the nature of the corporate entity to recognise that the large corporation depends in large measure on widespread feelings of loyalty to the corporation for its commercial success. In the case of regulatory offences these feelings can be put in issue by imposing a sanction against the corporation. Such sanctions are of doubtful efficacy where the corporation is used as a vehicle for intentional acquisitive crime.

The issue of sanctions

The utility of corporate criminal liability as a deterrent to intentional acquisitive crime appears even more doubtful when one considers the sanctions which may be imposed upon the corporation. For the sanction to be efficacious, it must in some fashion adversely affect those officers of the corporation who are assumed to be using the entity in order to perpetrate criminal offences.

In the endocratic corporation one may assume that offences are perpetrated in order to benefit the corporation and, indirectly, the officers concerned. It may be that if commission of the offence enures to the commercial benefit of the corporation, the officers will benefit by increases in status and remuneration. In the case of smaller corporations it is likely that the benefit which the officer hopes to derive will be more immediate. Where the officer has himself an appreciable shareholding in a small corporation, it is likely that the corporation will simply be manipulated for his personal ends. In the case of the endocratic corporation, law enforcement agencies may meet an opaque facade. The problem lies in devising a sanction which will effectively pierce the facade to the detriment of the officers concerned.

The manner of operation of the sanction

The sanction must in some measure affect the officers concerned. It must at least remove the motive underlying the commission of the offence. The sanction must therefore ensure that the officer will derive no benefit from the offence. Ideally, it should go beyond this and have a distinct adverse affect. Otherwise, it cannot remove an inducement to gamble in the future. The corporate sanction does not impose a direct fine against the officer concerned. The sanction of imprisonment cannot operate. The sanction must therefore prejudice the officer's position in the corporation from which he draws his livelihood. Only in this fashion will it introduce an element of personal detriment to the offender. Here however, certain characteristics of the modern large corporation militate against its effectiveness.

The corporate sanction must stimulate the shareholders to take action against the officers concerned. Its purported efficacy depends for validity upon the assumption, by no means new, that the shareholders can choose an honest management and supervise such management adequately in the exercise of its function.[102] It will be recalled that this is the very assumption upon which Lord Denman CJ relied in 1846, and which even then, appeared to be fictional.[103] There are few if any indicia by which a shareholder can determine in advance what personal qualities a candidate for a directorship possesses. The *Directory of Directors* is not particularly informative. It is probable that shareholders at general meeting have little personal knowledge of the candidates for office who present themselves. In most cases, it would seem that they do little more than ratify the choice of the existing board.

Secondly, the individual shareholder in a large company has little control over its operations unless perhaps he is an institutional shareholder with a large shareholding.[104] His rights can be exercised only at a general meeting.[105] He has neither detailed knowledge of the routine operation of the company in which he holds shares nor the opportunity of acquiring it. The executive of the corporation may exercise a continuing control even though their shareholding in the particular corporation is minute. Where shareholding in a corporation is diffuse, shareholders seeking to exercise control must combine with others. Here however, the existing management enjoys substantial tactical advantages. It has for example, a very large measure of control over the corporation's proxy machinery.[106] It has detailed knowledge of the corporation's operations and it thus has a full opportunity of displaying its operations in a favourable light. Berle and Means, in *The Modern Corporation and Private Property* point out that in the corporate system[107]:

... the 'owner' of industrial wealth is left with a mere symbol of ownership while the power, the responsibility and the substance which have been an integral part of ownership in the past are being transferred to a separate group in whose hands lie control.

They state that while a revolt against existing management is possible, managerial control though resting on no legal foundation is comparatively secure when stock is widely distributed. A similar aggregation of managerial control has been observed in England.[108]

The ineffective character of shareholder control at the general meeting has posed a dilemma to those committees on company law reform which have considered the matter of reform in this area.[109] The dilemma has yet to be satisfactorily resolved. There is an interest also in allowing management a reasonably free hand. Furthermore, it is not clear whether a duty of close supervision should be imposed upon shareholders. One of the attractions of corporate investment is that it affords a means by which persons, not competent to manage business concerns, can invest capital. In the result, provisions have been inserted in the Companies Acts, of 1948 and 1967 giving shareholders the right to request the Board of Trade to intervene and investigate the management of a company. The Acts further give power to the Board of Trade to initiate an investigation itself under certain circumstances including suggested fraud.[110] The most recent committee on company law reform noted however, that the Board of Trade rarely intervened unless the interested party could present considerable evidence showing that such a procedure was warranted.[111]

These factors militate against any assumption that shareholder control will be sufficiently effective to ensure that a sanction against the corporation will result in substantial detriment to the officers concerned. Winn, writing in 1927, sought to meet this argument by arguing for what might be called a corporate Ombudsman who would exercise rights of inspection and supervision on behalf of the shareholders.[112] This duty is performed at present in only a modified form by the auditor who is in law the sole officer directly responsible to the general meeting.[113] It is questionable how useful such an official would prove to be. If the conditions which Winn assumed to exist were of common occurrence, the idea would have considerable merit. If corporate crime is in general clandestine rather than resolved upon in the board-room, the idea must be less enticing. If the problem relates to the activities of middle-range officials such as department managers, the shareholders' representative would in effect be duplicating with the same sources of knowledge the ordinary managerial functions of existing corporate officers. His activities, while perhaps useful, might produce less impressive results than one might expect. He would of course perform a useful function where management essentially was turning a blind eye to the actions of subordinates. If the conduct of top management is in issue, the shareholders' representative might well discover that the task of investigation due to the concealment of material facts by those in control of the corporation, posed considerable difficulties. It is questionable whether Winn's suggestion would prove sufficiently efficacious in practice to warrant the imposition of a duty of supervison on shareholders. Unless the scheme were workable shareholder control would remain an aspiration rather than a fact.

It is submitted therefore, that any system of sanctions which depends for its efficacy upon stimulating shareholder control as a means of ensuring that managerial officers will suffer detriment as a result of criminal conduct is unlikely to prove satisfactory. At the very least, substantial detriment to the corporation will have to occur before any substantial reaction on the part of shareholders can be anticipated. Probably substantial measures would also have to be taken in order to ensure that a conviction for an offence was publicised. The shareholders would have to be made aware not only of the fact of conviction, but of the circumstances in which the offence took place. As previously stated, the same problems are unlikely to exist with respect to the small corporation. But there in any event it is probably possible to obtain evidence sufficient to convict the officer. In such circumstances, corporate criminal liability would seem to involve an unnecessary and undesirable circuity.[114]

Existing sanctions in English law

In the light of the above considerations, the sanctions presently available against corporations in English law can be explored. The common penalty imposed upon the corporation is the fine. Formally, the possible severity of the fine must depend upon the status of the offence. Statutory offences normally carry a fine, the maximum amount of which is determined by the statute. Most offences are now finable.[115] Non-arrestable offences, which can be either common law or statutory offences, may be punishable by fine, imprisonment, or both. No statutory maxima apply to non-arrestable offences punishable at common law. The penalty lies entirely within the discretion of the court. The fine which it may impose need bear no relation to the statutory penalties applicable to convictions for the substantive offence. *Regina* v. *Blamires Transport Services Ltd.* provides a good illustration of this.[116] The corporation and its managing director were convicted of a conspiracy to violate certain sections of the Road Traffic Act, 1930, the Road and Rail Traffic Act, 1933 and the Road Traffic Act, 1960.[117] The corporation was ordered to pay costs of £2,000. The managing director was fined £1,000 on one count, and £5 on the other. The maximum fines which could be imposed

F

for each substantive offence under the Road Traffic Acts, 1930 and 1960 were £20 for a first offence, and £50 for each subsequent offence.[118] Under the Road and Rail Traffic Act, 1933 the maximum fine for each offence was £20.[119] The prevalent practice of charging corporations with conspiracies to commit summary offences, perhaps suggests that the prosecution is not entirely happy with the statutory maxima imposed in respect of regulatory offences and is bringing charges of conspiracy in order to attract a higher penalty.[120] The prosecution can in this way also avoid limitation periods applicable to the substantive offences.[121] The practice continues in spite of judicial protest against charging a conspiracy in circumstances where commission of the substantive offence can be proven.[122]

Whether the maximum fines specified for violations are generally high enough to serve a real deterrent purpose is questionable. Great flexibility existed under wartime regulations. Provisions directed towards ensuring that the offender derived no benefit from the commission of an offence were a common feature under the Defence (General) Regulations, 1939. At present, these aspects of flexibility have largely disappeared. Regulations falling under the provisions of the Emergency Laws (Re-Enactments and Repeals) Act, 1964 attract penalties of both fine and imprisonment. Furthermore, by section 13(2):

> ... no provision limiting the amount of the fine which may be imposed shall apply, and the body corporate shall be liable to a fine of such amount as the court thinks just.

This presumably reflects the fact that certain offences proscribed by the regulations, such as the unlawful trading of strategic materials, offer an enticing field for acquisitive crime.[123]

The efficacy of existing sanctions: the fine
The fine has serious practical weaknesses as a deterrent to intentional acquisitive crime on the part of corporate officers. This seems particularly true of American experience in the anti-trust field. A fine imposed against the corporation seldom results in substantial detriment to the officers. One must therefore rely on it to diminish substantially the profit motive underlying the commission of offences. But here, as the author of a recent note in the Yale Law Journal points out, it is ' ... totally ineffective as a profit diminishing sanction'.[124] In general, the fine levied is simply not

sufficiently large to deprive the corporation of profits made as a result of criminal conduct. Professor Glanville Williams argues that at any rate, the fine will simply be recouped by higher prices.[125] The authors, rightly, do not accept this as universally valid. They point out that some industries are so highly competitive that price-raising cannot safely be undertaken and that some industries fearing governmental intervention, would not raise prices, even if they could. Their conclusion; that even the largest corporation cannot entirely avoid the loss of revenue which a criminal fine entails, seems eminently sound.

This however, does not mean that the offender has been reached by the deterrent. If the fine does not place his personal position in jeopardy, he may be prepared to attempt to commit another offence at some future time. Essentially, he has simply lost a gamble. A corporate conviction has really shielded him from responsibility. The response must then be to increase the fine in the hope that the corporation will suffer sufficiently to induce the shareholders to remove the officer from his position of responsibility. Shareholders, as has been said, tend not to interest themselves in the actual management of the business. Consequently, the corporation will have to suffer considerable detriment both initially from the fine and from any publicity following upon conviction before any successful move to oust management can confidently be anticipated. Examples of provisions imposing higher fines upon corporate offenders do exist as we have seen. In general however, they relate to wartime conditions. Under ordinary circumstances it is doubtful whether this is an entirely appropriate response. In normal times, considerations of fairness can be allowed scope. We must consider to what extent it is justifiable to inflict a substantial detriment on shareholders in order to induce them to penalise those persons whom we assume to be responsible for the commission of the offence. It is at least doubtful whether such a solution represents a sound or a just policy. Furthermore, as such provisions presumably would relate generally to all corporations, they would relate to the close as well as the endocratic corporation. An amount which would represent a severe fine to an endocratic corporation might well be annihilating to a close corporation. Although the officers of a close corporation are likely to have a substantial interest in it, it cannot be said that they are the only persons likely to do so. Employees and dependants may well for example, have had their pensions provided by an issue of non-voting shares. Basically, the fine is a clumsy and indirect method of deterrence. At present, the corporate fine does not deter acquisitive crime and any potential which it may have is limited by notions of fairness.

The injunction

In respect of statutory offences, the injunction may have a useful role to play as a supplementary sanction. The Attorney-General is entitled to sue for an injunction to protect the public at large from an invasion of its rights. An early and common example is the restraining of a public nuisance. He can sue to restrain a wide range of illegal acts of a character apt to injure the public generally, to restrain breaches of statutory duties, and to restrain excesses of powers conferred by statute or charter.[126] In this context, he has a useful power to sue for an injunction where the ordinary sanctions of the criminal law in relation to petty offences have proven incapable of deterring the commission of offences. This power has been exercised against corporations. In *A.G.* v. *Premier Lines Limited*, it was used to restrain the continuing operation of motor express coaches by the defendant which had failed to obtain a road service licence as required by the Road Traffic Act, 1930. A conviction against the corporation had not prevented repetition of the offence. Eve J stated the basic principle[127]:

And if those who are acting in breach of them (Acts of Parliament) persist in so doing, notwithstanding the infliction of the punishment prescribed by the Act, the public at large is sufficiently interested in the dispute to warrant the Attorney-General intervening for the purpose of asserting public rights.

Disobedience to an injunction so issued may be visited by a fine the amount of which lies in the court's discretion. This may be enforced against the corporation by sequestration.

Recent decisions of the courts have strengthened the Attorney-General's position. There has been apparently no disposition to restrict the granting of injunctions to cases in which a small and inadequate penalty alone may be imposed for continuing offences. Furthermore, the Court of Appeal held in *A.G.* v. *Harris* that injury to the public need not be proven. It held further that only in exceptional cases will the court decline the relief asked for by the Attorney-General.[128] It would be undesirable were the injunction to become a common device, but in certain cases, where statutory fines are an insufficient deterrent, it may have a useful supplementary role to play.

As stated, the injunction while useful, must be relegated to a supplementary role. The issues here have been noted by Professor S. A. de Smith who states[129]:

Disobedience to an injunction may result in imprisonment of indefinite duration without the benefit of trial by jury. If the offence is triable by jury, the criminal law should be allowed to take its course; the award of an injunction to repress a public nuisance could well remain as a special exception to this principle. Even if the offence is triable only summarily and the penalty is inadequate, the most suitable remedy will generally be to increase the penalty by statute.

While imprisonment is not primarily in issue in the case of corporations, it is surely undesirable that the ordinary criminal law should be circumvented by the use of injunctions. The corporation can, as a result of disobedience to an injunction, be visited with a fine far in excess of that provided for the substantive offence in issue. The danger is that penalties for breach of injunctions will be imposed in a spirit of primitive retribution. Furthermore, there is a problem of possible abuse of power. As a result of recent decisions, particularly *A.G.* v. *Harris*[130] the court may not adequately scrutinise the Attorney-General's contention that the actions of the defendant have resulted in substantial detriment to the public. And of course there is a danger that if injunction procedure becomes a common mode of proceeding against corporations it will gradually relate back to and become more common in the cases of individuals. The injunction can therefore properly be regarded only as a supplementary sanction to be exercised with caution.

Other possible sanctions directed to the corporation

In the United States an additional sanction bearing some similarity to the injunction has been devised. Stemming from the ancient writ of *quo warranto* which has a history of use in this country to prevent corporations incorporated by Royal Charter from abusing their franchises, it has become in the United States an additional sanction which may be applied to cases of corporate crime.[131] Its development indeed preceded the development of corporate criminal liability as such.[132] It has been said to be a far more efficacious deterrent than the fine.[133] The result of *quo warranto* proceedings in the United States may be forfeiture of the corporate charter or, more commonly, ouster from the right to carry on certain activities. It is similar to the injunction, in that the remedy is essentially civil and is granted only in cases where the activity complained of has been continuous. What is tried is not the issue of guilt or innocence but the right of the corporation to continue to exercise its franchises. Continuous breaches of penal laws are regarded for this purpose as a perversion of the purposes for which incorporation was granted.[134]

Quo warranto is however, a remedy which American courts use sparingly. In few cases, seemingly, has forfeiture actually been decreed.[135] In *People* v. *North River Sugar Refining Co.* Finch J, drawing attention to the commercial importance of large corporations, remarked that corporations were not to be destroyed without clear and abundant reason.[136] Similar expressions of caution occur in other American decisions.[137] So far as a foreign observer can judge, *quo warranto* procedure is made to cover much the same ground as the injunction. The usual decree is to 'oust' the corporation from doing the acts complained of, perhaps coupled with an injunction to comply with the relevant statutory provisions.[138] In addition, it has been used to prevent corporations from carrying on certain professions such as medicine, a function which, as has been seen, is performed in England by the injunction.

The retention of the *quo warranto* sanction is a feature of the *Model Penal Code*.[139] The rapporteurs consider it to be a useful sanction. It was subjected to a strong attack at the 1956 meeting of the American Law Institute. Two grounds of objection were advanced. It was argued that were a large corporation to be dissolved, the result would be economic chaos. The remedy therefore would, in practice, be directed to the small corporation where it was less necessary. Secondly, the remedy was said to be a potential source of grave injustice to shareholders.[140]

These objections are, it is submitted, sound. There is a possible element of shareholder prejudice. It is not clear, as has been indicated, that sound policy dictates that a duty of supervision should be imposed upon the shareholders. Secondly, the history of *quo warranto* procedure does indicate that its use is generally confined to small corporations. The history of the cognate divestiture remedy under the Sherman Anti-Trust Act is revealing. This remedy, requiring a monopoly to divest itself of a portion of its business activities in order to open to competition an area which its activities have closed, has been sparingly applied. The courts have been reluctant to use so extreme a measure in restructuring the economy.[141] The case for restraint is even greater where, as in the case of *quo warranto*, it is the possible destruction of an industry which is in issue. Furthermore, against the small corporation, *quo warranto* is an extravagant remedy. It could result in the destruction of the means of livelihood of persons who are in no sense parties to the offence.

The stigma of conviction as a sanction

It has been argued that the fine, and other formal sanctions, must not be viewed in isolation. The social stigma associated with conviction must also be taken into account. Sutherland, for example, argues that while the fine is an ineffective deterrent taken in isolation, the fine together with the stigma of conviction provides a useful sanction against corporate criminal liability.[142] Here too however, the sanction, to be effective, must reach the individuals concerned.[143]

The primary factor governing the efficacy of the stigma as a sanction is public awareness of the fact that a conviction has been registered. It may be doubted how widespread this awareness is. There is some warrant for believing that historically it was efficacious with respect to food and drug offences. Apparently, the expedient of publicising the names of vendors of adulterated foodstuffs was employed in Canada in 1890. It was sufficiently unpopular to be soon dropped.[144] In England, it has an earlier history under the Bread Act, 1836, by which the magistrates had power, on conviction for a second offence, 'to cause the offender's Name, Place of Abode, and Offence to be published in some Newspaper' printed or published near the place where the offence had been committed. This sort of provision has become less useful in the light of more widespread business operations, and perhaps, the increased size of newspapers. A very real problem lies in bringing home the fact of conviction to the public in the context of a dynamic rather than a relatively static community.

Some of the problems are exemplified by the famous General Electric anti-trust case to which reference has already been made. It was the most publicized American anti-trust prosecution in recent years. A note in the Yale Law Journal states that of thirty representative newspapers, over half kept the news off the front page. Although a number of corporations were implicated, only one was mentioned. Most publicity was given to certain corporate officers who were sufficiently unfortunate to receive prison sentences. This did not include the top officials of the corporations. The reaction of the American public was said to be one of mute acquiescence.[145] Admittedly, as a result of that case, certain executives of the General Electric Corporation suffered a loss of prestige. The case was however highly exceptional. It would be naive to assume that lesser cases affect management so adversely.

Those studies which do stress the value of publicity in law enforcement, tend to stress the results achieved by regulatory agencies in discouraging the purchase of certain commodities. Publicity, if employed imaginatively, may cause the public to boycott a product. In general however, this result occurs where the product may be dangerous to health.

Rourke, in a useful article in the University of Chicago Law Review argues persuasively that adverse publicity has an impact as part of the total punishment received by persons who violate regulatory legislation.[146] Public support can be enlisted to support legislative aims. It is a malleable factor which can be shaped by the agency concerned. He sees a public attitude hardening towards offenders. This may reflect a change of attitude on the part of the American judiciary. The findings reported in the Yale Law Journal cast doubt upon the general validity of the proposition. The public seemed to have no strong feelings with respect to anti-trust violations. At any rate, it is questionable whether the same techniques can usefully be applied where the offence is of a major character and enforced through the normal criminal courts. Here, one must make another exception with respect to the American anti-trust laws which, while prosecuted criminally in the ordinary courts, are prosecuted by a central agency which might well use publicity as an adjunct to other sanctions.

As a general proposition, publicity, and the stigma of conviction are likely to prove useful with respect to regulatory legislation, the purpose of which is to ensure adherence to proper standards, particularly with respect to foodstuffs, drugs, and other articles of consumption. Otherwise, it is likely to go unnoticed.[147] Yet to be effective, the stigma would have to be such that the corporation's clientele were much less ready to deal with it. If this were the case, the corporation would obviously suffer a detriment additional to that formerly imposed. The effect of a conviction upon a corporation is at the moment unknown. There is some doubt whether its effect is generally appreciable. We know little of the impact of such publicity upon public opinion. In all probability as respects most crimes the stigma has little effect upon the corporation. Under these circumstances its effect upon management cannot be great. It would seem at present to have little functional role in deterrence. And of course the fact that the conviction has been made against the corporation leaves to management the solace of anonymity.

Corporate criminal liability cannot be regarded as a satisfactory method of deterring acquisitive crime perpetrated by corporate officers essentially for their own ends. It is an indirect sanction. Its validity depends upon the presumed effect of the application of certain sanctions. These, to be effective, must stimulate shareholders to activity. But shareholders are not in a position to exercise detailed control over the operation of the business, even were it considered desirable that they should do so.

None of the justifications advanced for the imposition of corporate criminal liability is particularly impressive, save and except the assumed difficulty of proving that the highest range of managerial officer was implicated in commission of the offence. Here some considerable difficulty has been faced. But here the corporate sanction has proved to be an inefficient deterrent. Its characteristics, and the characteristics of large company organisation and contol, militate against its effectiveness. In some measure corporate criminal liability may prove actively harmful. It may be that one result of such liability is, in practice, to lead to the exemption of corporate personnel free from individual responsibility. This cannot be considered to be desirable. In addition, corporate criminal liability may prove to be capricious in its incidence. Under existing law the corporation may be held liable for acts which its officers did not in fact command or tolerate. Widespread liability may be imposed for acts performed in violation of company policy.[148] This too is surely undesirable. At the very least, reform of the sort envisaged in chapter 8 should be undertaken.

Corporate criminal liability does not discriminate between various types of corporation. A need for it may have been felt in the case of the endocratic corporation. This proposition can scarcely be advanced with respect to the small or close corporation, where the guilty officers can in most cases be identified. Here the danger is that the corporation will be charged simply because it is an easy target. It is noteworthy that most English cases involve relatively small corporations, and, in each case, the responsible officers were charged and convicted as well. The case of the public corporation is even stranger. It is hard to see what useful purpose is achieved by fining a public corporation occupying a monopoly position. The explanation once ventured by an Attorney-General, that it was intended thereby to demonstrate that such corporations were subject to the criminal law, is not entirely convincing.[149] The result of such a conviction may simply be to fine the public at large. The *Model Penal Code*, as a result of Professor Williams' persuasive advocacy, has excepted state-owned corporations from criminal liability.[150] In general there is no need to proceed against the Crown corporation in Great Britain. In the statutes setting up the nationalised industries, directors' liability clauses were for the most part inserted[151] and the prosecution could charge only the directors. In the famous *Yorkshire Electricity Board* case in 1951, the board and its officers were punished for unauthorised building contrary to the Defence Regulations.[152] The effect of the fine levied on the board could simply have been to raise electrical rates in Yorkshire.

One partial justification may be advanced. Where a Crown corporation does not occupy a monopoly position a conviction made against such a body can have the useful effect of demonstrating to the industry at large that certain conduct is prohibited by law. This however justifies only a modest fine.

The arguments against corporate criminal liability for major crimes do not apply in the case of public welfare offences. The ends to be served by such prosecutions are different. There corporate criminal liability may have a useful, perhaps indispensable, role to play. But in that area it is not a *sui generis* phenomenon. General principles of strict and vicarious liability are simply applied to the corporation as to any other master. The problems which may be encountered in enforcing the legislation are not specifically corporate problems. They involve wider problems of law enforcement generally.

Simply to reject corporate criminal liability however is not enough. The problems which have been felt throughout the field must be solved in some fashion. In the following chapter therefore, some attempt is made to indicate how the present position might be improved, and a more effective system of sanctions devised.

1   See *New York Central and Hudson Railway Company* v. *United States* 212 US 481 (1909); *Cotter* v. *United States* 60 F 2d 689 (1932); *Rex* v. *Michigan Central Railroad Company* (1907) 17 CCC 483; *Rex* v. *McGavin Bakeries Ltd.* (6) (1951) 101 CCC 22
2   Glanville Williams, *Criminal Law: The General Part* (2nd ed. 1961) pp 862-865
3   Winn 'The Criminal Responsibility Of Corporations' (1927) 3 Camb. LJ 398
4   e.g. 'Criminal Responsibility Of Corporations' (1946) 62 Sc. L. Rev. 212; Burrows 'The Responsibility Of Corporations Under Criminal Law' (1948) 1 Jo. Crim. Sc. 1; Welsh 'The Criminal Liability Of Corporations' (1946) 62 LQR 345
5   Yarofsky 'The Criminal Liability Of Corporations' (1964) 10 McGill LJ 142; but cf. Heerey 'The Criminal Liability Of Corporations' (1962) 1 Tas. Univ. L. Rev. 677
6   Brett, *An Enquiry Into Criminal Guilt* (1963) pp 122-123, 'There is just about as much to be said for this . . . as there is, in time of war, for visiting upon the whole community collective punishment for some offence against an occupying force. And that is—almost nothing.' cf. The more balanced view in Friedmann, *Law In A Changing Society* (1959) p 195 'It is entirely to be welcomed that the sphere of possible criminal responsibility of the corporation should have widened in recent years'
7   Backman, *Rationing And Price Control in Great Britain* (1944); Hadden, *The Control of Company Fraud*, P.E.P., 1968
8   Hartung 'White Collar Offences In The Wholesale Meat Industry In Detroit' (1950) 56 Am. Jo. Sociol. 25
9   *Russell on Crime* (12th ed. edited by Turner, 1964) vol 1, pp 96-97
10   Baldwin, *Antitrust And The Changing Corporation* (1961) pp 282 *et seq.;*

Ball & Friedman 'The Use Of Criminal Sanctions In The Enforcement Of Economic Legislation; A Sociological View' (1965) 17 Stanford L. Rev. 197

11 See Berge 'Remedies Available To The Government Under The Sherman Act' (1940) 7 L & CP 104

12 For example, the giving of rebates in interstate commerce struck at by the Elkins Act, the constitutional validity of which was upheld in *New York Central and Hudson Railroad* v. *United States* 212 US 481 (1909)

13 Note 'Liability Of Corporations To Exemplary Damages For The Torts Of Their Agents' (1893) 7 Harv. L. Rev. 45

14 See Lane, *The Regulation Of Business Men* (1954) pp 21 *et seq.*

15 See Smith 'The Incredible Electrical Conspiracy' In: Wolfgang, ed. *The Sociology Of Crime And Delinquency* (1962); Berle, *The Twentieth Century Capitalist Revolution* (1954) page 50. But in securities regulation it has been suggested that there has been an increasing tendency towards mutual understanding between government and business. See M. A. White in 'Self-Regulation', in *Conference On Securities Regulation* (1964, ed. Mundheim) at pp 23 *et seq.*

16 *Thorne* v. *Motor Trade Association* [1937] AC 797

17 See the discussion of the rise of public welfare legislation in chapter 3

18 Much difficulty had been experienced in the enforcement of such legislation. The history of enforcement of the Factories Acts is dealt with by Howells, *Priestly* v. *Fowler And The Factory Acts* (1963) 26 MLR 367

19 *Report Of The Company Law Committee* 1962 Cmnd. 1749, at page 3, paragraph 11 drawing attention to and endorsing the findings in this respect of two previous company law committees

20 (1946) 144 H. L. Deb. cols. 1006-1007 (Lord Jowitt LC); cols. 1049-1050 (Lord Simonds); and cols. 1066-1067 (Lord Chorley)

21 *Share-Pushing; Report Of The Departmental Committee Appointed By The Board of Trade* (1936-37) Cmd. 5539

22 Crossland 'The Private And Public Corporation In Great Britain' in: Mason, ed. *The Corporation In Modern Society* (1959)

23 Mays, *Crime And The Social Structure* (1963) is a British work which treats the subject at length. Unfortunately, the discussion is largely derivative, relying on published American material

24 *Regina* v. *Grunwald* [1963] 1 QB 935; *Board of Trade* v. *Owen* [1957] AC 602

25 Much of the following discussion owes a debt to Mr. J. Trapnell, Assistant Solicitor, Board of Trade

26 *Regina* v. *St. Margarets Trusts Ltd.* [1958] 1 WLR 522

27 *Regina* v. *Lincolnshire General Finance Co. Ltd.* 1965 no. 2759/64 (DC); *Regina* v. *Lombard Banking Ltd.* 1957 (Cent. Crim. Ct.) unreported cited by Goode, *Hire-Purchase Law And Practice* (1962) at page 460

28 'White Collar Criminality' (1940) 5 Am. Soc. Rev. 1

29 Sutherland 'Crime And Business' (1941) 217 The Annals, 112

30 Sutherland 'Is "White Collar Crime" Crime?' (1945) 10 Am. Soc. Rev. 132 at page 136

31 Sutherland 'Is "White Collar Crime" Crime?' (1945) 10 Am. Soc. Rev. 132 at pages 137-138

32 Kramer 'Criminal Prosecutions For Violations Of The Sherman Act: In Search Of A Policy' (1960) 48 Georgetown L. Rev. 530; Attorney-General's National

Committee to study the Anti-Trust laws, *Report* (1955) at page 349 *et seq.*
33 (1965) LR 5 RP 315
34 Tappan 'Who Is The Criminal?' (1947) 12 Am. Soc. Rev. 96; Caldwell 'A
Re-Examination Of The Concept Of White Collar Crime' (1958) 22 Fed. Prob. 30
35 Some examples of fraud given in the last chapter of his book, *White Collar Crime*
(1949) seem for example typical of the marginal operator rather than of business
practices generally
36 Clinard 'Criminological Theories Of Violations Of Wartime Regulations' (1946)
11 Am. Soc. Rev. 258 *et seq.; The Black Market* (1952)
37 Lane 'Why Business Men Violate The Law' (1953) 44 J. Cr. L. Crim. and PS 151;
Lane, *The Regulation Of Business Men* (1954)
38 Clinard, *The Black Market* (1952) found that total violations of wartime price
regulations from Feb. 11, 1942 to May 31, 1947 in respect of which some action
was taken totalled 289,966 cases of which 19,126 cases or some 6% were disposed
of by prosecution
39 Clinard, *The Black Market* (1952) at page 232
40 Note 'The New Federal Trade Commission' (1955) 65 Yale LJ 341
41 Clinard, *The Black Market* (1952) stresses this factor, noting that by 1945
governmental policy had changed from one of co-operation to a policy of coercion
42 Clinard, *The Black Market* (1952) and Dession, *Criminal Law, Administration
And Public Order* (1948) page 200
43 The term 'endocratic corporation' has been used in the United States to signify
a large corporation with a diffused shareholding. It is employed in the same manner
here
44 *Standard Oil Company* v. *State* (1907) 100 SW 705
45 Dolan & Rebeck 'Corporate Criminal Liability For Acts In Violation Of
Company Policy' (1962) 50 Georgetown LJ 547
46 See the discussion in chapter 8
47 Winn 'The Criminal Responsibility Of Corporations' (1927) 3 Camb. LJ 398,
traces of this view seem evident in Welsh 'The Criminal Liability Of Corporations'
(1946) 62 LQR 346
48 Winn it will be recalled, wrote at the time of the General Strike, and the case of
Rex v. *Cory Brothers Limited* [1927] 1 KB 810. Mueller 'The Criminal Liability Of
Corporations' (1957) 19 U. Pitt. L. Rev. 21 gives further examples of action taken
during periods of industrial unrest, but none is recent and the situation is not
typical of those in which corporate criminal liability is generally imposed
49 See the discussions in chapters 4 and 6
50 See Baldwin, *Antitrust And The Changing Corporation* (1961); Smith 'The
Incredible Electrical Conspiracy' In: Wolfgang, ed. *The Sociology Of Crime And
Delinquency* (1962)
51 The extent to which top management was implicated in the General Electric
Company case is a hotly disputed issue. Baldwin, *Antitrust And The Changing
Corporation* (1961) at pp 238-240 cites statements made by some of the convicted
officers which suggests that they had derived a fairly clear impression that they
were expected to enter into clandestine price-fixing operations. Smith, *The
Incredible Electrical Conspiracy* (1962) considers that management may have been
unaware of what transpired at a lower level. Galgay, in a symposium in 19, The

Business Lawyer, 637 (1964) recognises that some offences of this character do originate among lower echelon personnel who seek to stabilize the market in order to secure their personal position. He argues that management has a duty to set a moral tone for the organisation at large. The extent of managerial impication in these offences will remain in doubt until further case studies are undertaken
52 Florence, *Ownership, Control And Success Of Large Companies* (1961) points out that the board frequently exercises an approval function, leaving detailed management to the managing director who thus becomes the key figure in management. Gordon, *Business Leadership In The Large Corporation* (1944) points out that substantial responsibility may be further diffused throughout the organisation, stating in part that ' . . . decisions of considerable significance for the firm as a whole may be at least initiated, and sometimes approved, by department heads and other subordinate officials'. The General Electric Company affords an example of such widespread decentralisation. See Donnelly, Goldstein & Schwartz, *Criminal Law* (1962) p 1086 citing a statement from the President of the company to its shareholders. For an English example (chosen at random) see the Annual Report of the Plessey Company Limited, in The Economist, Nov. 16, 1963
53 These points in no way seek to deny that management may so conduct the affairs of the corporation that a subordinate may feel that management will tacitly condone certain criminal conduct. See Simon, *Administrative Behavior* (2nd ed. 1957) at pages 129-133
54 See the discussion in chapter 10
55 *United States* v. *Krupp et al.* (1948) 10 L. Trials of Major War Criminals 69; *United States* v. *Flick et al.* (1947) 9 L. Trials of Major War Criminals 1
56 Note 'Increasing Community Controls: A Problem In The Law Of Sanctions' (1962) 71 Yale LJ 289
57 And these persons may, especially in the case of the close corporation be former employees or their dependants whose pensions may for example, be secured by a non-voting issue
58 See the discussion in chapter 8
59 Lee 'Corporate Criminal Liability' (1928) 28 Col. L. Rev. 1 stresses this point
60 Kadish 'Some Observations On The Use Of Criminal Sanctions In Enforcing Economic Regulations' (1963) 30 U. Chi. L. Rev. 423 at page 433
61 *Model Penal Code*, TD 4, Notes at page 150
62 Remarks of Chief Judge Ganey, cited in Donnelly, Goldstein & Schwartz, *Criminal Law* (1962) at pages 1087-1088
63 Smith 'The Incredible Electrical Conspiracy' In: Wolfgang, ed. *The Sociology Of Crime And Delinquency* (1962)
64 See the discussion in chapter 10
65 *Model Penal Code*, TD 4, Notes at page 149
66 *Model Penal Code*, TD 4 Notes at page 149; Mannheim, *Criminal Justice And Social Reconstruction* (1946) at page 31 citing remarks of the late Chief Justice Taft
67 *Model Penal Code*, TD 4 Notes at page 150
68 The *Model Penal Code* rightly does not stress this purported justification. Under the Defence Regulations 1939-1945 the courts were empowered to fine offenders against certain regulations an amount sufficient to ensure that they derived no

benefit from the offence. The measure was purely deterrent. See Backman, *Rationing And Price Control In Great Britain* (1944); *Sarna* v. *Adair* 1945 JC 141

69 The *Model Penal Code* does not list compensation as a general principle governing the imposition of punishment. See Section 1.02

70 Edgerton 'Corporate Criminal Responsibility' (1926) 36 Yale LJ 827 at page 830

71 Laski 'The Personality Of Associations' (1915) 29 Harv. L. Rev. 404 at page 408

72 *Model Penal Code* TD 4, Notes at page 149

73 212 US 481 (1909)

74 Sharfman, *The Interstate Commerce Commission* (1931) vol 1, p 37

75 212 US 481 (1909) at page 495

76 212 US 481 (1909) at page 495

77 212 US 481 (1909) at page 496

78 (1909) 17 CCC 483

79 (1951) 101 CCC 82

80 60 F 2d 689 (1932) at page 694

81 See the discussion in chapter 10

82 The entire subject was raised in 1951 on a private member's motion. The debates are remarkable for the lack of information which they contain. No attempt was made to inform the House of Commons in what circumstances or how frequently such provisions have actually been invoked. See H. C. Deb. (5th ser.) 1951 vol 488 col. 647. I am informed that the Board of Trade have not found it necessary to utilise such provisions

83 Information supplied by the prosecutions branch, Board of Trade

84 *United States* v. *Wise* (1962) 82 Sup. Ct. 1354, and see Berge 'Remedies Available To The Government Under The Sherman Act' (1940) 7 L & CP 104 noting that a bill was introduced in the 1940 Congress to bar officers convicted of anti-trust violations from acting for a period of time in the corporation's service

85 Lee 'Corporate Criminal Liability' (1928) 28 Col. L. Rev. 1 citing House *Report* No. 1297, 66th Congress (3rd Sess.) (1920-1921)

86 'Increasing Community Controls, A Problem In The Law Of Sanctions' (1962) 71 Yale LJ 289

87 *United States* v. *Wise* (1962) 82 Sup. Ct. 1354

88 Dession, *Criminal Law, Administration, And Public Order* (1948) at page 200

89 Kadish 'Some Observations On The Use Of Criminal Sanctions In Enforcing Economic Regulations' (1963) 30 U. Chi. L. Rev. 423

90 See Galgay, 19 The Business Lawyer 637 (1964) for a statement of American enforcement policy in this field. See also the General Electric Company case in Donnelly, Goldstein & Schwartz, *Criminal Law* (1962) at pages 1086-90, and *United States* v. *Standard Ultramarine Company* 137 F. Supp. 167 (1955)

91 Smith 'The Incredible Electrical Conspiracy' In: Wolfgang, ed. *The Sociology Of Crime And Delinquency* (1962)

92 e.g. *Regina* v. *Russell* [1953] 1 WLR 77; *Board of Trade* v. *Owen* [1957] AC 602; *Regina* v. *Grunwald* [1959] 1 QB 935

93 See 'Watches plot a sore in side of trade', The Times Jan. 29, 1964; 'Tax case will cost £250,000,' The Times Dec. 18, 1965, in both of which cases individuals and their corporations were charged. The reason may have been to establish their *prima facie* liability to tax

93a This seems to be the explanation for *D. P. P.* v. *Automatic Telephone & Telegraph Co. Ltd.* [1968] Crim. LR 214. The decision is not entirely satisfactory. See Restrictive Trade Practices Act 1956, ss. 14 and 16 and the commentary in [1968] Crim. LR 215

93b [1958] Crim. LR 809

94 Booth, *Criminal Aspects Of Corporation Law, State And Federal* 12 U. Miami L. Rev. 44 (1957) contains much information concerning American prosecution practices

95 See also the discussion in chapter 5 dealing with the practical incidence of liability

96 See *United States* v. *Magnolia Motor Company* 264 F 2d 950 (1959) (larceny); *State* v. *Graziani* 158 A 2d 375 (1959) (attempted false pretences), for recent examples, and in England, the recent prosecution of *Northern Strip Mining Construction Co. Ltd.* for manslaughter at Glamorgan Assizes. The corporation was acquitted on the merits, The Times, Feb. 4-5, 1965

97 See Lord Devlin, *Samples Of Lawmaking; Statutory Offences* (1962) at pages 76-81

98 See Baldwin, *Antitrust And The Changing Corporation* (1961) pp 282 *et seq.*

99 This factor is stressed in American writings, reflecting the vague character of some anti-trust laws. See Kadish 'Some Observations On The Use Of Criminal Sanctions In Enforcing Economic Regulations' 30 U. Chi. L. Rev. 423 (1963)

100 Leigh 'Statutory Offences And Vicarious Criminal Liability' (1964) 27 MLR 98

101 See *Minutes of Evidence* (Report of the Company Law Committee, 1962, Cmnd. 1749) Appendix xi page 259 in which *The Economist* in its memorandum to the committee points out that management works primarily for the company rather than for the shareholders as such

102 See Winn 'The Criminal Responsibility Of Corporations' (1927) 3 Camb. LJ 398; Edgerton 'Corporate Criminal Responsibility' 36 Yale LJ 827 (1927); Note 'Corporate Criminal Responsibility In New York' 48 Col. L. Rev. 794 (1948)

103 See the discussion in chapter 3

104 Berle & Means, *The Modern Corporation And Private Property* (1933) is the classic study in this area. See also Rostow 'To Whom And For What Ends Is Corporate Management Responsible' in: Mason, ed. *The Corporation In Modern Society* (1959); Pickering 'Shareholders' Voting Rights And Company Control' (1965) 81 LQR 248

105 *John Shaw & Sons (Salford) Ltd.* v. *Shaw* [1935] 2 KB 113 at page 134 per Greer LJ; *Scott* v. *Scott* [1943] 1 All ER 582

106 *Peel* v. *L & NW Railway Co.* [1907] 1 Ch. 5

107 Berle & Means, *The Modern Corporation And Private Property* (1933) at page 67

108 Florence, *Ownership, Control And Success Of Large Companies* (1961)

109 *Report of the Company Law Committee* (1962 Cmnd. 1749) pages 37-40

110 See the discussion in chapter 10

111 *Report of the Company Law Committee* (1962 Cmnd. 1749) pages 78-82

112 Winn 'The Criminal Responsibility Of Corporations' (1927) 3 Camb. LJ 398

113 *Re Kingston Cotton Mills*(2) [1896] 2 Ch. 279

114 It should be remembered that not only may a guilty officer be visited with the normal punishment; he may also, if convicted on indictment, be forbidden by the

court from being concerned in the management of a company for a period of up to five years from the date of conviction. See section 188 of the Companies Act, 1948
115 See chapter 5 pp
116 [1963] 3 WLR 496
117 The relevant sections were Road Traffic Act, 1930 section 19; Road Traffic Act, 1960 sections 73 and 186; Road and Rail Traffic Act, 1933 section 16
118 Road Traffic Act, 1930 section 113; Road Traffic Act, 1960 sections 73(3) and 186(6)
119 Road and Rail Traffic Act, 1933 section 35(2)
120 e.g. *Regina* v. *Stanley Haulage Ltd.* (1964) 114 L. Jo. 25; *John Henshall (Quarries) Ltd.* v. *Harvey* [1965] 1 All ER 725
121 *Regina* v. *Blamires Transport Services Ltd.* [1963] 3 WLR 496
122 Query whether in the light of *Regina* v. *Griffiths* [1965] 3 WLR 405, the practice will continue
123 See e.g. *Board of Trade* v. *Owen* [1957] AC 602
124 'Increasing Community Controls, A Problem In The Law Of Sanctions' 71 Yale LJ 289 (1961) at page 285
125 Glanville Williams, *Criminal Law, The General Part* (2nd ed. 1961) at page 864
126 S. A. de Smith, *Judicial Review Of Administrative Action* (2nd ed. 1968) pp 470-472
127 [1932] 1 Ch. 303 at page 313
128 [1961] 1 QB 74
129 de Smith, *Judicial Review Of Administrative Action* (2nd ed. 1968) at page 472
130 [1961] 1 QB 74
131 Two excellent general discussions are Rosenzweig 'Quo Warranto', 13 Cornell LQ 92 (1927) and an unsigned Note 'Quo Warranto And Private Corporations', 33 Yale LJ 237 (1928)
132 See e.g. *People* v. *North River Sugar Refining Company* 24 NE 834 (1890) (NY Ct. of App.)
133 Hornstein, *Corporation Law And Practice* (1959) vol 2, page 49
134 Rosenzweig 'Quo Warranto', 13 Cornell LQ 92 (1927)
135 An example is *Standard Oil Company* v. *Missouri* 224 US 270 (1912) in which the Supreme Court declined to relieve from a State decision decreeing forfeiture for violation of the state anti-trust statute
136 24 NE 834 (1890)
137 e.g. *State ex rel. Crabbe* v. *Thistle Down Jockey Club Inc.* 114 Ohio State 582, 151 NE 709 (1926); *Commonwealth ex rel. Woodruff* v. *American Baseball Club of Pennsylvania* 53 ALR 1027 (1921)
138 *State ex rel. Crabbe* v. *Thistle Down Jockey Club Inc.* 114 Ohio State 582, 151 NE 709 (1926); *Commonwealth ex rel. Woodruff* v. *American Baseball Club of Pennsylvania* 53 ALR 1027 (1921); *State* v. *Brotherhood of Friends* 247 P 2d 787 (1952); *State* v. *United Royalty Company* 363 P 2d 397 (1961)
139 *Model Penal Code,* section 6.04
140 *Proceedings* (1956) American Law Institute, pp 197 *et seq.*
141 The Report (1955) of the Attorney-General's *National Committee to study the Antitrust laws,* pp 353-358 points out that in the first fifty years of anti-trust enforcement, only 24 divestiture decrees were made

142 Sutherland, *White Collar Crime* (1949) at pages 42-51
143 At least this is true so far as the sanction is designed to have an immediate operation. This factor seems with respect, to be sometimes overlooked. See e.g. Friedmann, *Law In A Changing Society* (1959) pp 196 *et seq.*
144 Curran, *Canada's Food And Drug Laws* (1953) page 151
145 'Increasing Community Controls, A Problem In The Law Of Sanctions' 71 Yale LJ 289 (1961)
146 Rourke 'Law Enforcement Through Publicity' 24 U. Chi. L. Rev. 225 (1957)
147 McKay 'Sanctions In Motion, The Adminstrative Process' 49 Iowa L. Rev. 441 (1963)
148 The issues are of course different where crimes of vicarious liability are in issue, but such a duty would be anomalous in the case of major crimes
149 See Heuston, *Essays In Constitutional Law* (2nd ed. 1964) at page 45
150 *Model Penal Code,* proposed official draft, section 2.07; see Glanville Williams' comments in *Proceedings* (1956) of the American Law Institute at page 179
151 See the discussion in chapter 10
152 The Times, November 17, 1951

Chapter 10

Future developments in the law

In the previous chapter it was suggested that corporate criminal liability is not an adequate response to the problem of crimes committed by or at the instigation of corporate management. In this context it would be undesirable to attempt to draw a distinction in kind between regulatory offences and crimes generally. There can be no unitary category of regulatory offences exhibiting characteristics peculiar to them alone.[1] The distinction is one of degree, and the degree in question must necessarily be cast in terms of an assumption whether the offence in question is most likely to be committed wilfully, or whether the problem is one of ensuring adherence to standards by conducing to a proper standard of care. In the latter case strict and vicarious liability may be sufficient weapons of enforcement. Under these circumstances one can hope to treat the corporation in the same manner as any other employer with the like prospect of success or failure.[2] The employment of the criminal sanction against corporations is probably both useful and necessary. At any rate until such time as our system of sanctions becomes more sophisticated, its continued use is to be expected.[3]

The problem becomes more acute when wilful violations occur. It is not helpful to attempt to delimit in advance what these are likely to be. The issue will be decided in terms of predictions associated with particular pieces of legislation, and in the light of any assumed inducement to commit them arising from the possibility of gain, difficulties of compliance, and response to commercial factors. An adequate system of sanctions must take account of the possibility that even regulatory offences may be committed wilfully and seek to deter against this possibility. It is here that the corporate sanction proves fallible. The scale of corporate enterprise both precludes adequate identification of the individuals involved, and protects them from the stigma from which otherwise they would suffer. In some fashion, a rule of personal responsibility must be evolved.

It is easier to condemn corporate criminal liability than to devise an acceptable alternative. An attempt has been made to do so in the *Model Penal Code* and under much legislation in the United Kingdom. The efficacy of the resulting provisions is not however the only issue.

Exceptional means are employed to identify the individual, and the resultant sweep of the legislation has been very wide. Inevitably, such provisions give rise to civil liberties issues. Measures reversing the onus of proof have been common for some time, but their departure from accepted legal concepts and the values underlying them requires their continued justification. The problem is the more acute when sweeping provisions are drafted not as supplementary but rather as primary powers. In evaluating alternatives, these considerations must be attended to.

This chapter examines primarily the personal responsibility of officers at common law, under the *Model Penal Code*, and under a number of English statutes which contain clauses designed to enforce a personal responsibility against directors and officers of corporate bodies. As a preliminary matter vicarious liability under the *Model Penal Code* is discussed. No English statute has attempted to enunciate the circumstances under which such liability should be imposed, or to indicate what offences should attract this form of liability. The *Model Penal Code* does not touch the latter problem.[4] It does contain some interesting ideas with respect to the former.

Vicarious criminal liability under the model penal code

The *Model Penal Code* attempts to indicate under what circumstances vicarious liability may be imposed upon corporations. Generally speaking the Code envisages corporate responsibility where a legislative intention to penalise a corporation appears, and the act in question is performed by an agent acting in the scope of his office or employment on behalf of the corporation.[5] Agent is widely defined in the Code to include any director, officer, servant or employee of the corporation.[6] In effect this reflects the present rule employed in the United States Federal Courts. The wording is further designed to surmount the difficulty presented by *Moore* v. *I. Bresler Ltd.*,[7] that a corporation might otherwise be held liable for offences essentially committed for the purpose of defrauding the corporation.[8] This latter limitation has now been laid down by the Federal Courts as a matter of common law.[9]

The solution so adopted seems generally satisfactory. It is apt to impose vicarious liability in any case in which *mens rea* is not an element. The lack of any reference to delegation as an occasion for the imposition of liability, is clearly correct. Delegation should be used as an occasion for liability only when the statute is specific in its address to some particular person. When a corporation delegates its function to some other person, and then vacates the field, it can be held liable under already accepted principles. When the corporation continues to act, albeit through the instrumentality of some person in its employ to whom performance of its functions has been delegated, the course of employment test is apt to comprehend the situation.[10]

In one respect at least, the *Model Penal Code* formulation goes beyond what is desirable. If the purpose of liability is to make management ensure that standards will be enforced throughout an industry it is unsound to restrict liability to instances where acts are committed with intent to benefit the corporation. The object here is to ensure that regulations will be complied with. Infractions by corporate servants may reflect simply negligence on their part, or a conscious desire to shirk the due performance of their duties. Under such circumstances it could hardly be said that they acted with intent to benefit the corporation. It would be preferable to restrict liability only where the servant acts contrary to orders which are generally adequately enforced. Corporate benefit itself should not be essential to liability. The *Model Penal Code* formulation is a response to decisions in which the imposition of corporate liability was clearly unwarranted.

A very useful provision exculpating the corporation where due diligence has been employed by corporate agents appears in section 2.07(4) which provides, in part:

> . . . it shall be a defence if the defendant proves by a preponderance of the evidence that the high managerial agent having supervisory responsibility over the subject matter of the offense employed due diligence to prevent its commission.

It is perhaps unfortunate that the section proceeds to exclude from the ambit of exculpation those cases where such exculpation is at variance with the legislative purpose in defining the particular offence. In few cases will legislation indicate with any clarity that this is not a desired result. The section as drafted invites a restrictive judicial interpretation.

Measures designed to deal with wilful offenders

It is now necessary to consider what measures may be taken in the case of wilful violations. It seems clear that sanctions directed towards the officers concerned will succeed best. Criminological researches have shown that the personal stigma of conviction and punishment are particularly feared by offenders enjoying a rather superior social status.[11] In theory, there is no reason why such persons could not be prosecuted.

Personal liability at common law

Corporate criminal liability has always been viewed as cumulative. Its advent has not affected the rule that officers, servants or agents who commit offences which can be attributed to the corporation for which they act are themselves primarily liable criminally. An officer servant or agent may be convicted either as principal, or as a party to the offence. The latter assumes particular importance in cases in which only the corporation is subject to a duty or prohibition, and therefore alone can be convicted as principal.[12] Before an officer can be convicted of an offence, it must be shown that he knowingly participated in its commission.[13] The guilt of such an officer in no way depends upon the existence of a special statutory provision deeming the violation in question to be that of the individual directors and officers. It has been held both here and in the United States that corporate personnel who were actually concerned in the commission of an offence cannot protect themselves behind the facade of the corporate entity.[14]

It is clear that corporate officers are not placed in the same jural position as the corporation. They are not liable vicariously for the offences of other corporate personnel.[15] In the case of public welfare offences liability attaches to the corporation alone as employer. The officers are not made liable for the offences of other and lesser servants and agents.[16]

Generally speaking, directors and officers of a corporation are not liable at common law for omissions by the corporation to perform its duties. In the leading case, *Regina* v. *Tyler and International Commercial Company*, Bowen LJ drawing attention to the need for proceeding against corporations by indictment in cases of omission states[17]:

> The directors and officers of the company, who are really responsible for the neglect of the company to comply with the statutory requirements might not be struck at by the statute, and there would be no way of enforcing the law against a disobedient company.

The same rule has been enunciated in Canada. Corporate officers, it has been held, cannot be prosecuted in respect of an omission to perform a statutory duty laid upon a corporation. The distinction drawn is between misfeasance and nonfeasance. Where the offence is one of misfeasance, any officer participating in the commission of the offence may be made liable. Where the offence is one of nonfeasance, only the corporation upon which the statutory duty is imposed may be held liable.[18]

It has been suggested that corporate directors should be liable where neglect of their duty to the corporation in causing it to perform its statutory duties results in the death of some member of the public.[19] Unfortunately perhaps, such a liability involves substantial problems both with respect to the duty involved and with regard to causation. In cases where a duty of care on the part of the corporation is required in order to found liability, it may be difficult to show that any given officer should have been concerned in the matter. The problem may further be exacerbated by problems of knowledge of a duty to act arising from the circumstances. As stated earlier, not all the directors and officers of a corporation are or can be fully conversant with the day to day affairs of the corporation. There is therefore a primary problem in the selection of appropriate persons to be prosecuted. A further problem arises with respect to management's knowledge of the danger posed by the condition in question. In the case of large corporations, a dangerous condition may not be brought to the attention of the board or of the officer within whose sphere of duty the matter falls, or may not be brought forward with due emphasis.

The real problem underlying this whole field is the difficulty of proving that the highest echelons of managment were aware of and party to offences. Quite commonly, the actor who has performed the *actus reus* can be identified. It may prove impossible to identify the person from whom it is assumed that his instructions emanated. Certainly, this difficulty has been encountered with respect to anti-trust offences in the United States.

The Model Penal Code has attempted to surmount some of these difficulties. Section 2.07(5) provides:

(a) A person is legally accountable for any conduct he performs or causes to be performed in the name of the corporation or unincorporated association or in its behalf to the same extent as if it were performed in his own name or behalf.

(b) Whenever a duty to act is imposed by law upon a corporation or an unincorporated association, any agent of the corporation or association having primary responsibility for the subject matter of the duty is legally accountable for an omission to perform the required act to the same extent as if the duty were imposed by law directly upon himself.

(c) When a person is convicted of an offense as an accomplice of a corporation or an unincorporated association he is subject to the sentence authorized by law when a natural person is convicted of an offense of the grade and degree involved.

The purpose of this section is explained in the notes to Tentative Draft 4.

Paragraph (a) surmounts the difficulties caused where the statute is cast in such a form that only the corporation can commit the offence. The rapporteurs cite *People* v. *Strong*, an Illinois decision where officers and directors could not be convicted of embezzlement of purchase tax, the only person having received the money being the corporation.[20] Furthermore, the section is designed to surmount the difficulty caused where only the corporation could be liable, but for some reason cannot be convicted. This would seem to be a useful provision. While this particular difficulty seems not to exist in England, by reason of *Rex* v. *Daily Mirror Newspapers Ltd.*,[21] nonetheless, the nature of limitations to corporate criminal liability is not always clear. Were a court to hold that in a given case, a corporation could not commit an offence, it would follow that there would be no principal whose actions the officers could aid and abet.[22] Such a defence would be a defence on the merits. Paragraph (b) deals with the question of liability for omissions. A substituted duty is now cast on corporate officers. The remaining problem is practical; of identifying the person who ought in the circumstances to have acted, and to prove that his omission to do so was culpable. This particular difficulty is not entirely resolved by the *Model Penal Code* formulation. Paragraph (c) relates to a difficulty not encountered in England. It has been held in the United States that an accessory cannot be subjected to a penalty greater in kind than the principal. In effect, if the corporation is the principal, the accessory can only be fined.[23] No such limitation has been enunciated by the English courts, and the statutory provisions relating to secondary parties directs that they shall be punished as principals.[24]

It would surely have to be shown that the directors were aware of the nature and extent of the danger. As respects liability of lower echelon personnel, one would be met with the difficulty of proving that they failed to fulfil a duty to the corporation. This might well be difficult in the case of a large corporation in which responsibility is diffused. Consequently, as a practical matter, personal liability at common law of directors and officers for omissions cannot be of great importance.[25]

Common law liability therefore, is not always a practical deterrent, because of the difficulty of reaching corporate personnel. Parliament has therefore devised a statutory method of accomplishing this. It has further sought to emphasize the duty that directors and officers of corporations owe not only to their corporation, but to the public at large.[26] The result has been a spate of directors' liability clauses in regulatory legislation.

Liability under statute

A wide statutory duty is commonly found today in many English statutes dealing with regulatory offences, in which the directors and officers of corporations are made liable for offences attributed to the corporation. These provisions have as their object a singling out of the officers concerned as well as the corporation, as criminally responsible for the conduct of their corporation. Several of these statutes are post-war developments, governing the conduct of nationalized industries. The legislature has provided an additional means of enforcement, the potentialities of which are still largely unexplored. From a comparatively early period, these clauses seem to have been thought necessary for the enforcement of regulatory legislation.

The statutory forms employed

Early enactments of this character were couched in terms penalising any director who knowingly acted as a party to a prohibited transaction. This left the Crown with the ordinary burden of proving that the accused possessed guilty knowledge.[27] It was not long however, before the legislature began to employ a wording requiring directors and officers to disprove complicity on their part. This development began with the Official Secrets Act, 1920, section 8(5) of which states[28]:

Where the person guilty of an offence under the Principal Act or this Act is a company or corporation, every director and officer of the company or corporation shall be guilty of a like offence unless he proves that the act or omission constituting the offence took place without his knowledge or consent.

A similar provision next appears in section 2(2) of the Dangerous Drugs and Poisons (Amendment) Act, 1923, and since that time, provisions penalising directors and officers in both the forms mentioned above have passed into common usage.

Enactments passed prior to World War II reveal a luxuriant differentiation in phraseology. Mr. Lieck in an article in the Justice of the Peace magazine noted that these provisions had been extended to the officers of local authorities by the Civil Defence Act, 1939, and, reviewing the then existing statutory provisions, noted that the common element of them all was that the corporation must have committed or in some cases have been convicted of an offence before the officers could be penalised.[29] He also pointed out that the culpable elements required varied from statute to statute. Some required consent and connivance, while others required in addition neglect of duty. Negligence 'facilitating' commission of the offence and negligence to which commission of the offence was 'attributable' appeared. In *Dean* v. *Heisler*[30] it was held that these sections were not apt to incriminate a person who, while purporting to act as the officer of a corporation, had never been validly appointed. As a result, the language employed was extended to cover the case of a person purporting to exercise an office in the corporation.

Since the war, the statutory forms employed have been largely standardized. In the first case, the onus of proof that the director was implicated is left upon the Crown. A modern example is the Consumer Protection Act, 1961, section 3(3) of which provides:

> Where an offence under this section committed by a body corporate is proved to have been committed with the consent or connivance of, or to be attributable to any neglect on the part of, any Director, manager, secretary, or other similar officer of the body corporate, or any person purporting to act in any such capacity, he as well as the body corporate shall be deemed to be guilty of the offence.

Provisions similar to this are found in a wide range of statutes, and it appears to be the dominant form at the moment.[31] Akin to these provisions is section 414 of the Companies Act, 1948 dealing with failure to comply with the provisions respecting registration of foreign companies. The culpable elements there employed are 'knowingly' and 'wilfully' authorising or permitting the default. The Rivers (Prevention of Pollution) Act, 1951 subjects officers to increased penalties including imprisonment if the offence of which the corporation has been convicted is a repetition or continuation of an earlier offence.[32]

Statutory provisions in which an onus is placed on corporate officers to disprove guilt are also common. A typical provision is section 69(2) of the Gas Act, 1948 which provides that where an offence has been committed by a body corporate, every person who was a director, general manager, secretary, or other similar officer or who was purporting to act in any such capacity shall be deemed guilty:

> unless he proves that the offence was committed without his consent or connivance and that he exercised all such diligence to prevent the commission of the offence as he ought to have exercised having regard to the nature of his functions in that capacity and to all the circumstances.

This form of clause was used extensively in the post war nationalization legislation, although earlier examples are to be found.[33] Following an attempt to pass a private members' bill in 1951 which would have placed the onus of proving complicity upon the Crown throughout the statute book, this particular form of wording began to be used less frequently.[34] It is to be found under the nationalisation statutes, and is usually extended to members of the governing boards of nationalised industries.

It should be noted that the modern form of clause does not require that the corporation be first convicted before proceedings against the officers can be instituted. The usual form adopted is 'committed' which permits the court to investigate both the guilt of the corporation and the complicity of the officers in the course of the same proceedings. Confusingly however, the Film Act, 1960 has adopted the word 'guilty' of an offence. There is Canadian authority holding that where the word guilty is used, it is necessary that the corporation be first convicted before proceedings against the officers can be taken.[35]

There is little authority construing these sections. What Parliament apparently intends is that not only shall corporate officers not commit or facilitate commission of regulatory offences, but that they shall also police the corporation to the extent that the nature of their functions permits, and shall be held personally liable for a failure to do so. Under both the modern forms, the duty owed by a director for breach of which he can be held personally liable is greater than at common law. Not only is he liable where the offence was committed with his consent or connivance, but he is also liable where the fact of commission of the offence can be attributed to neglect of his duties as an officer of the corporation.

It is not clear what persons are intended to fall within the ambit of these sections. The Trading Stamps Act, 1964[36] attempts to define the word 'officer'. Section 10(2) provides:

For the purpose of this Act, a person shall be deemed to be a director of a corporation if he occupies in relation thereto the position of director by whatever name called, or is a person in accordance with whose directions or instructions the directors of the corporation or any of them act.

Under this wording, the officers of a parent corporation giving directions to the board or to the officers of a subsidiary would be comprehended. The wording is also apt to include, for example, a major shareholder who took an active, though not ostensible part, in the management of a corporation. Apart from the above Act, the word has not been defined for statutory purposes. It can include the corporation's solicitor.[37] Presumably it also includes the auditor,[38] at any rate if he holds a permanent office.[39] It has been held in Canada that an attorney appointed to represent a foreign company is an officer.[40] Otherwise the test appears to be functional, depending on the authority exercised by the person concerned over the work of the corporation.[41] In *In re Kingston Cotton Mills* (2)[42] it is intimated that those persons who perform duties specified under the articles of association may be considered officers, but this may be too narrow.

What will constitute culpable neglect is a question which cannot be answered in the abstract. The duty of a director, for example, does not necessitate the giving by him of his full attention to the corporation, or attendance at all meetings of the board. In order to ascertain the duties of a director in a given company, not only must the nature of the company's business be considered, but also the manner in which the work of the company is in fact distributed between the directors and other officials of the corporation. A rough yardstick might be that the larger the corporation concerned, the less likelihood there is of the directors being held liable. The form of statutory wording which places the onus of disproving negligence upon the directors puts the duty affirmatively, but, as respects the majority of company directors, is unlikely to lead to wider liability in practice. The brunt of liability will probably attach to the managing director, secretary, and other like officers.[43] Nonetheless, no director can afford to assume that a court will regard him as purely ornamental.[44]

One may assume that the commonly used terms 'consent' and 'connivance' will bear the same construction as they do in matrimonial law.[45] 'Connivance' in matrimonial law clearly involves intention on the petitioner's part, which may be coupled with an active conspiracy or a standing by without taking any active steps to intervene. The quality of intention involved may be[46]:

. . . either intentional in the simple sense of knowing, promoting and encouraging a thing to happen before it happens . . . or, perhaps in the somewhat philosophical sense of knowledgeable concurrence, concurrence with intention in the sense of knowledge of all the circumstances.

In effect, a like definition under these statutes would incriminate any corporate officer who, knowing the circumstances, takes no steps to prevent commission of the offence. Consent similarly involves knowledge, coupled with perhaps a standing aside.[47]

The apparent liability imposed on directors and officers is wide. If, as a result of his functions, the director or officer ought to have been aware that an offence was about to be committed he will, unless he can show that he took steps to prevent it, be held liable personally. If, because he has neglected his duties, the commission of an offence has been made possible, he will equally be liable. Seemingly, in practice, the effective ambit of liability must be greater if the onus of disproving fault rests upon the directors and officers. If the Crown must prove negligence, it will have to prove what system the corporation used in delegating its work, what the position and functions of the officers were, and in what manner his neglect enabled the offence to be committed. In practice this could prove to be inordinately difficult. If the onus rests upon the directors and officers then, once it has been shown that the corporation committed an offence they will have to prove that they were not parties, and that they exercised due diligence. This need not be an impossible onus. Presumably the onus is cast in terms of a balance of probabilities.[48] This type of section has not surprisingly met with little favour among lawyers.[49] The author of a book on the functions of the company director not unnaturally castigates this type of section as incriminating persons for the sake of administrative convenience.[50] No doubt there is much truth in this, but the alternative is to rely primarily on the fine or injunction as a deterrent since in many cases the Crown will not be able to prove the precise functions of corporate officers. The impact of these provisions is to enforce a rule of personal responsibility, and so must be welcome to those who regard punishing the corporation itself as imposing a vicarious liability upon the shareholders. Furthermore, it may well be that the proper enforcement of regulatory and administrative statutes, particularly in the sphere of economic regulations, must involve some interference with traditional rights and liberties, if not in the substantive criminal law, then in the realm of procedural powers vested in the police or in other regulatory agencies.

Naturally, there ought to exist a clear necessity for so wide a spectrum of powers. In the case of much regulatory legislation, such necessity probably cannot be shown. To the extent that it does exist, this type of provision may be justified. In fact we know little of the enforcement problem to be surmounted. The practical reasons which justify directors' liability clauses have never been made apparent. This comparative secrecy must remain the greatest danger inherent in the use of such sweeping devices.[51] Nonetheless in some areas of the law no doubt they have a place, and are becoming of increasing importance.

It is clearly not necessary that these sections be brought into play on every occasion in which a corporation is convicted of an offence under one of these statutes. Their use might well be reserved for cases in which the violation was apparently wilful or the result of apparent gross negligence, as where the offence was a second or third offence against the regulatory provisions of the same statute. In that case, they would be reserved for use by the prosecution in situations in which it was clear that fining the corporation had failed to act as a deterrent. They should be used essentially as supplementary powers. It is probably desirable that these provisions should be cast in such a form as to ensure their effective operation, and this involves, it is submitted, reliance on an onus-reversing type of section. Nonetheless, it is undesirable that such provisions should be passed in so routine a fashion. It may be that they should be drafted explicitly as supplementary powers.

Criminal discovery

Although at common law no person is obliged to answer incriminating questions or to produce incriminating documents, substantial inroads into this position have been made by statute. A number of statutes require persons, the subject of administrative investigations, to answer questions, produce records or both under penalty for refusal.[52] In commercial matters these powers are quite extensive. Under the Companies Acts of 1948 and 1967 for example, the Board of Trade may investigate the affairs of a company where it appears to them that there are circumstances suggesting *inter alia* that its business is or has been conducted with intent to defraud creditors or for a fraudulent or unlawful purpose or in a manner oppressive to any part of the members.[53] In conducting its investigation the Board may require the company's officers to produce to the inspector all books and documents of the company which are in their power, to attend before the inspector and answer questions, and renders it an offence to refuse to do so.[54] Similar powers exist in relation to the insider trading provisions of the Companies Act 1967 and enable subsidiary and holding companies and dealers in securities to be investigated.[55] These powers are designed not only to facilitate administrative inquiries but also prosecutions.[56] These powers are exercisable only when an investigation arising from the circumstances noted above has commenced. In addition the Companies Act 1967 contains provisions requiring the production of books and documents and the giving of explanations regarding them under penalty if the Board of Trade at any time thinks that there is good reason so to order.[57] Any statement made by a person in compliance with these provisions may be used in evidence against him.[58] Even without the latter provision answers compellable by statute are admissible in subsequent criminal proceedings provided that the requisite formalities have been observed and no statutory immunity has been conferred.[59] Supplementary powers enable a magistrate to issue a warrant for the seizure of books and papers of which production has been required and which have not been produced.[60] It is an offence to destroy or mutilate documents.[61] Documents and information so obtained may be used for criminal proceedings arising from the Companies Acts, the Insurance Companies Act 1958, the Protection of Depositors Act 1963, the Exchange Control Act 1947 or for any criminal proceedings for an offence entailing misconduct in connection with the management of the body's affairs or misapplication or wrongful retention of its assets.[62] Similar wide powers exist under Schedule 1 to the Emergency Laws (Re-Enactments and Repeals) Act 1964 which applies to trading in strategic materials.[63] There can be little doubt that extensive powers of this character are vitally necessary in the case of commercial fraud. They have been employed in both England and many Commonwealth jurisdictions.[64] In addition such provisions enable essential administrative inquiries to be made before prosecution is commenced in complicated commercial fraud cases, some of which may well now fall within the new extensive definition of theft contained in the Theft Act 1968. It is perhaps disturbing that so few formal safeguards for investigatees and witnesses have been included. In the United States for example an investigatee may inspect, photograph and copy any document seized from him or from another if these are material to the preparation of his defence.[65] Safeguards against the abuse of extensive administrative powers to order inquiries which may prove detrimental to companies and individuals ought to be formulated lest their employment prove to be intolerable. Unfortunately while criminal discovery is a well-developed field in the United States, it has attracted little discussion in Great Britain.[66]

Directors' liability under the companies act

Fraudulent directors are specifically dealt with under the Companies Act, 1948. Section 188 gives the court jurisdiction to make an order that any person who has been convicted on indictment of any offence in connection with the promotion, formation or management of a company, or a person who, it is discovered on a winding up, has been guilty of an offence under section 332 of the Act or of any fraud in relation to the company, or in breach of his duty to the company, shall not, without the leave of the court, ' . . . be a director of or in any way, whether directly or indirectly, be concerned or take part in the management of a company for such period not exceeding five years as may be specified in the order'.[67] Violation of such an order may be visited with a two year term of imprisonment if the offender is convicted on indictment, or, on summary conviction, for a term not exceeding six months, or to a fine not exceeding five hundred pounds, or to both.

It is to be noted that the director must be convicted not simply of an indictable offence, but must actually be convicted on indictment. The court therefore cannot make an order if he has been convicted of an indictable offence on summary conviction.[68] It should also be noted that for the purposes of this section, the term 'public company' includes a private company.[69] The reference in the section to section 332 of the Act refers to offences connected with trading by the company with intent to defraud creditors. If a company's articles reproduce Table A of the Companies Act, the effect of the making of an order by the court under section 188 is that the director's office is automatically vacated. In such case the remaining directors may, if Table A articles are employed, either fill the vacancy until the next annual general meeting[70] or the company may, in general meeting appoint a person to fill the vacancy thus created.[71] The Board of Trade indicates that the court is usually asked to make an order under section 188, and views it as a potent weapon against fraud.[72]

In this connection, the recommendations of the Jenkins Committee on company law reform might be noted. The committee recommends in section 85(b) of its report that[73] :

Section 188 should be extended to cover:–
(1) persons convicted on indictment of any offence involving fraud or dishonesty whether in connection with a company or not; (2) persons who have been persistently in default in complying with the provisions of the Companies Act; (3) persons who have shown themselves when acting as directors of companies or when otherwise concerned in their management, to have acted in an improper, reckless or incompetent manner in relation to the companies' affairs.

In effect, this extension, together with the extensive powers to obtain documents and information from corporate directors and officers when an investigation is proceeding under the investigation provisions of the Companies Acts, should conduce to a very considerable measure of control over corporate affairs by the Board of Trade. Furthermore, the Jenkins Committee also recommends in paragraph 85(c) of its report that:

> In cases where the person concerned is sentenced to a term of imprisonment for the offence for which he is also disqualified from acting as a director the Court should have express power to direct that a disqualification should continue for not more than five years after the end of his term of imprisonment.[74]

This is designed to surmount the present difficulty that the date of suspension must run from the date of conviction.[75] These provisions must act as a very strong disincentive to the commission of criminal offences under the guise of the corporation. The court's power however, is discretionary, and one would not expect it to be exercised except perhaps in circumstances where continued neglect of duty could be shown. The Jenkins Committee itself envisaged the use of such machinery in grave cases only.[76]

Conclusion

Until the Theft Act 1968 such novel provisions had never made an appearance with respect to traditional criminal offences. Under that Act there is a director's liability clause pertaining to the offences of criminal deception, obtaining pecuniary advantage by deception, and false accounting. The relevant section (sec. 18) requires proof that the officer consented to or connived at the commission of the offence. It is therefore narrower than the normal type of clause and may not extend liability much beyond that which pertains in cases of aiding and abetting.[77] It is not clear why such a provision was required, though doubtless it will conduce to greater managerial care in an area where civil law standards are rather lax, and it seems unlikely that the provision, directed as it is towards commercial frauds, discloses a need for such clauses generally. It has been seen that convictions are rarely made against corporations for traditional offences against the person or property. Such offences are perhaps adequately dealt with by traditional means. They are clearly supported by the mores, and they would not appear to pose any problems of enforcement, as respects corporations, justifying the use of extreme measures. The enforcement of the traditional criminal law does not, with the exception of offences connected with fraud, require either corporate criminal liability or the use of provisions deeming directors, agents or officers, liable for 'corporate' crimes. The factors rendering enforcement of much modern regulatory legislation difficult, such as its novelty, ambivalent public attitudes toward it, and failure to enforce provisions systematically by use of the criminal process, do not apply.[78] Hence, in the area of most traditional criminal offences, there is no need for novel machinery to contend with 'corporate' crimes. The need rather is to recognise that these matters can be dealt with traditionally, and to recognise that the problem of 'corporate' crime lies elsewhere.

While corporate criminal liability is a general principle of English criminal law, it seems true to say that Parliament has preferred to lay considerable stress on the rule of personal responsibility. This seems eminently sound. An examination of the weapons of enforcement open to the prosecution seems to indicate that, as respects wilful infractions of much modern legislation relating to the regulation of trade and commerce, and in particular variants of commercial fraud, the aim has rather been to punish management directly, than to punish the corporate entity. To this end legislative devices have been fashioned which, for comprehensiveness and scope, are apparently unrivalled elsewhere.[79] The assumption has apparently been that crimes accomplished through corporate media have been the work of a minority of dishonest or negligent businessmen.

No convincing case can be made out for the retention of corporate criminal liability as a general principle of criminal law. In England at least, other and sharper weapons for dealing with the commonly advanced difficulty of identifying corporate personnel for the purpose of prosecution have been devised. Admittedly, directors' liability clauses. and provisions relating to criminal discovery represent a departure from the commonly accepted framework of criminal law and its enforcement. An accused may be required to defend himself from a *prima facie* imputation of guilt. He may be required to incriminate himself. That they should have aroused hostility is perfectly understandable.[80]

Corporate criminal liability itself however, also involves a similar departure, although the fact of departure and its precise significance are concealed from view by the use of traditional legal methodology in attaining the result. In the end we must choose between vicarious liability, bearing with it factors, at least as respects intentional crime, militating against its effectiveness, and personal liability involving a departure from the normal onus of proof and presumption of innocence. The choice then,

G

is between alternatives each of which depart from commonly accepted
norms. The argument here advanced is that the choice should tend towards
effective personal liability. The real issue is not whether an entity should
be made criminally liable; it is, granting the existence of a problem in the
enforcement of modern legislation, what sanctions ought the legal system
to employ in the struggle for enforcement. Here a host of considerations
present themselves. Chief among these are the dimensions and character
of the enforcement problem. We must know more about the reasons
underlying infractions. We require to know much more about the efficacy
of different forms of enforcement, about possible sanctions and about
their employment. In a sense the apparent issues posed by corporate
criminal liability are really non-existent. The real issues are issues not of
criminal responsibility, but of procedure, evidence and sanctions. When
this is once realised, at least the true problem is apparent and the
conceptual niceties of corporate criminal liability can usefully be relegated
to the attention of history.

1   Ball & Friedman 'The Use Of Criminal Sanctions In The Enforcement Of
Economic Legislation; A Sociological View' (1965) 17 Stanford L. Rev. 197
2   See the discussion in chapter 9
3   In the United States at the present time there is considerable controversy
respecting the desirability of enforcing much modern regulatory legislation
through the criminal courts. For recent discussions, see Ball & Friedman 'The
Use Of Criminal Sanctions In The Enforcement Of Economic Legislation; A
Sociological View' (1965) 17 Stanford L. Rev. 197; and Kadish 'Some Observations
On The Use Of Criminal Sanctions In Enforcing Economic Regulations' (1963)
30 U. Chi. L. Rev 423
4   The issue is begged by enunciating as a criterion for the imposition of such
liability a legislative intention to penalise corporations. Such an intention is rarely
expressed on the face of the legislation, but is left to judicial emendation. The
Model Penal Code states in section 2.07(2)(a) that a legislative purpose to impose
liability on a corporation will be assumed where the offence is one of strict
liability. Here too, the issue is usually left to judicial construction. Hence, in
many cases, the issue will still be doubtful
5   *Model Penal Code* section 2.07(1)(a)—the text of the section is set out in
Appendix I
6   *Model Penal Code* section 2.07(2)(b)
7   [1944] 2 All ER 515
8   *Model Penal Code* TD 4, Notes at p 147
9   *Standard Oil Company of Texas* v. *United States* 307 F 2d 120 (1962);
United States v. *Carter et al.* 311 F 2d 934 (1963)
10   See the discussion in chapter 6
11   Clinard, *White Collar Crime* (1952) chapter 9, especially pp 252 *et seq.;*

Dession, *Criminal Law, Administration And Public Order* (1948) p 200 citing the
Office of Price Administration Manual
12 *Graham* v. *Strathern* 1927 JC 29; *Glasgow Corporation* v. *Strathern* 1929 JC 5;
People v. *Strong* 363 Ill. 602, 2 NE (2d) 942, and see *Rex* v. *Daily Mirror
Newspapers* [1922] 2 KB 530
13 *Rex* v. *Hendrie* (1905) 11 OLR 202; *Dellow* v. *Busby* [1942] 2 All ER 439;
Rex v. *Sorsky* (1944) 30 Cr. App. R. 84
14 *United States* v. *Wise* 82 Sup. Ct. 1354, 370 US 405 (1962); *State* v. *Graziani*
158 A 2d 375 (1959 NJ); *State* v. *Shouse* 177 So. 2d 724 (1965 Fla.) and cases
cited therein; *State* v. *I. & M. Amusements Inc.* 226 NE 2d 567 (1966 Ohio);
Reg. v. *Ovenell* [1968] 1 All ER 933
15 cf. Lee 'Corporate Criminal Liability' (1928) 28 Col. L. Rev. 1 who advanced the
view, based on *Rex* v. *Medley* (1834) 6 C & P 292 and certain American decisions,
that corporate officers, like the corporation, could be made liable for the offences
of minor servants
16 *Mallon* v. *Allon* [1963] 3 WLR 1053; *Rushton* v. *Martin* [1952] WN 258;
Booth v. *Helliwell* (1914) 30 TLR 529
17 [1891] 2 QB 588
18 per Riddell JA in *Rex* v. *Michigan Central R.R. Co.* (1907) 17 CCC 483
19 See 'Criminal Liability Of Negligent Directors' (1903) 17 Harv. L. Rev. 377.
There seems no reason in law why a person, who, in breach of his duty to a
corporation acts negligently in such a manner as to endanger the public could not
be held criminally liable for, e.g. manslaughter—See *Rex* v. *Pittwood* (1902) 19
TLR 37
20 363 Ill. 602, 2 NE (2d) 942
21 [1922] 2 KB 530
22 See the discussion in chapter 5. Where the offence is of that rare type in which a
corporation cannot, as a matter of law commit the constituent elements of the
crime, e.g. perjury in the face of the court, there would be no principal capable of
committing the offence. Therefore there could be no accessory, *Rex* v. *Tyler and
Price* (1838) 8 C & P 616, but cf. *Rex* v. *Bourne* (1952) 36 Cr. App. Rep. 125.
However, there are, as explained previously, few offences of this character, bigamy
being another possibility. In most cases, inhibitions to a finding of corporate guilt
are not based on the view that a corporation cannot perform the constituent
elements of the offence, but are based on a view that the relevant statute was not
intended to penalise corporations
23 See *People* v. *Duncan* 363 Ill. 495, 2 NE (2d) 705 (1936) and *Model Penal
Code* TD 4, Notes at page 155
24 Criminal Law Act, 1967 sec 1. Accessories and Abettors Act, 1861, section 4.
Where the acts in question amount to the offence of assisting an offender contrary
to sec. 4 of the Criminal Law Act, 1967, the maximum penalties are as specified
in sec. 4(3) thereof
25 Furthermore, Hughes 'Criminal Omissions' (1957) 67 Yale LJ 590, classifies
those situations in which a duty to act is imposed by the criminal law. Only two
have real relevance to corporations, namely, duties imposed as a result of the
accused's exercise of a privilege to practice a calling, and duties arising from a
decision to participate in some permitted sphere of activity. In these fields, as will
be seen, Parliament has resorted quite commonly to directors' liability clauses.

26 Thus the Attorney-General stated, in a debate over a clause of this character; 'When persons accept office as directors of companies they ought to take upon themselves the burden of making reasonably sure that their companies conform to the law . . . We take the view that directors must take all reasonable care to know that their companies conform to the law.' H. C. Dec. (5th ser.) vol 422, col. 2012

27 Trading with the Enemy Act, 1914, section 1(3); Registration of Business Names Act, 1916, section 19

28 The phrase 'Principal Act' refers to the Official Secrets Act, 1911

29 Lieck 'Corporations As Criminals' (1939) 103 JP Jo. 80

30 [1942] 2 All ER 340

31 See the statutes cited in Glanville Williams, *Criminal Law; The General Part* (2nd ed. 1961) at page 867, note 10; and in addition, Betting, Gaming and Lotteries Act, 1963, s. 53; Weights and Measures Act, 1963 s. 50; Offices, Shops and Railway Premises Act, 1963 s. 65; Drugs, Prevention of Misuse Act, 1964 s. 8; Emergency Laws (Re-Enactments and Repeals) Act, 1964 s. 12(1); The Protection from Eviction Act, 1964 s.1(5); The Industrial Training Act, 1964 s. 6(8); Harbours Act, 1964 s. 10(2); National Insurance Act, 1965 s. 93(3); Nuclear Installations Act, 1965 s. 25; The Rent Act, 1965 s. 44; Trading Stamps Act, 1964 s. 10(2); Redundancy Payments Act, 1965 s. 52(1); Selective Employment Payments Act, 1966 s. 8; Prices and Incomes Act, 1966 s. 22(5); Agriculture Act, 1967 s. 71; Sea Fish Conservation Act, 1967 s. 12; Theft Act, 1968 s. 15

32 1951, section 29, but note the provisions to this section by which an officer may not be subjected to increased penalties (1) if he was not aware of the previous offence and was not then acting as an officer, and (2) that the repetition occurred without his consent or connivance and that he exercised all due diligence to prevent its occurrence

33 See for example, Official Secrets Act, 1920 s. 8(5); Theatrical Employers Registration Act, 1925 s. 6(3); Disabled Persons (Employment) Act, 1944 s. 19(4); Electricity Act, 1947 s. 62(2); Coal Industry Nationalization Act, 1946 s. 59(1)

34 See Parl. Deb. (HC) (5th Ser.) vol 488, col. 647. Statutes passed since 1951 utilising a reverse onus clause include Dangerous Drugs Act, 1951; Therapeutic Substances Act, 1956; Betting Duties Act, 1963; Dangerous Drugs Act, 1965

35 *Rex* v. *Hawthorne* [1944] OWN 237

36 The wording is apparently taken in part from sections 195(10) and 328(3) of the Companies Act, 1948

37 *Ex parte Valpy* (1872) LR 7 Ch. App. 289

38 *In re Kingston Cotton Mills Company* [1896] 1 Ch. 6

39 *Regina* v. *Shacter* [1960] 2 QB 252

40 *McNeil* v. *Lewis Brothers* (1908) 16 OLR 652 (Ont. HC)

41 See *Mulligan* v. *Lancaster* [1937] 1 DLR 404 (Alberta App. Div.)

42 [1896] 1 Ch. 6

43 See remarks of Lord Goddard CJ in *Rex* v. *Yorkshire Electricity Board,* The Times, Nov. 17, 1951

44 See remarks of Lord MacKay in *Edwards & Sons Limited* v. *MacKinnon* 1944 SLT 120 (Justiciary) ' . . . I refuse to accept the submission that three persons who accepted directorships and acted as such for fifteen full years were excusably ignorant of the nature of the business from which they accepted director's fees. Such propositions are wrong and dangerous'

45 A suggestion advanced in Glanville Williams, *Criminal Law; The General Part* (2nd ed. 1961) at page 867 and accepted here

46 *Lloyd* v. *Lloyd and Leggeri* [1938] P 174, 184

47 See Glanville Williams, *Criminal Law; The General Part* (2nd ed. 1961) at page 867, as to the construction of both terms

48 The onus of proof on the defence would thus be the same as that obtaining in cases of insanity: that is, the defence would have to be proven on a balance of probabilities

49 In *London and Country Commercial Properties Investments Ltd.* v. *Attorney-General* [1953] 1 WLR 312. Upjohn J said of such a clause, at p 318 ' . . . It indeed, I suppose, represents the high-water mark of Parliamentary invasion of the traditional rights of the subjects . . . '

50 Read, *The Company Director* (3rd ed. 1967) at pp 76-81

51 Glanville Williams, *Criminal Law; The General Part* (2nd ed. 1961) at page 868, is prepared to accept that the safety of the State might have been a valid reason for the reverse onus section contained in the Official Secrets Act, 1920. It is difficult to see to what other Acts this justification is pertinent, save perhaps the Emergency Laws (Re-Enactments and Repeals) Act, 1964. Even here, one is asked to presume a great deal in favour of the judgment of the executive. It is no doubt desirable to insert provisions to meet anticipated abuses, but the paucity of prosecutions under these provisions, and their use throughout so large an area of the statute book, leads one to conclude that their inclusion is simply 'common form', albeit a common form which does present dangers

52 See generally *Phipson on Evidence* (10th ed. 1963) paras. 620-622 and in particular the provisions of the Bankruptcy Act 1914

53 Companies Act, 1948 sec. 165(b) as amended by Companies Act, 1967 sec. 38

54 Companies Act, 1948 sec. 167 as amended by Companies Act, 1967 sec. 39

55 Companies Act, 1967 sec. 32

56 Companies Act, 1967 secs. 36 and 41

57 Companies Act, 1967 sec. 109. The power is virtually unlimited. For a decision on a similar provision see *International Claim Brokers Ltd.* v. *Kinsey and A.G. B.C.* (1966) 55 WWR 672

58 Companies Act, 1967 sec. 109(5)

59 *Reg.* v. *Harz* [1967] 1 AC 760; *Reg.* v. *Leathem* (1861) 3 El. & El. 657

60 Companies Act, 1967 sec. 110(1)

61 Companies Act, 1967 sec. 113

62 Companies Act, 1967 sec. 111

63 Emergency Laws (Re-Enactment and Repeals) Act, 1964 Sched. 1 sec. 1 and 2. This Act also contains in sec. 12(1) a directors' liability clause and in sec. 13(2)(a) a provision that where an offence is committed by a corporation, the corporation shall be fined such amount as the Court thinks just

64 e.g. under the Canadian Securities Acts. See Securities Act (Ont.) 1966 sec. 21(6) and compare Securities Act RSO 1960 c. 363 sec. 21(3). The investigation provisions of the Australian Companies Acts are very wide indeed. See Companies Act (Vict.) 1961 secs. 168-180

65 See *Federal Rules of Criminal Procedure* Rule 16. As to the construction of the rule see 'Discovery in Criminal Cases', 33 FRD 74 (1963) and *Bowman* v. *United States* 341 US 214 (1951). A similar but less extensive provision appears in

the Securities Act (Ont.) 1966 sec. 21(7). This latter statute serves as a model for most Canadian jurisdictions save perhaps Quebec and the Maritime provinces
66 *Justice* has considered some of the issues. See for a brief account (1967) III. Sol. Jo. 442
67 Companies Act, 1948 section 188(1)
68 *Hastings and Folkestone Glassworks Ltd.* v. *Kalson* [1949] 1 KB 214. There however, the articles provided that a director vacated his office if convicted of an indictable offence. It was held that this comprehended convictions for an indictable offence made on summary conviction
69 *Regina* v. *Davies* [1954] 3 All ER 335
70 Companies Act, 1948, Table A, Article 95
71 Companies Act, 1948, Table A, Article 97
72 Information kindly supplied by the Prosecutions Branch, Board of Trade
73 *Report of the Company Law Committee* 1962, Cmnd. 1749 at pages 29-30
74 Cmnd. 1749 (1962) at page 30
75 *Regina* v. *Bradley* [1961] 1 WLR 398, cf. *Regina* v. *Cohen & Smith* [1954] Crim. LR 221. The practice there followed must be taken to be improper
76 Cmnd. 1749 (1962) at pages 27-28
77 See generally, Smith, *The Law Of Theft* (1968) at pp 92-94
78 See Sutherland, *White Collar Crime* (1949) chapter 3; Clinard, *The Black Market* (1952) chapter 9
79 See 'Increasing Community Controls; A Problem In The Law Of Sanctions' (1962) 71 Yale LJ 289, where it is suggested that the United States might consider the introduction of such legislation
80 It is of course true that these presuppose the liability of the corporation, but this difficulty could be surmounted by a drafting amendment to make it clear that what is objectionable is the manipulation of corporate forms and assets leading to breach of the law

Appendix 1

Model penal code: tentative draft number 4

Section 2.07 Liability of Corporations, Unincorporated Associations and persons Acting, or Under a Duty to Act, in Their Behalf.

1 A corporation may be convicted of the commission of an offence if and only if:

a) the offense is a violation or the offense is defined by a statute other than the Code in which a legislative purpose to impose liability on the corporation plainly appears or the offense is defined by sections of the Code, and the conduct is performed by an agent of the corporation acting within the scope of his office or employment in behalf of the corporation, except that if the law defining the offense designates the agents for whose conduct the corporation is accountable or the conditions under which it is accountable, such limitations shall apply; or

b) the offense consists of an omission to perform an act which the corporation is required by law to perform; or

c) the commission of the offense was authorized, requested, commanded or performed by the board of directors, or by an agent having responsibility for formation of corporate policy or by high managerial agent having supervisory responsibility over the subject matter of the offense and acting within the scope of his employment in behalf of the corporation.

2

a) When absolute liability is imposed for the commission of an offense, a legislative purpose to impose liability on a corporation shall be assumed, unless the contrary plainly appears.

b) 'Agent' as used in this section, means any director, officer, servant, employee or other person authorised to act in behalf of the corporation or association and, in the case of an unincorporated association, a member of such association.

c) 'High managerial agent' means an officer of a corporation or an unincorporated association or, in the case of a partnership, a partner,

or any other agent of a corporation or association having duties of such
responsibility that his conduct may fairly be assumed to represent the
policy of the corporation or association.

. . .

4 In any prosecution of a corporation or an unincorporated association
for the commission of an offense included within the terms of subsection
1(a) or subsection 3(a) of this Section, other than an offense for which
absolute liability has been imposed, it shall be a defense if the defendant
proves by a preponderance of the evidence that the high managerial
agent having supervisory responsibility over the subject matter of the
offense employed due diligence to prevent its commission. This paragraph
shall not apply if it is inconsistent with the legislative purpose in defining
the particular offense.
a)   A person is legally accountable for any conduct he performs or
causes to be performed in the name of the corporation or an
unincorporated association or in its behalf to the same extent as if it
were performed in his own name or behalf.
b)   Whenever a duty to act is imposed by law upon a corporation or an
unincorporated association, any agent of the corporation or association
having primary responsibility for the subject matter of the duty is legally
accountable for an omission to perform the required act to the same
extent as if the duty were imposed by law directly upon himself.
c)   When a person is convicted of an offense as an accomplice of a
corporation or an unincorporated association, he is subject to the
sentence authorized by law when a natural person is convicted of an
offense of the grade and the degree involved.

Appendix 2

Combines investigation act RSC, 1952, c 314

41

1 In this section,

a)   'agent of a participant' means a person who by a document admitted in evidence under this section appears to be or is otherwise proven to be an officer, agent, servant, employee or representative of a participant.
b)   'document' includes any document appearing to be a carbon, photographic or other copy of a document, and
c)   'participant' means any accused and any person who, although not accused, is alleged in the charge or indictment to have been a co-conspirator or otherwise party or privy to the offence charged.

2 In a prosecution under Part V,

a)   anything done, said or agreed upon by an agent of a participant shall *prima facie* be deemed to have been done, said or agreed upon, as the case may be, with the authority of that participant;
b)   a document written or received by an agent of a participant shall *prima facie* be deemed to have been written or received, as the case may be, with the authority of that participant; and
c)   a document proved to have been in the possession of a participant or on premises used or occupied by a participant or in the possession of an agent of a participant shall be admitted in evidence without further proof thereof and shall be *prima facie* evidence
i)   that the participant had knowledge of the document and its contents,
ii)   that anything recorded in or by the document as having been done, said or agreed upon by any participant or by an agent of a participant was done, said or agreed upon as recorded and, where anything is recorded in or by the document as having been done, said or agreed upon by an agent of a participant, that it was done, said or agreed upon with the authority of that participant,

H

iii)   that the document, where it appears to have been written by any participant or by an agent of a participant, was so written and, where it appears to have been written by an agent of a participant, that it was written with the authority of that participant. 1949 (2nd Sess.), c. 12, s. 3; 1952, c. 39, s. 8.

Table of cases

H*

Table of statutes

1964

The industrial training act, 1964 (c 16) sec 6(8)

Agriculture and Horticulture act, 1964 (c 28) sec 18

Harbours act, 1964 (c 40) sec 10(2)

Emergency laws (re-enactments and repeals) act, 1964 (c 60) sec 2(1); sec 12(1); sec 13(2); Schedule I sec 1; sec 1(3)

Drugs, prevention of misuse act, 1964 (c 64) sec 8

Trading stamps act, 1964 (c 71) sec 10(2)

The protection from eviction act, 1964 (c 97) sec 1(5)

1965

Dangerous drugs act, 1965 (c 15) sec 19

National insurance act, 1965 (c 51) sec 93(3)

Nuclear installations act, 1965 (c 57) sec 25

Redundancy payments act, 1965 (c 62) sec 52(1)

Rent Act, 1965 (c 75) sec 44

1966

Selective employment payments act, 1966 (c 32) sec 8

Prices and incomes act, 1966 (c 33) secs 13, 16, 22

1967

Agriculture act, 1967 (c 22) sec 6(5); 71

Farm and garden chemicals act, 1967 (c 50) sec 3

Criminal law act, 1967 (c 58) sec 1; 4; 5

Criminal justice act, 1967 (c 86) sec 10; 33

Companies act, 1967 (c 81) sec 16; 20; 32; 36; 41; 109; 110; 111; 113 Schedule 2

Sea fish (conservation) act, 1967 (c 84) sec 12

1968

Theft act, 1968 (c 60) sec 15; 18

Canadian Statutes

13   Geo. VI (2nd Sess) c 12 (An act to amend the Combines Investigation Act, 1949)

RSC 1952 c 314 (Combines investigation act) sec 41

2 & 3   Eliz. II c 51 (Criminal Code, 1954) sec 470; sec 528; sec 707

The securities act, 1966 (Ontario) c 142 sec 21(7)

American Statutes

(All references are to the official edition of Federal statutes at large)

Sherman act, 26 Stats 209 (July 2, 1890)

Elkins act, 32 Stats 847 (Feb. 19, 1903)

Hepburn act, 34 Stats 584 (June 29, 1906)

Clayton act, 38 Stats 730 (Oct. 15, 1914)

Espionage act, 40 Stats 217 (June 15, 1917)

Capper-Volstead act, 42 Stats 388 (Feb 18, 1922)

Index